WHITE FLIGHT/
BLACK FLIGHT

WHITE FLIGHT/ BLACK FLIGHT

The Dynamics of Racial Change
in an American Neighborhood

Rachael A. Woldoff

CORNELL UNIVERSITY PRESS   ITHACA AND LONDON

First published 2011 by Cornell University Press

First printing, Cornell Paperbacks, 2011
Printed in the United States of America

Library of Congress Cataloging-in-Publication Data

Woldoff, Rachael A. (Rachael Anne), 1973–
    White flight/black flight : the dynamics of racial change in an American neighborhood / Rachael A. Woldoff.
        p. cm.
    Includes bibliographical references and index.
    ISBN 978-0-8014-4918-5 (cloth : alk. paper) —
    ISBN 978-0-8014-7728-7 (pbk. : alk. paper)
    1. Ethnic neighborhoods—United States—Case studies.   2. African American neighborhoods—United States—Case studies.   3. Residential mobility—United States—Case studies.   4. Social change—United States—Case studies.   5. United States—Race relations—Case studies.   I. Title.
    HT221.W65   2011
    307.3'362—dc22   2010047279

Cornell University Press strives to use environmentally responsible suppliers and materials to the fullest extent possible in the publishing of its books. Such materials include vegetable-based, low-VOC inks and acid-free papers that are recycled, totally chlorine-free, or partly composed of nonwood fibers. For further information, visit our website at www.cornellpress.cornell.edu.

Cloth printing   10 9 8 7 6 5 4 3 2 1
Paperback printing   10 9 8 7 6 5 4 3 2 1

For my husband, Robert Litchfield, and for baby Roscoe, who fill me up and make me smile in the morning

Contents

Acknowledgments

This research project would not have been possible without the encouragement and assistance of my husband, Rob Litchfield. I extend my loving thanks to him for collaborating with me on this endeavor, as with everything. He indulged me in my daydreams about embarking on a project like this and urged me to dive in and get started. He was my companion in travel, my trusted listener and reader, and my dutiful editor. Of course, he is also so much more. I would also like to thank my parents, Myra and Paul Segal, for sparking my interest in neighborhoods at a young age by raising me in the city. Thanks also to my late grandmother, Estelle Zeldin.

This work was supported by a grant from West Virginia University. I would like to thank Fred King and my colleagues in the Division of Sociology and Anthropology at West Virginia University for their assistance and support. I am also grateful for the effort and interest of my research assistants, who helped me to transcribe many hours of interviews: Larisha Campbell, Katelyn Casten, Seth Cox, Katie Davis, Jamie Farren, Loren Friend, Christina Kress, Katasha Leggett, Dawn Lozzi, Victoria Marra, Jennifer Mitchell, Robyn Popper, Teresa Sparklin, and Melissa Tressler. Thanks also to Andrew Cognard-Black and Sarah Woldoff-Kern, whose careful readings of chapters yielded significant improvements.

I extend thanks to the following colleagues from other institutions, who were very helpful throughout the process, offering encouragement, providing comments, engaging in insightful discussions, and sharing their support during the writing of the book: Elijah Anderson, Korrie Edwards, Herbert Gans,

Seth Ovadia, and Mary Pattillo. I am thankful to have colleagues who share my passion for neighborhood and urban research and who boost my efforts at quality work.

I especially want to thank my editors from Cornell University Press. Peter Wissoker listened to my ideas at an early stage in the process, and Peter Potter provided guidance toward the end. Their interest, dedication, support, and advice have been invaluable. Ange Romeo-Hall managed the editing and production of the book, John Raymond copyedited the manuscript, and Victoria Baker carefully and thoughtfully indexed the content.

Above all, I wish to express my deepest gratitude to the residents of Parkmont for generously sharing their precious time and trusting me with their stories.

WHITE FLIGHT/
BLACK FLIGHT

WHAT HAPPENS TO A NEIGHBORHOOD AFTER WHITE FLIGHT?

The change was quick. The only thing I can tell you is I wasn't even aware of anything. A few black families moved onto our street, and it didn't bother me. And suddenly, I walk up to the bank, and when I'm in line, I'm the only white person there. I get on the bus, and I'm the only white person getting on the bus. Plus, I can tell you one other thing that also surprised me. The stores on the strip—a lot of them closed up. For instance, the beauty shop I went to for so many years, they closed. He retired.

—Rose Berger, stayer, aged seventy-five

As more houses went up for sale, people began to run, I guess because they were afraid of the values of their property. Mainly though, it was younger people that were moving, not the older people. The younger people moved, and they said if they're gonna move, they're gonna do it now.

—Dolores Duskin, stayer, aged seventy-nine

It is a typical afternoon in Parkmont. I am there for the day, visiting with residents in their homes, on their patios, on the streets, in schools, at barbershops and hair salons, and at the local synagogue. As I move around the neighborhood, I notice real estate agents showing homes to black families.[1] As recently as 1990 the community was only 2 percent black and yet today, ten years after the collection of 2000 census data, it appears that the community contains very few white residents.

Parkmont[2] is a modern U.S. community that has experienced firsthand the phenomenon of white flight. Settled in the late 1940s as a white working-class

---

1. I primarily use the word "black" in the text, to reflect the language of the residents themselves and because recent data suggest there is "no strong consensus" in the black community about a preference to be described as African American versus black (Newport 2007).

2. I use the ethnographic convention of a neighborhood pseudonym to comply with the intent of human subject protections, as well as to elicit more honest answers from informants about the sensitive topics of race, crime, disorder, and neighbor conflict. Accordingly, I have changed the names

neighborhood in a northeastern city, it is not far from downtown, and it is close to the wealthy suburbs. In the 1980s whites began to leave in the wake of the city's efforts to enforce racial integration. The exodus was most pronounced in the 1990s, and by the year 2000 white flight was largely complete (see table 1 in appendix) with only a small number of remaining whites, mostly senior citizens, immigrants, and unemployed or disabled people. In short, Parkmont had become a majority-black neighborhood by the start of the new millennium.

The story of Parkmont is a familiar one to those living in U.S. cities, from Boston and Baltimore to Cleveland and Detroit, that have seen residential areas abandoned by middle-class and working-class whites. Between 1990 and 2000, American cities lost white population. For the first time in history, non-Hispanic whites now represent less than half the population in the largest central cities of the United States, going from 52 percent in 1990 to 44 percent in 2000.[3] Analyses of neighborhood data show that out of the 5,753 census tracts in which more than 60 percent of the residents were non-Hispanic whites in 1990, slightly more than one out of every five (20.1%) experienced a decline of more than 20 percentage points in the proportion of whites between 1990 and 2000.[4] When whites leave the city, they also leave neighborhoods, fundamentally changing the character of entire communities.

In this book I present an ethnographic study of Parkmont, focusing on the changing racial makeup of the community. I explore what happened in Parkmont after white flight had largely run its course and the blacks who had arrived first, often called "pioneers," were forced to adjust to their new residential environment. Confronted with the loss of relationships with their longer-term white neighbors, alarming signs of community decline (including a failing school that was demographically transforming), and conflicts with newer incoming black neighbors, many pioneers decided to flee Parkmont (if they could) and move to other neighborhoods. This led to a second wave of change that has received less attention in the scholarship on urban communities—what I (and others) call "black flight." Taking my cue from Parkmont, my argument is that we cannot

---

of informants in order to conform to ethical standards about confidentiality. In addition, I have reluctantly opted to conceal the name of the city in which Parkmont is located, although I do provide important context, such as the fact that the city is in the Northeast region and is known as a "black-white" city. Had I revealed the city's name, it would have been far easier to identify the name of the neighborhood (and its residents), which would place their confidentiality at risk. Also, by keeping the name of the city confidential, I was able to provide readers with crucial and honest information about the informants' biographies, as well as descriptive and factual details about Parkmont's historical, demographic, social, and cultural landscape. The trade-off is, I believe, worthwhile because the neighborhood-level details are crucial to this particular story.

    3. Berube (2001).

    4. See analyses by Ovadia and Woldoff (2008).

fully understand white flight and its ramifications without first coming to terms with the cultural and social dynamics that occur in the aftermath of white residents leaving a community.

Updating and Extending the White-Flight Narrative

White flight is a familiar theme to just about anyone who has read news stories, articles, or books about the plight of American cities since World War II.[5] Because it touches on race, class, urban/suburban divisions, and a host of other structural and cultural issues, white flight has the potential to generate controversy from all quarters. Some view it as a concern from a bygone era when suburbanization was a new mode of living, offering a respite for whites fleeing both urban crisis and black in-migration.[6] Indeed, much of the research on white-flight communities focuses on historical incidents of black-white ethnic tensions in the period between 1950 and 1980,[7] and this work often foregrounds the perspectives of whites who felt "left behind" or "dominated by fear."[8] A number of studies examine extreme situations, such as sexually violent "wilding incidents" and "ghettoization" in the South after white flight.[9] Despite the fact that many cities and neighborhoods remain entrenched in segregation or else turn over rather quickly when integration occurs, some research has highlighted the declines in racial segregation, albeit slow, that have occurred in multiethnic cities and neighborhoods.[10] Recent cases of wealthy whites reentering urban neighborhoods have even led some optimists to proclaim "the end of white flight."[11] The story of Parkmont reminds us that even today, when whites see people of color entering their communities, they flee. Whether because of racial factors or nonracial suburban pulls and urban pushes, white flight, "a massive migration of whites to the suburbs," is still occurring.[12] But Parkmont also reminds us that white flight is only one part of the story.

---

5. See especially, Carr and Zeigler (1990); Charles (2003); Clark (1987); Clotfelter (1976); Crowder (2000a, 2000b); Crowder and South (2008); Frey (1979, 1994a, 1994b); Galster (1990); Greenbaum and Tita (2004); Harrison (2002); Jonas (1998); Krysan (2002); Lee and Wood (1991); Renzulli and Evans (2005); Wilson and Taub (2006).

6. Seligman (2005).

7. See, for example, Levine and Harmon (1992).

8. Quotations from Cummings (1998) and Ginsburg (1975).

9. See, for example, Cummings (1998).

10. Ellen (2000, 2008).

11. Dougherty (2008).

12. Quotation from Frey (2002, 21).

Yet Parkmont poses a challenge to the common wisdom on white flight because it is a community where residents live and interact with each other under relatively normal conditions. It did not descend suddenly into violence and ghettoization but neither is it a stable, integrated community. Unlike many historical accounts of white flight that have circulated, this story is not about the loss of a great Jewish or white, ethnic neighborhood and the subsequent advent of a crime-ridden ghetto.[13] Too often, such accounts translate to overly simplified discussions of the "old neighborhood" in decline and overtaken by deep race and class divides.

Instead of emphasizing the perspectives of the whites who left for the suburbs, I examine the experiences of the three groups who remained in Parkmont—the whites who stayed (stayers), the first blacks who moved in (pioneers), and the blacks who arrived after resegregation (second wavers). These groups have experienced the atmosphere of a transformed neighborhood where few residents know each other, residential stability is low, and social cohesiveness is minimal. During my three years of fieldwork in Parkmont, I conducted more than ninety interviews with stayers, pioneers, and second wavers, as well as with local business owners and community members—including police, librarians, teachers, and school administrators. I asked residents why they chose to live there, what they like and dislike, their perceptions of change, why they stay, and whether or not they plan to leave.

The findings point to important features of new, predominantly black neighborhoods that emerge in the aftermath of white flight. Neighborhoods such as these can be found in cities that historically have had a large black presence or a mainly black/white population, including Baltimore, Boston, Buffalo, Cleveland, Detroit, Philadelphia, Pittsburgh, several New York City boroughs, Washington, D.C., and Wilmington, Delaware. Though many view racial change as a visible sign that a neighborhood is becoming "bad," the reality is that these are not places that can be so simply categorized by looking at the racial composition of the residents. On warm evenings, residents can be seen enjoying the neighborhood, homeowners are outside tending to their lawns, most properties appear to be in good condition with a convenient business district, and there is minimal violent crime. In short, these communities are not the "ghettos" that many people have come to associate with white flight.

My account of Parkmont begins with the first stage of racial change, the crucial period of transition in the 1990s when many white residents still remained,

---

13. Cummings (1998); Gamm (2001); Ginsberg (1975); Gordon (1959); Lassiter (2007); Levine and Harmon (1992); Osofsky (1966); Pritchett (2002); Rieder (1985); Seligman (2005); Suarez (1999).

though in diminishing numbers. Instead of focusing on the whites who left, I offer insight into the lives of the pioneers and whites who chose to stay in the community after white flight had already taken over. At first, the new black residents are greeted by friendly neighbors, and they learn about the norms of the community: trash day, mowing the lawn, shoveling snow, where to vote. Soon, however, the pioneers notice that more and more houses are on the market. Having paid a considerable amount of money for their homes, a financial leap for most pioneers, they become concerned when they notice the early signs of white flight. Still, they carry on, continue to get settled, and make plans for their families.

Then comes the second stage of racial transition. As white faces become fewer and white neighbors load their moving trucks with the pretense of searching for "bigger homes with more space," "smaller homes for empty nesters," or "lower taxes," black residents become doubtful of whites' stated motives for leaving. After all, why do all of the whites want to downsize or upgrade right now? The pioneers who have saved and taken the risk to buy homes in an unfamiliar community often wonder what their futures hold. Some decide to join the white leavers who are moving away, resulting in more houses going on the market. This, together with the passing of many older white residents, contributes to a new stage of turnover in the community as a second wave of blacks arrives into an increasingly resegregated neighborhood.

The remaining pioneers make peace with the fact that they will once again live in a segregated black neighborhood. These residents hope that the newest black families moving in will be similar to them and share their values, and that together, they will maintain the amenities and character of Parkmont. At first, this hope seems justified, as houses continue to sell for good prices and neighbors keep to themselves. Soon, however, problems become apparent. Noise, loud music, and hanging out become daily occurrences; litter lingers on neighbors' lawns; broken screen doors are not repaired; and children begin to outnumber adults on the streets. To some black residents, these concerns are minor. After all, Parkmont is far better than many black neighborhoods in the city, including the communities in which the black residents once lived. Still, many pioneers view the neighborhood's problems with increasing alarm. The second wave of blacks and their children appear to have fewer resources, less to offer, and possess different community values than the pioneers.

This new Parkmont is a far cry from the violent urban neighborhoods too often depicted in the headlines, but also absent are the markers of a strong community. Residents have little time for socializing so they barely get to know each other. Moreover, missing are many of the basic institutions that build durable ties and relationships, such as community centers, playgrounds, and churches.

Because it was only recently a Jewish neighborhood, the community lacks influential social institutions that cater to blacks. Parkmont is not an oasis of harmony where all black residents enjoy close-knit relationships with one another and function as an extended family. Instead of feeling unified in their experience as relatively new residents in a desirable urban community, Parkmont's blacks are divided: their shared culture and historical experience of racial exclusion cannot bridge their more proximate conflicts over social and community values in their new neighborhood. Divisions among Parkmont's black residents in terms of financial and family stability and value systems also translate to different reactions to the signs of decline. Many pioneers ruminate about the changes they see, view the community as being in trouble, and wish they could move to the suburbs. In contrast, many second wave black residents think Parkmont is fine for now and feel that they have little obligation or incentive to help improve the neighborhood.

It was in these circumstances that I came to know Gene and Margaret Meadows. One afternoon, while Margaret's husband, Gene, slept upstairs after a busy night working as an emergency medical technician (EMT), I talked with Margaret in her small living room cluttered with children's toys, backpacks, and a thick statistics textbook. A nurse with three jobs and one of the first black residents to move to Parkmont, Margaret was working on a statistics paper for a graduate school class while she intermittently checked on her younger children, Marcus and Latanya, who were playing outside. Margaret's oldest son from her first marriage had just graduated from college and was living in the basement while he searched for a job in the communications field.

According to Margaret, the Meadows family was excited to purchase their first home, leave the violent crime of their former neighborhood, and settle down in the reputable community of Parkmont. Intending to make this their final home, they became friendly with the white neighbors and learned the norms of life there. However, Gene and Margaret soon observed a disturbing phenomenon: large numbers of houses on their block began to display "for sale" signs. Surprised and saddened by this, Gene and Margaret came to accept the resegregation of Parkmont and began to focus on making the best of their new community. Afraid of decline, they wanted to make sure that the neighborhood's integrity remained intact. Along with some of the remaining white neighbors and new black residents, they worked to ensure that Parkmont continued to be a "good" neighborhood with clean, maintained properties, a good school, and quiet, crime-free streets. The couple became block captains, participated in the town watch, and went to civic association meetings. However, as more whites left or died, and some of the pioneers moved away, things changed. Some homes became rentals, some underwent foreclosure, and a second wave of blacks migrated to the community. Rapidly, Parkmont was transformed. Within fewer than ten years, the only remaining white neighbors were elderly. Additionally, the black residents who formed the second wave appeared to have more struggles, different values, and seemed far less involved in community life. With very little financial flexibility and having city jobs that anchor them to the urban core, the Meadows family now has few options for upward residential mobility. Like so many black families in congested, crime-ridden, segregated cities in the United States, they feel stuck.

Lara Bianco, who arrived in Parkmont as part of the second wave of black residents, purchased her home for a very low price with the aid of a government program for low-income, first-time homeowners. Lara, a single biracial woman, lives less than a block away from the Meadows family. Though she gets frequent visits from her mother, she lives alone and is not working due to a mental health disability. The outside of Lara's home shows signs of disrepair, but because she has only a modest income, she prefers to put her money to uses other than home improvements. She does not know her neighbors and has never even heard of the local civic association. Lara sees her Parkmont home as temporary and is aware that the area has seen better days.

Nearby are stayers Lorna and Abe Rothman. At ninety and eighty-seven years old, they are "originals," the first to own their Parkmont home. They are highly aware of changes in the neighborhood and are devastated that the local synagogue is due to close in a few weeks, but they have no plans to move. The Rothmans became frustrated when their neighborhood friends moved during the height of white flight, but they are more understanding about the more recent moves of their elderly friends who have become sick or unable to climb steps. Comfortable in the home they love and where they raised a family, their hope is to live as long as possible in Parkmont on their own terms, surrounded by their possessions, eating their own kosher cooking, and enjoying each other's company.

These three families exemplify the unique population mosaic that is left after the dust of white flight settles. Together, they introduce key aspects of the stories of white flight and black flight. The ideas that I elaborate upon in this book develop a new trajectory for understanding multiple stages of neighborhood racial change and the ways that older and newer residents are affected.

Plan of the Book

In the book's first chapter I provide a portrait of Parkmont. I set the stage for my analysis by describing the racial and ethnic history of the community in the context of urban housing after World War II and implementation of school integration policies in the 1970s. I then examine the demographic, cultural, and physical changes that occurred in Parkmont over time and provide a description of the area as it looked during the time of the study. I proceed by introducing readers to the three key groups in the book—the stayers, the pioneers, and the second wavers.

Chapter 2 shifts the focus to the first phase of racial change in Parkmont: white flight. When middle-aged and elderly whites moved out of Parkmont in droves and new whites failed to plant roots there, an unusual mix remained: elderly white stayers and striving black pioneers. This chapter profiles the two groups and describes how they came to co-reside. I describe the elderly whites who continue to live in Parkmont, many of whom refer to each other as "originals," and the blacks who first moved into the neighborhood. What do we really know about these so-called pioneers? This chapter highlights their desire for integration and their perception of white flight. The selective white flight of the 1990s and selective black in-migration that followed produced a black neighborhood with two populations who are distinct in several ways. The details of their stories complicate what we think we know about race, as we see two very different groups who have come to identify with each other.

Chapter 3 is the first of the three vignette chapters that provide portraits of the residents themselves and demonstrate how members of these groups interpret their respective places in the community. After describing the history of Parkmont and the relationships between stayers and pioneers, I introduce readers to Stella Zuk, an eighty-seven-year-old Jewish stayer who has resided in Parkmont since 1950. The setting of her story moves from Parkmont's synagogue to Stella's home, where she describes her personal experience of aging in place in Parkmont over the years. Stella wants to stay in the neighborhood for as long as possible. She shares vivid memories of the white neighbors who left and recalls the factors that led them to leave the community:

> My neighbors, an Italian woman and her sister, moved to the suburbs. Their son lived across the street. One of the sisters was single; she never married, and then she got sick. She was in a nursing home, and she died. Then, when the neighborhood changed, they left. I think, because the neighborhood changed to black, they moved out.

Stella's chapter highlights the reasons that elderly white stayers view their decision to remain in a black community as a logical choice as well as an assertion of independence. Her vignette also reveals white stayers' sophisticated understandings of neighborhood racial change and their awareness of the ways that people view elderly whites who live in black communities. As I will explain, it is possible for most stayers to move, but they choose to stay for a variety of reasons.

Chapter 4 continues the focus on relationships between Parkmont's white stayers and black pioneers. Here, I examine the interracial ties between residents in order to explain how elderly white stayers and black pioneer residents affect each other, and by extension, the culture of the neighborhood. This chapter points toward grounds for hope, interracial cooperation, and agency, all of which are important factors in devising solutions to neighborhood problems. Relationships between blacks and whites in integrated neighborhoods are often portrayed in simplistic ways, so I develop a more nuanced view of cross-racial neighboring. Using interviews from white stayers and pioneers, I examine the range and intensity of cross-racial neighboring in white-flight neighborhoods. Parkmont's pioneers are sensitive and responsive to their elderly white neighbors' losses (isolation, illness, and death) and offer support to them. This chapter reveals that pioneers' participation in helping and service occupations and their cultural norms of respect for elderly people are particularly important for interracial neighboring behaviors with stayers. Many black residents assist stayers with their daily living needs as well as with emergencies, and they usually do so without economic compensation. In most cases, white stayers gain the most from these interactions, but stayers can also be the givers who provide childcare, emotional support, social exchange, and a sense of community history and continuity.

Chapter 5 presents a second vignette, the story of a forty-seven-year-old pioneer named Ken Wilkinson who is a married father of two teenaged sons. Ken, a city worker who once served in the U.S. Air Force, is what some researchers would describe as a "watcher" in that he views himself as a guardian of the neighborhood. As one of the first black residents on his block, Ken witnessed Parkmont's white exodus firsthand and believes it was racially motivated. Like many pioneers, Ken is an active community member who is frustrated with the way that the neighborhood's social character has declined, though he acknowledges that Parkmont remains far better than the other residential neighborhood options available to him in the city. For Ken, desperate neighborhood conditions such as violent crime are not a concern, but the values, norms, and behaviors of the incoming second wave black residents are. He believes that, along with the population change and loss of whites and pioneers, there are major values differences between the pioneers and second wavers. He believes that Parkmont's black residents are divided on a range of issues, from parenting to community well-being:

> I think some of the differences is like, attitude, more of a hip-hop attitude. I mean, I think of myself as more family-oriented, whereas they may not. Maybe, just because it's a younger attitude. Like, they just don't care, they're not concerned. They're more concerned with just themselves....I believe that some people think that they move someplace, and it takes care of itself, but I know that's not true.

Ken's story provides a basis for understanding the conflicts within Parkmont's black community, as well as the affinity shared by stayers and pioneers. His narrative serves as a bridge between the two stages of neighborhood change and provides insight into pioneers' experiences from the time that Parkmont first integrated, into the period of resegregation and the era of black flight. His stories foreshadow the changes to come.

Chapter 6 begins the second section of the book with the focus now squarely on black flight. I explain the changes that have occurred as the second wave of black residents has begun to replace the pioneers. The continuing flight of black pioneers and the arrival of their replacements mark a second shift in Parkmont's population transition. This chapter highlights the similarities and differences between the pioneers who first moved into Parkmont when it was white or integrated and the second wave of blacks who moved in after it had already become predominantly black. The pioneers differ from the second wave in several important ways. Expecting to live in a white or integrated community with a stellar school, the pioneers are relatively economically stable, but increasingly have low satisfaction levels with Parkmont since it has resegregated. In contrast, the second wave only arrived after resegregation and their direct knowledge about the community is limited; this group has only heard about the large presence of whites that recently characterized Parkmont. This difference in timing of arrival between the two groups is a factor in both their *selection* and *socialization* into the community. The second wave has fewer financial resources, lower community expectations, and often different fundamental values about lifestyle, family, and community behaviors. Further, this group feels detached from the celebration of Parkmont's history, the legitimacy of its norms, and a stake in its future, at least in part because the second wave families did not benefit from living in Parkmont while the original long-term residents were still there. With no memory of another Parkmont, no socialization from elderly white neighbors, and strained relations with pioneers, they are seen as a neighborhood problem by stayers and pioneers. These more established residents believe that, at best, the second wave fails to notice local problems; however, more often, they are the source of disorderly behavior, school conflict, and crime. To the second wave, Parkmont is a just a black neighborhood that is *relatively* good for city living. This group assigns little meaning to community life in Parkmont and seems unmotivated to become acquainted with neighbors or participate in day-to-day opportunities for involvement.

Billy's story in Chapter 7 is the final vignette. As a nineteen-year-old second wave resident, Billy represents the group whom the pioneers blame for lowering Parkmont's status and degrading its quality of life. Billy's family epitomizes the destruction of Ken's hopes for a calm, peaceful, involved sense of community.

Billy's narrative begins in the barbershop owned by his father, with whom he was once estranged. The story takes readers on a journey revealing the social problems and cultural values that families like Billy's carry with them when they arrive in Parkmont. For instance, Billy explained how his father's work at the barbershop exposes his father to the underworld of crime, and despite the fact that he is raising a family and running a business in Parkmont, his father is reluctant to take the initiative in contacting the police or even to be seen at the local crime watch meetings:

> The only difficult part for my dad, I don't know how to put it....We got so much clientele that's into stuff [crime]. Most of our clientele are working people, but then we got a lot of clientele that is into stuff like that. So my dad definitely don't want to look like he goes to those meetings. That's why it's hard, especially with a barbershop. It's hard for businesses like that. Because you got so many different type of people, you just got to stay humble, man. You won't believe what people talk about, but my dad likes to know what's going on.

Clearly, Billy's story provides a stark contrast between the second wave families and pioneer families such as Ken's.

Of course, the story of change in urban neighborhoods in the United States is closely tied to patterns in city school systems. All three groups in Parkmont share some concern about one local institution: Lombard Public School. In chapter 9 I continue the discussion of factors that have triggered the black flight of pioneers by examining the role of Parkmont's school in the neighborhood's decline. This chapter describes the ways in which pioneer parents, children, and teens cope with Lombard, the failing school in Parkmont. Pioneer parents seek to remove and separate their children from Lombard's changing student body, some of whom travel from neighborhoods all over the city, but most of whom are the children of their own neighbors. I show how pioneers attribute school decline to a complex web of factors, including the inferior values and parenting of their second wave neighbors. It becomes clear that Parkmont's divisions extend to Lombard and have consequences for the future of the school and for continued population churning in the neighborhood.

In the final chapter I review and discuss the book's key findings as an example of a two-stage model of neighborhood racial change. I explain why and how neighborhoods that experience white flight work the way they do in the current era of white population loss in many U.S. cities. I also highlight the reasons that these neighborhoods are vulnerable to black flight. Finally, I discuss the implications of the findings for maintaining racially integrated neighborhoods and sustaining more viable, stable black communities.

1

THE PARKMONT ENVIRONMENT

White flight remains a relatively common pattern in U.S. cities. In fact, data on neighborhood racial change show that white flight is still far more widespread than white in-migration into mixed areas (see appendix).[1] On a very basic level, we know that many urban blacks seek a better place to live and that white and integrated communities tend to have more amenities than segregated, inner-city black communities, where poverty and disadvantage tend to be more concentrated.[2] However, we also know that whites often leave integrating neighborhoods. The evidence suggests that there are three major reasons that white residents leave neighborhoods

---

1. Evidence suggests that the pattern of white in-migration to mixed areas, a common feature of gentrifying areas (see Maurrasse 2006), is far less widespread than the pattern of white flight from mixed areas. In examining white flight in the 1990s, Ovadia and Woldoff (2008) found that, out of the 5,753 census tracts in which more than 60% of the residents were non-Hispanic whites in 1990, slightly more than one out of every five (20.1%) experienced a decline of more than 20 percentage points in the proportion of whites between 1990 and 2000. For white in-migration, they found that, out of the 3,922 census tracts in which less than 30% of the residents were non-Hispanic whites in 1990, 4.5 percent experienced an increase of more than 5 percentage points in the proportion of whites between 1990 and 2000. Thus, it is clear that white flight did not cease in the 1990s and that white in-migration is a far less common urban event (see figures 1 and 2 in appendix). These analyses also demonstrate that there is a substantial amount of intercity variation in the frequency of white flight. For instance, in Memphis, white flight took place in more than half of the central city tracts that had more than 60% white residents in 1990. However, in Seattle, white flight occurred in only three out of 167 possible neighborhoods.

There are, of course, exceptions to these patterns. See Ottensmann (1995) and Ottensmann and Gleason (1992) for cases of racially mixed neighborhoods in which whites continued to move in at rates sufficient to maintain integration.

2. See Massey and Denton (1993) for an in-depth discussion of the ways in which urban segregation concentrates disadvantage for blacks and interferes with the effectiveness of services and institutions.

after blacks have entered. First, some whites undoubtedly flee because of white prejudice and discrimination.[3] Since World War II, social science researchers and the public have drawn a connection between neighborhood racial change and racial prejudice. Second, many whites are concerned about legitimate "nonracial" problems related to crime, schools, services, and property values that often coincide with racial change.[4] In fact, policy and community efforts to maintain or stabilize integrated neighborhoods often respond primarily to this nonracial set of arguments, focusing on improving neighborhood quality, appearance, and services, rather than on encouraging residents to remain in the community, controlling rumors about decline, or promoting integration.[5] The fact that white flight often continues in the face of such efforts suggests that they may either come too late or target only part of the problem. Third, a subset of whites moves because their housing needs change at a time that just happens to overlap with a period of neighborhood racial change.[6] Whatever its causes, white flight is a persistent obstacle to racial and economic integration.

When white urban residents move away and new white families fail to replace them, neighborhoods undergo racial turnover, often called racial transition, tipping, or succession. However, what happens to these communities after the masses of whites leave? The most common narrative describes a post-white-flight tale of "ghetto" neighborhoods facing violent street crime, where residents live in fear. But is this the inevitable ending? In explaining what happens after white flight, the story of Parkmont provides a new look at the lifetime struggle for city residents to live in neighborhoods that meet their needs to feel safe, comfortable, and successful.

At first, the goal of this book was to further the understanding of white flight by extending the existing research into the new millennium and by providing a portrait of the ways that white neighborhoods change into black neighborhoods.

---

3. See Bobo and Zubrinky (1996) for evidence of white resistance to nontrivial numbers of black neighbors, and see Charles (2000) for evidence that out-group stereotypes interfere with integrationist attitudes. Also, see Charles (2006) for a discussion of the various theoretical arguments that link racial prejudice to segregation patterns.

4. These are sometimes called "racial proxy" or "race-associated" explanations rather than "racial" because they stem from race-based neighborhood stereotyping (see Charles 2006). See Krysan (2002) for evidence of whites invoking these kinds of responses when asked why they would flee an integrating community, and see Charles (2006) for evidence that some blacks use neighborhood racial composition as a proxy to avoid undesirable neighborhoods. Also, see Harris (1999) for evidence about the effects of racial versus nonracial traits on property values.

5. For research on social movements and other organized attempts (e.g., via residents' associations) at neighborhood stabilization or maintaining integration, see Goodwin (1979), Molotch (1972), and Saltman (1990). Also, see Nyden et al. (1998) for policy suggestions related to maintaining integration.

6. See Bures (2009) and Rossi (1955).

However, it soon became apparent that a second story of equal importance was unfolding: the rapid transformation of white flight into black flight. The stories of blacks and whites who are still living in Parkmont capture the multiple stages of neighborhood transformation that continue after the majority of white residents have departed. Most of what follows in this chapter is a history of Parkmont and a summary of the changes to its overall living environment.

Racial and Ethnic Aspects of Parkmont's History: 1940s to 1980s

A dense working-class neighborhood, Parkmont was built and settled in the late 1940s on the former site of a farm. It was part of the city's postwar building boom and larger efforts at residential development for the young families of the World War II generation. Homes were small, but they featured add-ons that were rare in the city at that time: one-car garages, small front lawns, and paved patios. Until recently, Parkmont was home to a large Jewish population. In fact, many white stayers reported that they sometimes referred to the neighborhood as "Little Tel Aviv" (and according to one Catholic resident, as "Kike's Peak"). According to locals, people viewed Parkmont as a "mini-suburb," and its school was considered the "gem of the city." Less than ten miles from the downtown area and close to wealthy suburbs, Parkmont had a very strong reputation as a convenient and self-sufficient community of working-class and lower-middle-class Jews with modest homes, small green yards, and a thriving, diverse retail district.

For its thousands of white ethnic residents, Parkmont seemed like paradise. Yet even though Parkmont was segregated and white, it was immersed in complicated race relations from its beginnings because, unlike other neighborhoods in the city, Parkmont did not have its own neighborhood public school. This was not a problem at first when the original families and their babies began to move in, but by the 1950s Parkmont's children were old enough to attend elementary school. Residents were forced to send their children to a school located in nearby Wynn Hill. Though it was inconvenient, Parkmont's Jews were comfortable with sending their children away to attend school in a more established and solidly middle-class Jewish neighborhood, surrounded by many large, stately single-family homes.

However, around the same time that Parkmont's first cohort of children began attending school in Wynn Hill, the city's changing population patterns began to alter the racial composition of Wynn Hill's school. An increase in the urban black population was characteristic of many cities during this period, causing many black neighborhoods and schools to become overcrowded. To many whites, it seemed that blacks were "taking over the city."[7] Soon, black families began to spill over into white neighborhoods and attend the white schools. Parkmont parents learned from their own observations, as well as from family and friends, that Wynn Hill's school was becoming integrated. In the racially charged atmosphere of the time, Parkmont's parents believed the school was no longer a desirable environment for their children's education. In this manner, race became the spark that fueled Parkmont residents' organized effort to build their own neighborhood school. Parkmont parents successfully lobbied the city to build Lombard, a new school offering classes from kindergarten through sixth grade to neighborhood children, most of whom were Jewish.

With Lombard established, Parkmont remained a solidly Jewish enclave in the 1960s, even though non-Jews (known to Jews as Gentiles) had become a presence. The newcomers comprised mostly first- and second-generation Italian Americans with a smattering of Irish Americans who had migrated to Parkmont from nearby communities and other parts of the city. To these new residents, Parkmont represented a high-status, white urban neighborhood that was in close proximity to jobs, extended family, and ethnic churches, peers, and organizations. In addition, Lombard was a main attraction, as it had quickly gained a reputation for academic excellence and for its successful, well-behaved, achievement-oriented students. The new Gentile residents filled the vacancies that appeared when small numbers of upwardly mobile Jews chose to move from Parkmont's ethnically integrated and modest row houses to the city's more spacious and prestigious Jewish first-ring suburbs.

The large segment of working-class Jewish families who remained in Parkmont learned to tolerate, and in some cases, embrace the Italian and Irish "goyim."[8] After all, Jewishness continued to dominate Parkmont's reputation, power structure, institutions, and cultural life. Parkmont residents were far more threatened by the black population that had crowded into the neighborhoods located just a few miles away. Like most of the city's whites, Parkmont residents were cognizant of the possibility of black encroachment; everyone knew someone whose neighborhood had "changed over." However, families in Parkmont took comfort in the fact that their community had remained solidly white. They felt protected in their defended community,[9] which was characterized by strong leadership and

---

7. See Hirsch (1983). Quotation from Early (2003, 81).

8. "Goyim" is the plural for the Hebrew and Yiddish word "goy," which refers to non-Jews or Gentiles. Although many argue that the word is not inherently offensive, it is often used in a derogatory fashion.

9. In Gerald Suttles's research (1972) on forms of neighborhood threat and resistance to neighborhood change, he referred to communities where residents attempt to protect their territory from the invasion of outsiders (e.g., immigrants, land developers) as "defended communities." His study

involved residents; in addition, they knew that the houses in their neighborhood were unaffordable or inaccessible to blacks.[10] Like so many white ethnic working-class areas, Parkmont had an unwritten code that prevented blacks from finding any affordable homes that might be for sale: lawn signs were banned. As one elderly stayer said of such signs, "One time somebody put a sign up, and the next night, there was no sign. Somebody took it off." This informal "no sign" policy helped to stave off racial change for a long time because blacks could not simply drive around and find homes for sale. Additionally, realtors knew that if they showed Parkmont homes to black families, they risked alienating white residents and sabotaging their own earnings and careers. Thus, Parkmont residents felt secure in their certainty that their neighborhood would remain unchanged despite the shifts in surrounding communities. As Susan Waxman, an eighty-year-old Jewish widow, said about her confidence in Parkmont's future:

> I thought I would live here until the day I die. It was so convenient to everything. Through our growing years, the community was one thing that I loved. The kids had a good education at one of the top schools in the city. I think that most of the people who lived here thought that this is where they were gonna stay forever.

Residents' feelings of security and satisfaction were threatened in the late 1970s when the city implemented a school busing program that would racially integrate Lombard's student body. The fear of blacks that had once motivated Parkmont's residents to organize and build a neighborhood school was once again reignited. White families strongly resisted the idea of a black presence in their school. Just as scary to whites was the possibility that black students would soon be spending their after-school time in Parkmont, whether at their library, in their streets, in their businesses, or on their playgrounds.

This time, Parkmont parents' efforts to avoid black students were unsuccessful, and Lombard did not remain a white school. The city's implementation of desegregation busing redistributed the student bodies of disproportionately black public schools to the many white schools in white neighborhoods across the city. In a short period of time, Lombard gained a sizable black student body. Many black students confronted hostility from white residents and classmates. For instance, one resident protested the noise made by black students who stayed in the recess yard after school by bending down Lombard's outdoor basketball

---

emphasized violent means of defense (e.g., gang formation), as well as institutional means (e.g., restrictive covenants).

10. For research on racial and ethnic differences in the effects of income and wealth on neighborhood attainment in recent years, see Woldoff (2006a, 2008) and Woldoff and Ovadia (2009).

hoops so that the black students who lingered after school would have no place to play a pick-up game. Some Parkmont families moved to the mostly white suburbs, but most could not afford to move there or else did not want to because of the convenience of the neighborhood and their emotional and social attachments to the city and community. Instead of moving, many white residents began to divert their children to "whiter" schools located outside of the neighborhood. With the city's large white ethnic Catholic population, as well as a sizable Jewish population, the region offered several alternatives to Lombard in the form of Catholic schools, highly selective college-preparatory magnet schools, and Jewish day schools. Thus, vacancies began to open up in Lombard, and by the 1980s the school had become majority black, gaining the paradoxical reputation of being a "black school in a white neighborhood" (see appendix for table 1, which shows that Parkmont had no black population in 1970 and was less than 1% black in 1980).

White Flight: The In-migration of Blacks as Residents, 1990s Onward

By the late 1980s, the integration of Lombard placed Parkmont on the radar for many striving black families in nearby segregated communities, leading them to seek residence there. Most of these early arrivals sought to escape the worsening crime and school conditions in a black community called Westside. At first, Parkmont's black residents were few in number, with fewer than two hundred blacks residing in Parkmont in 1989, making up only 2 percent of the total population. In this very early stage of neighborhood integration, the new black residents coexisted with Parkmont's white residents, who had by then become accustomed to seeing blacks in the community due to Lombard's largely black student body.

Interestingly, it was younger white families who seem to have spearheaded Parkmont's white flight. Unlike older and middle-aged whites, those with school-aged children were forced to confront the decision about whether to send their children to Lombard. The nearby first-ring suburbs, which have long been known for their concentration of old money and their streets lined with large, expensive homes and estates, were beyond the reach of Parkmont families. However, white "leavers" were unwilling to move too far away from Parkmont, as they valued the central location of their longtime neighborhood. Typically, the leavers moved to suburbs that are located less than ten miles away and that met two criteria: availability of affordable homes and largely white populations. Although the Jewish leavers had similar incomes to their Catholic neighbors, they tended to select a different set of affordable suburban neighborhoods, those known for having a significant Jewish presence due to the earlier Jewish exodus from city neighborhoods into the suburbs.

With younger white families on the move, the Parkmont housing market opened up to black home buyers, and soon they could be found on every block. The more tolerant or less prejudiced older white residents stayed put, but many other whites moved to Florida or relocated to condos in the nearby suburbs. As one white resident who left said: "It changed. People moved. Some people seemed like racial issues were always the thing. One person of color would move in, and they were out." Like weeds, "for sale" signs multiplied on the lawns of row houses. As leavers erected signs, residents could hear conversations among neighbors who frowned as they wistfully reminisced about the old days when Parkmont was solidly white. To them, the very existence of "for sale" signs that were blatantly displayed on lawns announced an irreversible loss of community. With few exceptions, black families were the ones who replaced white movers, as younger white families avoided the integrating neighborhood that contained a largely black school. As the scare spread, the in-migration of new black residents surged from a trickle to a steady stream. One black pioneer who moved in when Parkmont was still mostly white described the speed and cause of the racial change this way:

> Let me tell you something black people say to me. They'll say, "You know, your neighborhood changed." And I'll say, "Yeah." It's changed as far as being a white neighborhood to being a black neighborhood. It changed. And this is something that I've said. It was just like the plague was coming. Like, once the blacks started buying, it's like the plague. When we came up here, it was nothing to have ten or twelve "for sale" signs for a block. Whites didn't want to live around us, so they left. They were out of here. It was like, "We got to go. We got to go." As houses were going for sale all over the place, I told my husband one time, I'm like, "Damn. You know, we went to sleep, and we woke up, and the whole neighborhood is black." We didn't used to see that many blacks. It's like we went to sleep in the winter, and it changed. Just that quick.

In a short period of time, white panic took over, and a large number of homes in Parkmont became available. This period of white flight coincided with the pent-up demand for housing in safe, reputable urban neighborhoods among the city's upwardly mobile working-class black families from nearby communities. Because this period of time overlapped with a national trend in the rise of specialized mortgages and government programs to support first-time homeowners, even black buyers with only one income could make the leap to Parkmont.

Subprime loans enabled potential homeowners to put down very little money (as little as 2% of the value of a home) as a down payment. Many new residents also qualified for down-payment assistance programs through banks, jobs, the city, and other types of financing that became widely available to lower income groups and first-time homeowners. Thus, the 1990s and early 2000s represented a brief period of integration for Parkmont.

In this modern era of white flight, hostility toward Parkmont's blacks was not as overt as it had been in the 1970s when blacks first entered the community to attend school at Lombard. Charlene Lawson, a black police officer who was assigned to be a "community relations liaison" in Parkmont, asserted that the more overt racial tension occurred in the nearby Italian communities situated between Parkmont and the black neighborhood of Westside: "When I came out in '94, '95, '96, there was one street that was still the borderline. You couldn't really cross over there unless you lived there. We actually had to have a detail there because of the racial tension from the change."

Instead of the open resentment found in the nearby Italian communities, Parkmont's mostly Jewish residents talked quietly about "the change." They would discuss racial turnover only when it felt safe to do so, and even then, it was often in the context of other "nonracial" concerns such as schools, crime, and taxes. It would be dishonest to characterize Parkmont's remaining whites as enthusiastic about integration or eagerly anticipating the chance to interact with blacks in order to advance the cause of racial harmony. That said, many of the whites who chose to remain in Parkmont were the most tolerant of blacks and integration. These stayers were also active members of Parkmont's civic association and made concerted efforts to reach out to new black residents and help socialize them into community norms.

Like the whites leavers who moved away, the stayers were aware of the possibility that crime and disorder might accompany racial integration. After all, whites in the United States have long associated blacks with crime because of negative past experiences, gossip, local news stories, as well as the more general media representations and stereotyping that pervade U.S. culture and that are especially exaggerated in cities with large black populations.[11] Additionally, Parkmont's remaining whites had to endure the warnings of family members, friends, neighbors, and realtors who spoke of the inevitable "ghettoization" of Parkmont

---

11. In general, blacks are more segregated than Asians and Latinos, but the degree of segregation for these groups varies by place such that "black-white" cities tend to have segregation patterns that are distinct from more multiethnic cities (Frey and Farley 1996). The racial composition of cities and metropolitan areas shapes the character of interracial relations and the focus of individuals' racial attitudes.

and the associated risks to stayers' property investments and personal safety. Thus, crime and disorder soon became the focus of civic association meetings convened at the local synagogue. Keeping longtime residents in the community, preventing and controlling crime, and avoiding social and environmental degradation were the key goals of Parkmont's "block watch" groups and block captains. It was no coincidence that civic association leaders and members timed the prioritization of these goals to overlap with the onset of black in-migration. White stayers, many of whom were elderly, knew they needed the energy, skills, and interest of younger people to meet their goals, so they eagerly urged new black residents to get involved. Stayers correctly assumed that these young black newcomers with families would be interested in maintaining a stable, orderly community with property values that would continue to appreciate over time. So, for a brief time, Parkmont's whites and blacks actively worked together toward common goals.

However, when white residents, some of whom were civic association members, continued to sell their homes, and new whites failed to relocate to Parkmont, membership in the civic association dwindled. Many of the remaining members became disillusioned as complete racial change started to seem inevitable, and residents feared that economic and social decline might soon follow. Morale and organizational effectiveness slowly deteriorated as older white stayers and young black newcomers felt betrayed by their community leaders and neighbors. With resegregation well under way and seemingly unstoppable and the knowledge that Parkmont was not a violent community needing immediate intervention, it was easy for elderly white residents facing health deterioration and busy, hardworking pioneer families to cut back on their civic association involvement and refocus their attention on their personal lives.

As blacks continued to stream into Parkmont, pioneers remained aware and concerned about the racial factors contributing to white out-migration. When buying homes from whites, it was commonplace for black buyers to engage in awkward conversations with white movers. They would ask why the white sellers were moving, often with skepticism, and would hear a range of excuses. Since whites did not want to insult current black residents or scare off potential buyers, they mostly explained that Parkmont's housing was no longer meeting their changing lifestyle needs. Sam Wilson, one of the first pioneers to move to Parkmont, explained that even though whites were congenial when he first arrived, he still felt suspicious of the racial intolerance of white sellers:

> You felt welcome, but at the same time, you just assume that people aren't going to tell you the truth. [Laughs.] They put their "for sale" sign up and say, "Well, my grandkids moved." Or they'll tell you, "We

really don't wanna leave, but the bills are so high now." C'mon. They're just giving us an excuse. You don't have to tell me anything. You wanna move. You got to do whatever the hell you wanna do, but when you start giving me an excuse like that? That's definitely like you've got some sort of racial issue behind it.

Between 1990 and 2000, when Parkmont's white population declined by 59 percentage points, it was the second most active sale tract in the entire city. In contrast, suburban sales activity in the metro area was associated with increases in white population. By the 2000 census, Parkmont was a majority-black neighborhood. Soon, the only whites left were senior citizens and a group of middle-aged whites who lived on the fringes of society, such as those who lived with their older parents into adulthood and then inherited their homes, immigrants, the unemployed, and the physically and mentally disabled. Even with so few whites left, some black residents continued to hold on to the image of Parkmont as relatively integrated, probably because they had become so accustomed to living in neighborhoods with no racial diversity at all. Second-wave resident Ramell Worthy compared Parkmont to his last neighborhood and expressed the sentiment that even a tiny percentage of nonblack residents counts as "integrated" to him: "Ethnically, it's probably a little more mixed. Definitely. Even if it *is* just a small percentage of this neighborhood that's white. My last neighborhood was all African American."

Today, Parkmont is known as a black neighborhood. Most white senior citizens who remain are in their eighties, with some in their nineties. At the beginning of my fieldwork, many stayers were relatively healthy and mobile; many others were small, bent over, walking with canes, and had limited time left in an independent living environment. Stayers enjoyed talking about Parkmont and the feelings of family and community that they once felt in this close-knit community. They also discussed the shared histories of Parkmont's original residents. Many expressed gratitude that they were still able to walk to the local synagogue or "shul" (the Yiddish word for synagogue) where they could socialize, worship, and gain support services.

However, over the course of my research, the local temple had closed down and had become a black Christian church with very few Parkmont congregants. As older stayers talked to me, it was easy to imagine them as parents in young families starting out after World War II. Although the younger black families never knew them as fully engaged human beings and important authority figures in the community, many pioneers still made meaningful connections with stayers. Just as these elderly whites learned about and socialized with blacks at the end of their lives, the younger pioneers glimpsed the way that stayers had lived, learned of Parkmont's institutional history, and witnessed the role of the neighborhood in stayers' lives, successes, and their sense of community attachment, satisfaction, and identity.

Black Flight: Gradual Decline, Not Upheaval

Racial change need not result in continued population churning and decline, but this is frequently what happens to neighborhoods after white flight. Many communities that become integrated start off with a stable economic base of residents, low crime, quality local businesses and institutions, and successful schools. However, these neighborhoods often become segregated and conditions worsen. Some research on integrating neighborhoods shows that residents fear racial change, and if they want to prevent neighborhood decline, they must work aggressively and in an organized fashion to maintain racial integration, prevent the public perception that the neighborhood is unstable and that properties are losing value, and stave off rapid decline in the forms of crime, disorder, and poor educational opportunities.[12] Some strategies for reaching these goals could include maintaining or improving housing quality, revitalizing shopping districts, building effective community organizations that focus on quality of life issues, and "managing" integration through intervening in the real estate market to promote fair housing practices and prevent panic peddling.[13] Unfortunately, these interventions are not likely to occur in many of the urban communities that are most vulnerable to white flight. When racial change is rapid, the original population is elderly, and the organizational structure of a neighborhood has been significantly weakened, white-flight communities like Parkmont are in a poor position to mobilize.

Although some of Parkmont's decline is physical in nature and some is social, residents have an overall sense that conditions are getting worse, and many pioneers have an impending sense of doom about the future of the community. Both white and black residents must learn to live with the changes, but this does not mean that they do not care. They stay for several reasons. Since many black residents have jobs that keep them in the city and many cannot afford to move to a better urban neighborhood, they do not believe they have the option to relocate to an improved situation anytime soon. Furthermore, black residents are quite familiar with the truly dangerous parts of the city; they frequently remind themselves of the relative safety of Parkmont, taking solace in the popular urban

12. Maly (2005).
13. Ibid.

refrain that "crime is everywhere" in some form. Like the black residents, white stayers also compare Parkmont to worse neighborhoods. As eighty-two-year-old Aaron Schneider said when I asked about the noise levels on his block, "I'll tell you what you don't hear. You don't hear anything really bad here—at least not as much as you do in other places that have killings and shootings every night."

In addition to taking pride in its relative safety, Parkmont residents are comforted by and seek to maintain their reputation as a community of homeowners. In fact, Parkmont's 2000 homeownership rate was well above the city's average and remained unchanged during the massive white flight that occurred between 1990 and 2000. Although most whites have since left and the overall mobility rate of residents is now higher, almost three quarters of Parkmont's residents owned their homes in 2000. The average household, though working-class in terms of family members' occupations, brings in a lower middle-class income. The rapid and massive depopulation of whites allowed thousands of upwardly mobile blacks from poorer, less stable, and more dangerous neighborhoods to own a home in a community with the characteristics that most whites take for granted.

Yet at the same time, larger housing patterns have fueled a subtle decline in Parkmont. Research shows that the years between 1993 and 2004 marked a period of rapid homeownership for African Americans, with blacks experiencing a 7.7 percent increase in homeownership.[14] Specifically, the rapid shift in the profile of Parkmont's black residents is at least partly attributable to the fact that they took part in this national trend of increased minority homeownership. As is true of many neighborhoods with large minority populations, Parkmont subsequently experienced a wave of foreclosures, ranking high in the city's share of subprime loans. The mortgage strain was too much for many of Parkmont's black families and has taken a toll on the appearance of the area. In addition to financial struggles with mortgages, many second wave residents have struggled to keep Parkmont's older homes maintained and in good repair. The large inventory of homes and the availability of low-income housing programs have also led to an increased visibility of residents who earn lower incomes. Lower income residents have always had some presence in Parkmont, but they mostly lived in a few apartment buildings concentrated on a couple of blocks; now they are far more conspicuous and spread out. Thus, Parkmont's neighborhood disinvestment is much more evenly represented spatially, coming in the form of second wave residents who fall into one of several categories: those who live in rental housing; those who acquired homes with subprime mortgages; those who

---

14. See Herbert and Belsky (2008) and Herbert, Haurin, Rosenthal, and Duda (2005).

participate in low-income homeownership programs; and those who reside in homes that only became available after property tax defaults and foreclosures.

Even with all of these changes, Parkmont does not fit the tragic image of a white-flight neighborhood violently spiraling out of control. According to the typical tale of white flight, the older white stayers should have been trying to escape a black neighborhood in decline with falling property values. On the other hand, black residents were supposed to be content because they finally had access to the safety, good schools, orderly environment, and decent neighbors that they have always wanted. To my surprise, this was not the case. Many pioneers have fled, following in the earlier footsteps of white residents. Those pioneers who remain also want to flee, but not all will be able to realize their desires. Many purchased their homes as municipal employees, and while the city has rescinded some of its residency requirements, blacks are often tied to their homes by jobs, family obligations, and finances. To these public service and safety workers (e.g., teachers, police officers, EMTs, utility company workers, social workers, nurses, prison guards, sanitation workers, and firemen), white flight and the presence of the second wave of black residents have brought forth an obvious decline. The pioneers want to preserve the well-being of their children, their property investment, and their dream for a safe, peaceful, attractive, respectful community.

The Changing Streetscape

Though not plagued by liquor stores and public housing developments, the transformation of Parkmont can be gleaned from its appearance. More changes followed when housing stock started to turn over, and the neighborhood began to lose segments of the population. For instance, as is true in most major cities, stable small businesses lost ground when suburban shopping mushroomed and national chains began to buy out stores. Some store owners followed the white population out of Parkmont. Now the business environment contains many small, struggling stores that are new to the neighborhood. The withdrawal of established businesses has symbolized disinvestment to the many residents who are unhappy with the quality and stability of local stores and restaurants.

Most stayers and many pioneers reported that they can easily observe the changes in the neighborhood as they walk down "the strip." The strip is a two-way thoroughfare that is several blocks long, facing and intersected by long streets of brick row houses. On any given day, pedestrians walk on the strip to take children to school, pick up take-out food, shop for conveniences, run errands, or wait for the bus. There is a steady flow of traffic on the strip as buses and cars make their way to other parts of the neighborhood, to the suburbs, to the expressway, or toward nearby neighborhoods. Overflowing trash cans near the bus stops line the street, spilling garbage and debris to the ground. The businesses exude a bare appearance with limited signage and décor. They give onlookers the impression that the members of Parkmont's business community either do not care about the physical appearance of the neighborhood or else they are unable to afford the necessary improvements.

The men, women, and children of Parkmont consume and purchase a variety of items on the strip: Italian ices, front doors that are fortified with security bars, and sandwiches from take-out restaurants. They have access to chain drug stores and fast food restaurants. Residents also have the option of shopping in many of the shabby-looking, immigrant-owned small businesses, such as the large, cluttered Asian-owned dollar store that was formerly a bank. There is also an Asian-owned beauty supply store specializing in black hair care and cosmetics, an Italian tailor's shop with a sign in the door saying "out of business," a snack shop owned by an African man, and a tiny Caribbean-owned hair braiding salon. Two businesses are Israeli-owned: an auto repair garage and a shoe repair shop. On the strip, one may also see black children from the United States, Africa, and the Caribbean playing at a fenced-in local daycare center located near a barber-shop owned by a second wave family who rents a home nearby.

Absent from the strip are the businesses that mainly used to cater to Park-mont's white residents. There are no longer hair salons that cater to the needs of older white women, many of whom have thinning hair that they are used to having rolled and set. Optimistically, there are none of the telltale signs of ghettoization—no conspicuous public housing towers, pawnshops, liquor stores, bail bondsmen, check cashing agencies, or alcohol carry-outs. But the emergence of abandoned storefronts and the addition of a new Laundromat are indicators that the social class status of the community is slipping. The dearth of community pride symbols, murals, and institutions that cater to the younger, black family community is glaring and unfortunate.

Aside from the strip and a nearby shopping center, the streets of Parkmont are residential. The homes are set back from the street. Compared to suburban homes, the lawns are miniature, but city dwellers often remark on the "huge front lawns" here. In reality, the houses feature small squares of grass and little patios where residents feel the need to chain down their chairs, tables, and barbeques. Many homes have neatly kept lawns with manicured flower beds and bushes, but others have garbage strewn on the grass in the form of Chinese take-out advertisements, candy wrappers, and discarded cups. It is common to see homes that show signs of age with old, broken, or worn-out doors, peeling paint, bare lawns, cracked cement, and rusted railings along the front stairs. Often found on the doorposts of homes are the dirty, faded outlines of mezuzahs (Jewish orna-ments containing scripture), which symbolize that the house was once owned by someone of Jewish heritage. On any given block, a visitor may pass a house that is boarded up or one that is abandoned and surrounded by tall weeds, but these kinds of homes are not yet the norm. Second wave black residents tend to reside in the worst looking homes in the neighborhood. In general, they view the outside appearance of their homes as a low priority and only a slight source of embarrassment.

Pioneers blame the second wave for the decline in Parkmont's appearance. Even though pioneers know that it is likely that some of the second wave residents simply cannot afford to keep up their homes, they also think that these new residents have different values and choose not to make their homes a priority. Pioneers feel that they have little in common with their newest neighbors and have learned to keep their distance, leaving the neighborhood feeling withdrawn and antisocial at times. Though children can be seen all over Parkmont for most of the day, adult residents are at work or else just keep to themselves. On an average day, the curtains or blinds are drawn for privacy and few adults go outside to socialize or play with children. A thirty-year-old second wave resident named Aliya Sampson acknowledged the lack of close ties between black residents:

> Here, everyone kind of just minds their own business. I'm not sure if this *is* a neighborhood. I don't think this is a neighborhood where people have been on their streets, living here for as many years as the people were living on the streets that I used to live on. Literally, there were generations of people—people my sister's age, and my sister is thirty-eight. They've been there for that amount of time, so it was the same people, and everybody knows each other. Here, I think it's people from Westwood that have moved in. Now there's no real community feel. It's like people move in quietly. There's no "Hi. Welcome to the neighborhood. My name is such and such." They just mind their own business.

Stayers, Pioneers, and the Second Wave

In order to understand the development of this distinctive neighborhood and the relationships and conflicts found here, Parkmont must be considered in relation to the three groups who have made it their home.

The Elderly White Stayers

The first group to settle in Parkmont, the white stayers, is disproportionately composed of Jewish senior citizens, most of whom were the original owners of their homes. The stayers once lived in Parkmont in large numbers, and most of those who remain have been in the neighborhood for close to fifty years. Stayers' spouses are either living with them but in poor health or have died. Many stayers have adult children who live in other cities or states or else live in the suburbs, but others are childless and only have contact with nieces and nephews. The stayers have lost many of their closest friends; their longtime confidants and neighbors either fled from Parkmont when it "changed," or became so ill that they were forced to move into retirement homes, or, increasingly, they have died. Stayers' long lengths of residence in Parkmont and their status as "originals" have led them to decide to "age in place" for as long as possible and to resist the temptations and pressures to move. During my research, I met stayers who maintained their lifestyle for years, but many others became ill, died, or had to move into retirement communities that could better meet their needs.

In terms of social class, most stayers are from working-class backgrounds and have only high school degrees, but some had been teachers or once worked in retail. Most live on fixed incomes and are extremely careful with their finances. Even so, stayers tend to be economically stable and live modest lives in Parkmont. They have made peace with the racial change in the community and are relatively comfortable with having black neighbors. Although some stayers report that economic limitations have played a central role in their decision to stay in Parkmont, most say they had no desire to move and that they could have afforded to move earlier if they had really wanted to do so. Stayers recognize signs of decline in the neighborhood, but like many black residents they are quick to emphasize that "crime exists everywhere."

The category of "stayer" describes residents like Gerri Holtzman, an eighty-one-year-old Jewish widow. She and her husband purchased their home in 1951 after hearing about Parkmont from family and friends. They liked that it was Jewish, affordable, young, conveniently located, near her family, and close-knit. Gerri recalled that Parkmont neighbors were extremely close and lived in a "bubble" of safety and familiarity: "We used to walk up to the strip and park the baby carriages outside of Sal's Diner and go eat lunch. Sal would stand at the register, and he would say, 'The baby in the green carriage is crying.' He would tell us which baby was crying." Gerri's emotional investment in Parkmont stems from the community providing a good environment for her children, as well as from her continued involvement in the local synagogue. She has an active social life, visiting the local Jewish Community Center (JCC) several times a week to take aerobics classes and to walk on the track. She also enjoys the local library, which has a large collection of Jewish and Yiddish titles. For now, residents like Gerri can be found scattered on every block of Parkmont.

However, many other stayers are in far worse health and are fairly isolated. Edda DeLuca, an Italian immigrant who speaks broken English, reported that after arriving at Ellis Island, the only thing she wanted in a neighborhood was to be close to public transportation and live near a church that conducts the Catholic Mass in Italian. She stressed how important it was for her priest to understand her in confession and give her counsel in her own language. With no children and most of her original neighbors gone, Edda became very close with the first black neighbors who moved in, but these valued pioneers have since moved away.

Like longtime residents in most places, the stayers share a common history, but Parkmont's stayers are also joined by the shared experience of being the group of whites who lived through Parkmont's full arc of white flight. This means that many know about the history of businesses changing over, the metamorphosis of Parkmont's appearance, the decline of the local school, and most have heard neighbors' stories about episodes of local crime. As they have aged, they have become less "in the know" than they once were, and some of their interpretations of neighborhood changes seem to be based on outdated ideas. For example, stayers often notice that many of their new black neighbors have "improved" their homes by installing embellished screen doors. However, they fail to realize that many black residents have purchased these doors for security reasons. Coming from lower income and higher crime areas, pioneers have replaced Parkmont's older, flimsy screen doors with the kind of steel storm doors that are more commonly found in the higher crime parts of the city.

The Pioneers

The pioneers are the first black residents who moved to Parkmont in the 1990s. They are trying to get ahead in life. Mostly single women and families, they are not trendy, unattached urbanites looking for fun. They are focused on working at their jobs to earn enough money to pay bills, have some nice possessions, and provide their children with quality residential and school environments. Most pioneers work for the city in some capacity, although many admit that they have career ambitions to own a business. Up until the mortgages crisis, many wanted to get involved in the real estate industry by becoming realtors or by generating additional income through "flipping houses," or renting out properties nearby.

Pioneers have many positive things to say about Parkmont, and they emphasize that the neighborhood is far better than most in the city. They consistently compare Parkmont to worse areas where they or their loved ones have lived in the past. All pioneers filter their evaluations of Parkmont through this kind of comparison. They are relieved that visible drug houses, violent gangs, widespread vandalism, abandoned buildings, and "cheap stores" are not a major presence in their new community, and they are proud that "houses are selling in the low $100,000s." Janice, a thirty-seven-year-old nurse and mother of two teens, is typical of the striving pioneers. She purchased her home with her husband in 1998, but they split up, and he moved out. She sends her daughter to a charter school, and after a bad experience at Lombard, she now homeschools her younger son. She described the relative safety of Parkmont compared to the neighborhood where she was raised, explaining the violence that drove her away from there to Parkmont:

> Oh, it's horrible there. Horrible. Because of the drug trafficking. I've seen people using the stop signs for target practice. Young black men are dying, including my nephew. He got killed. They're just dying at a ridiculous rate. It's not a joke. I always say, "Who's gonna marry my daughter?" because there's just so many black guys dying. You can go as young as fifteen to twenty years old, and within that little age range, there were so many getting killed.

Despite pioneers' relative satisfaction with Parkmont, they also perceive significant decline in the community. When white flight was taking hold, they were troubled to watch Parkmont resegregate, and they continue to be saddened when older stayers pass away or grow ill. Pioneers have witnessed some Parkmont homes turn into low-income housing available for purchase, and believe that an increasing number of homes are also rented privately and through government programs. Many pioneers are extremely disturbed by the threat to their investment caused by homes on their block that are in disrepair or vacant. They complain about the daily incivilities and signs of crime, such as poorly controlled children, trash on the streets, abandoned cars, loud music, and even the occasional sounds of gunshots. Pioneers feel outrage and despair when they hear stories about disorder, drugs, and violence at Lombard school. They are sobered by any focus on Parkmont in newspaper and television stories about muggings, shootings, bank robberies, school attacks, and violent drug-related crimes. Pioneers are especially agitated when they see that in many news features about crime in Parkmont, the residents are not only the victims but also the perpetrators, as in recent cases of fraud scandals involving bad checks, gun-related aggravated assaults, kidnapping related to drug dealing, strong-arm robberies, gun sales, drug dealing, murders of innocent pizza deliverymen, and even the beating of Lombard's principal by a neighborhood parent.

Several pioneers told me that they feel as if they were victims of fraud, duped by a real estate "bait and switch." They moved to Parkmont as an integrated neighborhood, selecting it based on its reputation as a safe, quiet place with responsible homeowners and an outstanding school. Now, not only has the community resegregated but, more importantly, pioneers have noticed meaningful decline. As a reaction, many have begun to compartmentalize their social worlds and insulate their families. Most pioneers have fled violent neighborhoods, and with so much population churning in Parkmont, they feel distrustful of the newest people around them. They often try to minimize their contacts with newer neighbors, opting instead for neighbor relations with the white elderly residents they have come to know and trust. Parents are reluctant to send their children to Lombard, but in order to send them elsewhere they must spend hundreds of dollars a month on tuition or else figure out a way to get their children admitted and transported to magnet or charter schools. Pioneers see great room for improvement in Parkmont in terms of schools, recreation centers for children, and police presence, and feel pessimistic about the future of the neighborhood. Most would leave Parkmont if only their jobs, finances, and the nearby housing market would allow it.

The Struggling Second Wave

The recent wave of new black migrants to Parkmont represents a second phase of neighborhood transition and has contributed to black flight among pioneers. Like the pioneers, second wave blacks have come from higher crime and lower income neighborhoods. One second wave resident contrasted Parkmont's social class milieu to that of his last neighborhood: "This is a working-class neighborhood, but in my old neighborhood, there was a lot of illegal activity, a lot of drug dealing. Up here, it's like more our socioeconomic region, more advantaged than the other neighborhood." Unlike the striving pioneers, the second wave arrived in a community that was predominantly black with a very limited white presence. They know about the recent racial and social changes in Parkmont in more of a vicarious way, but have had very little contact with white neighbors and do not mix much with the pioneers, either.

Second wave residents seem to struggle far more than the pioneers in terms of economics and family instability. Some are single caregivers of older parents, some come from families shattered by drugs, divorce, or prison, some are immigrants from the Caribbean or Africa, and some are grandmothers raising their grandchildren for a variety of reasons, from drugs to parents' being soldiers in the war in Iraq. In contrast to the pioneers, the second wavers tend to send their children to Lombard for school. The second wavers find Parkmont to be relatively quiet and attractive, but with little to offer young people in terms of productive activities or recreation. With family members at work all day, second wave children have a great deal of unsupervised time in Parkmont after school. Many children tell of problems at Lombard, frustrations with learning, difficulties coping with family conflicts, the temptations to deal drugs, boredom in Parkmont because of a lack of free amenities for children, and the interpersonal conflicts and violence that they have seen or participated in as new residents. Even when they are not explicitly talking about it, one can observe the relative disadvantage of the second wave children compared to those of the pioneers.

I witnessed the difference between the two groups on one afternoon, when two second wave children, Imani and Jabril, approached me as I waited outside for their neighbor. They asked me to help them with their math homework, which I quickly learned was far too advanced for them. As they sat outside feeling helpless about the standardized test preparation workbooks that they had no idea how to complete, their grandfather's girlfriend appeared at the door in a nightgown and asked if they were bothering me. She informed me that their mother comes home from work after they are already asleep, and their older brothers usually fill in the answers for them in their notebooks when they get back from playing basketball.

At the local daycare center, Katie Kress, the white director, and Rhonda Hamilton, an African American school nurse and neighborhood resident, explained the social class and cultural changes that have occurred in Parkmont in recent years and the shift in the socioeconomic distribution of the youngest children in the community. According to Rhonda, "We get a lot of kids from the neighborhood. We had, when I began, a lot of 'private pay.' Now, we get a lot of subsidy because the area's changed." Katie thinks of the neighborhood as lower income based on her contacts with the children and their parents, many of whom are young single mothers and most of whom live in Parkmont or nearby. She says that the neighborhood feels safe, in general, but she admitted that she now keeps the school door locked all day. She shared the following bit of gossip to emphasize the fact that two conflicting groups call Parkmont their home: "It just so happened that there was a drug bust across the street, and we had parents who are police officers who showed up in their uniforms."

It is clear that Parkmont has experienced a great deal of change since its origins. U.S. Census Bureau data reveal the fact of racial change and the pace of it, but not the character or sentiments of the people who remain. The statistics demonstrate the reality of white flight, but conceal this second stage of black flight. The following chapters illuminate the worlds of the residents who lived though both white flight and black flight, exploring a neighborhood that is not the "urban ghetto" so often associated with white flight, but an interesting and changing black community with its own complicated social character, cultural strengths, and emerging troubles.

2

CHOOSING PARKMONT
Whites Staying and Blacks Pioneering

I have a nice home, and I don't intend to move out.

—Joanne Newcombe, stayer, aged ninety-one

Oh, I was excited. I was ready to go. My whole family lived on my old block—four houses in a row. So, I was ready to get away. I was ready to get off the block."

—Nina Jones, pioneer, aged thirty

The first phase of racial transition in Parkmont can be accurately characterized as white flight. Although many white residents sought to leave integrating Parkmont as soon as possible, others continued to find the community a desirable place to live. As younger, middle-aged, and even elderly whites moved out, Parkmont's demographics formed an unusual mix: elderly white stayers and black striving pioneers. This chapter introduces these two groups, explains how they came to share a community, and explores the role of choice and agency. In so doing, it complicates what we think we know about race, as we see two very different groups who have come to identify with each other in many ways. In part, this chapter presents a new look at elderly whites and pioneers in white-flight communities by examining their unique motives, decisions, constraints, and lifestyles. These stories challenge the commonly held assumption that people who stay behind after white flight are involuntary, marooned urbanites.[1] The narratives also bring into question any presumptions that black newcomers are indifferent to the loss of the white population, feel comfortable with resegregation, and are socially distant from elderly white stayers.

Eighty-four-year-old widower Joe Cassidy is one of the original Parkmont residents and is representative of many elderly white stayers who feel satisfied

---

1. I credit Townsand Price-Spratlen for introducing to me the concept of a "marooned urbanite," which may describe a city resident who is an "involuntary stayer" or a person who cannot carry out his or her mobility preferences (see Butler, McAllister, and Kaiser 1973). This concept is especially relevant in discussions of residents' agency and neighborhood population change.

with their decision to stay in Parkmont. When I first met Joe for an interview, he sat in a recliner in his Parkmont home, debating whether to microwave a frozen dinner or head to the local Greek diner, the Grapevine. The Grapevine has an inexpensive menu, and Joe has been eating there for decades. He felt tired after a round of golf at the nearby public course. He walks to this course several times a week because, as he said, "I've given up my driving pleasures and opportunities." Joe usually eats dinner at home and reserves the Grapevine for French toast breakfasts. But on this day, he felt like having a large, satisfying meal at the diner where the waitresses know him and where he is so familiar with the food options that he does not even need a menu. He decided to get dressed and go out. As we reached the front patio where he likes to read the paper in good weather, he spontaneously felt the need to defend his decision to live in an integrating neighborhood. He pointed to the cars parked along the street, "My kids want me to move, but look! Not one junky car. I love it here."

At the beginning of the twenty-first century, the U.S. population has been aging just as large cities have been losing sizable portions of their white populations.[2] In general, whites are overrepresented in the retirement-age population.[3] This is important because elderly whites are less likely to move than younger whites when their communities shift from white to black,[4] and neighborhoods with more senior citizens experience larger amounts of racial change.[5] The issues of neighborhood racial change and older people "aging in place" reflect a national trend. Not surprisingly, these demographic and social changes have trickled down and produced racial changes in many central city neighborhoods, affecting schools, local institutions, services, voting, and other aspects of community life.[6]

Why did Parkmont's elderly whites stay in their community at higher rates than their younger white neighbors? A substantial body of literature suggests that there are three factors about older people in contemporary society that make this situation so common. First, even though serious illness and disabilities become more likely with age, today's older people are healthier, wealthier, more educated, and live longer than was true in the past.[7] Second, along with these improvements, elderly people express a strong preference to "age in place."[8] Consistent with this desire, most seniors live in conventional homes by themselves or

---

2. Berube (2001).
3. Lee and Haaga (2002).
4. Fitzpatrick and Logan (1985).
5. Galster and Keeney (1993).
6. See Fasenfest, Booza, and Metzger (2004) and Rawlings, Harris, and Turner (2004).
7. He et al. (2005).
8. American Association of Retired Persons (1996).

with a spouse and in "natural" communities rather than in retirement settings.[9] And older people tend to live in homes to which they are quite attached, with almost half living in the same house for twenty-five years or more.[10] Third, the old and "oldest old" (i.e., those over eighty-four) are especially likely to live in metropolitan areas.[11] Thus, to summarize, it is common for older people to live independently, in metropolitan areas, and in their own homes, where they have lived for a very long time. With aging in place becoming an increasingly common trend,[12] it is important that we know more about the lives and views of older people who decide to stay in their homes even when their communities change around them.

The pioneers, like the stayers, have also served as witnesses to Parkmont's population changes. The pioneers form a distinct group in that these are families who, when they gathered their moderate resources to buy a first home, selected a historically white community. Depending on the definition chosen, the word "pioneer" may simply refer to an early settler, but the word also elicits images of people with more lofty aspirations: trailblazers preparing the way for others to follow into an unknown territory. The latter definition of pioneer aptly describes Parkmont's earliest black residents, many of whom knew very little about the terrain of the neighborhood before they settled in and found many surprises awaiting them. Pioneers' accounts provide a unique perspective on the transformations in Parkmont, while also communicating their place in the social and spatial hierarchy of urban blacks.

Parkmont's black pioneers may also be considered "strivers." The concept of the striver is well known in black history literature as a label for ambitious, upwardly mobile individuals who "want to get ahead."[13] For instance, in New York's Harlem neighborhood sits a block called "Strivers' Row," where many early black professionals once lived. Many pioneers in Parkmont fit the description of striver. In fact, one pioneer epitomized this identity when she distinguished the families who left their old neighborhoods to come to Parkmont from those who stayed behind: "I think we had what you would call the want to get a better education, like college, and keep children in positive things. Whereas there were certain blacks that they just tried to live. They were just trying to live."

Some of the most notable studies of black communities have focused on either the middle class or those who are extremely poor. These studies serve as a useful

---

9. Schafer (1999).
10. American Association of Retired Persons (1996).
11. He et al. (2005).
12. See Billig (2004) and Tinker (1997).
13. See Drake and Cayton (1945), Frazier (1957), and Singh (2004).

point of contrast to life in Parkmont. Mary Pattillo-McCoy's (1999) description of a black middle-class community called Groveland provided a memorable portrait of a long-standing black community in which residents functioned both as friends and family.[14] In fact, Groveland's neighbors were so close-knit that they even felt comfortable intervening on a personal level to stop social problems affecting the community, such as disorder, drugs, and violent crime. The relationships among four generations of Groveland's black residents have been characterized as "networks intertwined":

> At the neighborhood level, neighborly and family connections affect the management of youth behaviors, including crime. Residential stability is important for the creation and maintenance of social networks. Because Groveland is very stable, thick kin, neighborly, and friendship ties are the norm. These networks positively affect both the informal and formal supervision of youth.[15]

In Groveland, residents were unified, organized, and willing to intervene when problems emerged.

Elijah Anderson's (1999) ethnographic study of a low-income urban black community also points to a neighborhood that is distinct from Parkmont.[16] Although some of Parkmont's black residents struggle to pay their bills and some have lost their homes to foreclosure, very few are living in poverty. Additionally, pioneers' beliefs that the second wave blacks are inconsiderate toward neighbors and have a poor sense of community standards does not mean that a sizable share of Parkmont's residents would be considered "street" in the manner that Anderson describes. In Anderson's study, the presence of "street families" in the neighborhood is more extreme and omnipresent:

> Some people tend toward self-destructive behavior; many street-oriented women are crack-addicted ("on the pipe"), alcoholic, or involved in complicated relationships with men who abuse them....The seeming intractability of their situation, caused in large part by the lack of well-paying

---

14. Pattillo-McCoy's case study (1999) of the black middle-class enclave of Groveland is a strong contrast to Parkmont in terms of neighborhood type and subject matter. Parkmont is newly integrated, working class, and has few social connections among black residents, while Groveland has long been segregated, is middle class, and epitomizes life in established, close-knit black communities. Considering the differences between these neighborhoods is useful for understanding differences in social dynamics in black communities.

15. Pattillo-McCoy (1999, 70).

16. Above all others, Anderson and his works have provided a framework for understanding cultural divisions that exist within black communities. I am indebted to him for his focus on this topic and his courage and ability to convey such controversial ideas to readers.

jobs and persistence of racial discrimination, has engendered deep-seated bitterness and anger in many of the most desperate and poorest blacks, especially young people.[17]

Parkmont's pioneers are certainly not poor, but neither are they privileged in any absolute terms. This is not to say that the pioneers started out in life with nothing before reaching Parkmont, although some residents could be described in this way. But generally, in terms of socioeconomic status, most pioneers are working-class people who are better off than the average black family residing in the inner city.

To an outsider, it may seem that Parkmont's striving pioneers have arrived, but they have also been forced into the unfamiliar situation of entering a new community without the comfort of friends, family, and a familiar cultural milieu. Blacks who leave rough neighborhoods to move into white areas in the city may not do so under conditions that highlight the need for strong social ties. In making the move to Parkmont, pioneers made a trade-off because in a modern mass society where social networks seem increasingly unnecessary for a satisfying home life, they believed that the peace, safety, and quality of life would outweigh the absence of long-standing social ties with other families. However, the potential for white flight in Parkmont has left pioneers especially vulnerable to the forces of neighborhood resegregation, decline, and social distrust. In Parkmont, two specific sets of conditions have elevated the need for strong neighbor networks and social structures. First, pioneers must work long and unusual hours to make ends meet and need community members to help supervise children, maintain streets and homes, and organize the community to deal with local problems. Second, pioneers who relocate to white neighborhoods are heavily focused on the community as a financial investment. They have made great economic and social sacrifices to buy homes there and are having an extremely hard time watching the neighborhood slip away. To them, a home in Parkmont represented a chance to live in a mixed community, safe from serious crime, and with neighbors who share their desire for a quiet, well-kept, orderly, considerate environment.

Modern White Flight and Interracial Residential Lives

White flight conjures up images of overt white prejudice and community opposition of the 1940s, 1950s, and 1960s,[18] but it may be less obviously associated

---

17. Anderson (1999, 45).
18. Kruse (2005).

with contemporary urban change. This orientation to the past makes sense given that many blacks have suburbanized in recent years, and some urban neighborhoods have experienced increases in white population as whites have moved into central city neighborhoods to gentrify or live in high-rise luxury condos. However, these optimistic and highly publicized patterns are modest compared to the more dominant urban migration pattern of white flight, which remains a common phenomenon in many cities. Between 1990 and 2000, the one hundred largest U.S. cities lost extremely large shares of white population with whites in almost half of these cities losing "majority status."[19]

When cities lose white population, neighborhoods also experience racial turnover. One might imagine that white flight begins with the out-migration of the elderly, who are generally seen as having more old-fashioned racial attitudes. Yet the more typical trajectory of change from a white neighborhood to a black one begins with the exodus of middle-aged and younger residents, especially those with school-aged children, followed by an increase in the population of black residents who replace them.[20] Then, for a period of time, new black residents coexist with elderly whites. As older whites die or relocate to retirement communities, new white residents fail to replace them and the neighborhood population becomes almost completely black.[21] Although accurate, this depiction of white flight provides only a surface description of the very important period of time during which older whites and blacks co-reside.

Aging populations tend to be unevenly distributed across cities, forming enclaves.[22] A relatively small group of sociologists and gerontologists has focused on community-related factors that affect the elderly, including the effects of community settings and "elderly spaces" (e.g., retirement versus age-heterogeneous communities) on fear of crime, sense of community, quality of life, and neighborhood satisfaction.[23] Yet many community studies of older people take place in formal retirement settings.[24] Although retirement community studies are enlightening, it is common for senior citizens to be "stayers," many of whom co-reside with blacks.[25] The stayers and pioneers of Parkmont share a common desire to have control over their moving decisions and lifestyles. For the majority of residents,

19. Berube (2001).

20. See Krase (1982) and Taub, Taylor, and Dunham (1984).

21. See Krase (1982) and Taub Taylor, and Dunham (1984).

22. See Bryan and Morrison (2004) and U.S. Department of Housing and Urban Development (1999).

23. See, respectively, Akers et al. (1987), Faircloth (2002), Carp (1976), and Ward, LaGory, and Sherman (1988).

24. See Hochschild (1973), Keith (1977) and Young (1998).

25. See Wacquant (1997) for a critique of urban ethnographies that highlight extreme aspects of city life rather than more common urban phenomena.

living in this racially changing community is the result of a careful consideration of residential choices and a sense of ownership over their role as primary decision makers for themselves and their families.

The Realization of Mobility Preferences: The Role of Agency

The decision whether to move or to stay after white flight is just that: a decision. Researchers have long held that when making mobility decisions, residents weigh both the economic and noneconomic benefits and costs of moving by taking a good, hard look at where they live and what their other destination options are.[26] Yet scholarly literature and urban planning materials often take a passive tone when it comes to white flight, depicting such neighborhoods as naturally changing places where younger whites have simply moved on or "drifted away."[27] The view that racial aspects of white out-migration are of minimal import was echoed in an interview I conducted with a member of the city's planning commission. After listening to his comments about the prosperity of Parkmont and the "absolute minimum of problems" there, I asked about the obvious elephant in the room, Parkmont's racial change, and questioned him about why it had occurred. The city planner dismissed the topic, saying that Parkmont's racial change was "just migration patterns of people in this city."

These more passive formulations of the motives behind white flight are similar to ideas put forth by sociology's human ecology perspective, a paradigm that draws parallels between urban patterns and those processes that occur in the natural world (e.g., populations invade and dominate neighborhoods in the same manner that different species of plant or animal life compete to dominate habitats). Though today it is complemented by other theoretical points of view (e.g., new urban sociology or political economy),[28] human ecology continues to be an influential perspective and promotes the idea that the white suburbanization patterns are fully explained by "simple racial succession" factors related to variations in local housing stock and racial differences in housing affordability.[29]

As far as elderly white stayers' choices are concerned, sociological models of white flight that are grounded in the human ecology perspective suggest that

---

26. DeJong and Gardner (1981).
27. Bryan and Morrison (2004). See Meyer (2001), Taub, Taylor, and Dunham (1984), and Yinger (1995) for evidence of racial factors related to neighborhood change. See Aldrich (1975) and Lauria (1998) for an emphasis on the role of nonracial factors.
28. Woldoff and Gerber (2007).
29. Bickford (1997).

whites who remain in a community after a racial transition are there because they are economically disadvantaged. These whites are left behind by their counterparts who are better able to compete to realize the typical preference among whites to live in a majority-white neighborhood.

In addition to the economic competitiveness explanation for why some whites are left behind after white flight, it is also important to note that across many cultures, both Western and non-Western, societies hold negative stereotypes about the elderly, and people often pity them.[30] A common conception of older people, and one that is reinforced in popular culture and media, is that they are vulnerable in terms of their risk of suffering from health problems, injury, isolation, and criminal victimization. This characterization may be extended and applied to older people's mobility decisions. Stereotypes of the elderly as submissive, fragile, childlike, and passive[31] may also be reasons that this group is neglected or painted with too broad a brush in urban research on white flight and neighborhood transitions.

Like their white counterparts, black pioneers make decisions about where to live. Neighborhood integration partially occurs because of a process of self-selection by which the members of a minority group who have the resources and preference to live in a predominantly white or integrated community act to make it happen. On a structural level, when nonpoor black residents choose to exit ghettos, they take part in the creation, maintenance, and reproduction of community social inequalities.[32] However, for blacks living in segregated cities, the decision to move is a struggle for family survival, and the move to a white community holds the promise of better schools, less crime and disorder, and increased wealth, as well as social integration and social capital for children in the form of more normalized and frequent contacts with people outside of their own ethnic group. Yet unlike whites, who move in order to access better circumstances in other *white* neighborhoods, black pioneers' mobility decisions are complicated by the move across racial lines. This has the potential to create dissociation between some aspects of the new neighborhood cultural milieu, where pioneers may share common ground with whites but must also contend with the politically and socially charged issue of racial identity. Because of this possible dissociation between racial identity and aspects of culture, the way pioneers experience community integration and later resegregation calls for an in-depth

30. See Cuddy and Fiske (2002) and Cuddy, Norton, and Fiske (2005). Research on pan-cultural ageism suggests that stereotypes about the elderly (e.g., sweet/warm or feeble/incompetent) can even be found in collectivist cultures (e.g., Asia). Some research shows that these cultures actually may hold more negative views of the elderly than are found in the U.S.

31. Giles and Reid (2005).

32. Wacquant and Wilson (1989) have argued this point.

cultural understanding of the role of agency, in combination with structural constraints.

Since the 1970s, a growing number of urban scholars have departed from the strict ecological and life-cycle models of demographic change, emphasizing the need to more deeply understand the role of agency, racial preferences, and decision making as key aspects of residential life.[33] An exciting stream of qualitative urban community studies has focused on low-income populations and long-time black communities, documenting the ways that residents themselves understand their neighborhoods.[34] This research has provided insights into the diverse cultures and subcultures that characterize neighborhood life and citizens' active participation in their residential worlds, but the experience of white flight has not been a central topic of such investigations. Segregation scholarship asserts that in-depth interviews are a crucial research step for understanding how groups understand, justify, and experience their residential preferences.[35] At the same time that researchers want to better understand the role of choice in where people move, we must also acknowledge that few people desire or can afford to constantly change neighborhoods. In the wake of their choice to live in Parkmont, stayers and pioneers have learned that their agency is not inexhaustible, and that they have to live with what happens next.

Pioneers Taking the Leap: A Practical Transition and the Search for Integration

Many of Parkmont's pioneers have municipal jobs or else work in health care. Despite these relatively good jobs, one pioneer told me that many struggle a bit with expenses depending on "whether they have one or two incomes in the house." Before moving to Parkmont, when pioneers first initiated the search for new homes in better communities, many worried about their chances of finding a desirable neighborhood that would be located in the city for their jobs and that also would fit their need to adhere to a tight budget.

A typical pioneer story is that of Anne Jackson, a fifty-five-year-old operating room nurse and a mother of three. In 1996, she moved to Parkmont with her husband and her daughter, Carla. Carla, now twenty-four, is a social worker. She and her newborn baby continue to live with Anne. In the living room, I held Anne's granddaughter and listened as Anne explained her decision to "to take

---

33. See Charles (2006) and Krysan (2002).
34. See Anderson (1999), Duneier (1999), Freeman (2006), McRoberts (2003), Pattillo-McCoy (1999), and Venkatesh (1997).
35. Charles (2003).

the leap" into homeownership in Parkmont. Financially, it was a bit of a stretch for them, but she felt ready to take the chance that they could get by. Anne described her opinion of the people in her old neighborhood and whether they had the ability to make the same move: "I think it was a choice. They didn't know if they could make it financially. It's just a chance you have to take, and I knew that I could. Financially, I could just afford to buy the house, and I was ecstatic and happy about that."

As Anne has indicated, many pioneers had to stretch their finances to buy a home in Parkmont. For instance, many reported that Parkmont would have been an impossible destination without the option of tapping into mortgage programs and incentives provided by the military or their jobs. Most pioneers avoided the worst pitfalls of predatory lending, and many lamented to me that they had not qualified for the programs that target low-income, first-time homeowners. In buying a home, it was common for pioneers to have confined their search to the city limits since many have jobs that require them to reside in city neighborhoods. Even those who were not constrained in this way were still tied to the city by their practical need to be close to family and friends, as well as their jobs and churches. And for some pioneers, city neighborhoods provided the only affordable option for housing that they could even imagine.

When I first met Erma Williams, the sixty-seven-year-old working nurse had been living in her immaculate Parkmont row house for ten years. She moved to Parkmont alone, but has since taken in her elderly mother, a common lifestyle transition among Parkmont's black families. As a young woman, Erma was a single mother who later got married and bought her own house, but when her marriage ended she went back to renting in a black neighborhood. Located close to her job and shopping and stocked with affordable houses, Parkmont seemed like a good investment and offered the peaceful, orderly environment she wanted:

> I liked this neighborhood because it was close to work for me, so it was easy to get back and forth to work. So this neighborhood was important to me. I just drove around and used a realtor. It was convenient for work, and you had shopping that wasn't too far away and a couple of restaurants....I just thought it was a good choice because I was living alone at the time. My old neighborhood was different. If you're thinking about buying a home, then you want something that is going to appreciate in value. And I thought, since my old area was an older neighborhood, the houses here would hold value a little bit longer than a house would back there....It was the right price, and that just sealed the deal. I like the look of the neighborhood, how people try to keep their properties up. I like the back where there's no people around you. And guess what?

I've been here ten years, and I've never been to that creek, but people walk down there!

In the past few decades, the city's neighborhoods seem to have divided into two groups. There are the white or integrated areas that have gentrified and are now sprinkled with trendy stores, cafés, restaurants, bars, and condos. The properties in such neighborhoods can be prohibitively expensive, less family-friendly, and are usually off the radars of urban working-class blacks. The other prominent neighborhood type is the black segregated neighborhood that is plagued by poor schools, violent crime, physical decay, and abandonment. These are the neighborhoods from which pioneers are fleeing or are trying to avoid. It is in this housing climate that many of the city's black working-class citizens search for homes. With good jobs, close-knit families, and high hopes, pioneers carefully managed their finances to buy a home in a better place. So when large numbers of Parkmont houses went on the market and a few black families began moving in, the working-class blacks in nearby segregated communities took notice. This cohort of pioneers drove around on their own and with realtors and would happen upon "for sale" signs.[36] Then, usually through traditional mortgages, mortgage assistance programs that target members of the former or active military, or through "good neighbor next door" programs aimed at those who hold public servant jobs in the city (e.g., teacher, law enforcement officer, firefighter, EMT, and nurse), pioneers would begin the process of purchasing their first homes.

Pioneers were well aware that they were entering a white neighborhood, and for many, the choice of Parkmont was explicitly tied to the desire to raise their children in an integrated environment. Janice O'Neil, a thirty-seven-year-old nurse, moved to Parkmont with her husband, a heavy equipment operator who works for the city. Now a divorced mother of two, Janice personifies the views of many pioneer parents. Here, she described the role of racial composition in selecting Parkmont as a destination:

> It was all white....A lot of it is white flight, which is bad because part of the reason—when I've chosen or looked for places to settle down—I wanted a mixed neighborhood. I didn't want my kids in a predominantly black neighborhood because the world isn't predominantly black. I felt like they needed to interact with people of other ethnicities without feeling intimidated or anything. I wanted to move somewhere that was mixed.

It is noteworthy that Janice moved to Parkmont in the late 1990s after many pioneers had already arrived. By then, there was a visible black presence in the

---

36. According to Farley (1996), in searching for housing, blacks are less likely than whites to use real estate brokers and are more likely than whites to rely on informal search strategies such as conversations with friends, advertisements, and driving through neighborhoods.

homes, at the school, and on the strip where they patronized businesses and waited for the bus to go downtown. The importance of an apparent black population in attracting black residents is notable given that research on residential preferences shows that blacks are especially open to moving into white neighborhoods when their group is already represented in nontrivial numbers.[37] More highly educated blacks such as Janice (e.g., those with more than a high school degree), who are opposed to living in segregated black neighborhoods, commonly cite "diversity" and living with a "mixture" as reasons for their preference for neighborhood integration.[38]

In explaining their reasons for choosing Parkmont, pioneers Lamar and Clarice Nellis also highlighted the significance of teaching their son to feel socially and culturally comfortable with both blacks and whites. Lamar discussed his family's decision to move to a white community and the importance that he and his wife place on teaching their son to successfully adapt to or "sway" in white environments. This concept of swaying or "cross-cultural code-switching"[39] refers to the ability of individuals to intentionally modify their behaviors to accommodate social norms in new settings. Lamar elaborated:

> I feel that he should be exposed to certain elements because of the world we live in. But it's up to us, as parents, to teach him the difference. I'll put this out there, being African American, you have to understand how to sway. It's difficult. It's downright hard understanding the whole cultural aspect of it, and then understanding the terminology, understanding the code of ethics. I want him to have the best of both worlds.

One Sunday, I interviewed pioneer Nina Jones, a thirty-year-old first-grade teacher at Lombard. On her day off, she was wearing a colorful headscarf to protect her hairstyle until she was ready to go out. She is now married and has a baby son, but like many black women in Parkmont, she first purchased her home when she was still single. In general, the pioneers are distinct from the second wave of black Parkmont residents because they arrived in Parkmont with the knowledge that it was an integrating neighborhood that was recently all white. Many, like Nina, reported that the prospect of racial integration was a key feature that attracted them to the community:

> I don't want to just be in an all-black neighborhood. I guess from me just growing up, coming down here for school. Where we were, at the

---

37. Krysan and Farley (2002).
38. Krysan and Farley (2002).
39. See Molinsky (2007) and Pattillo-McCoy (1999).

time, Westside, was all-black, and then you come up here. It was nice. It was a nice mix. And then I went to a mixed college....I definitely want my son to be in an integrated area because that's the way of the world. When he gets older, he needs to be able to interact with everybody, and it's all different types of people. You can have the nicest white person, and you get the nastiest black person. But he needs to be able to know how to deal with all of them, and I want him in a place that's like that.

From the beginning, Nina wanted to live in an integrated community. She was excited about moving to Parkmont, a neighborhood she has known since she was eleven years old when she was bused in as a student to attend Lombard from fifth though twelfth grades. Nina's mother, also a teacher, carefully watched over her and made special efforts to send her to Lombard: "My mom didn't let me play outside. I was in the house, in the books, doing crafts." Nina was eager to start her career and teach at her alma mater, but finding an affordable home in an integrated community was difficult. As a public school teacher in the city, she was forced by the school district's residency requirements to purchase a home in a city neighborhood. For a single black woman just beginning a career as a teacher, few affordable integrated neighborhoods were available to Nina in the city, and, other than Parkmont, none was located near Lombard.

Joy Parker, a forty-two-year-old Jamaican "dietary hostess" at a hospital, moved to Parkmont from a nearby black segregated area to achieve social mobility, which to her, meant integration:

> I was living with my mama at that time, so I grew older, and I got out on my own....Nobody want to live in that same neighborhood. They wanna go higher. In fact, I'm trying to go to [the suburbs] now. Oh, I would love to. I want to go to different neighborhoods, better neighborhoods. After a while, it's going to be all-black around here.

When I asked Joy to elaborate on her concerns about Parkmont becoming an all-black neighborhood, she explained her suspicion that racial segregation leads to crime and a lack of neighbor involvement, which she fears could eventually take over in Parkmont.

During my interview with forty-two-year-old Sonya McCall, a postal worker and single mother, five family members sat around a large-screen television, enjoying the discussion of the changes they have observed in Parkmont. Sonya purchased her home from a young white couple with a child. She now lives in Parkmont with her daughter and her elderly father, who moved in after his wife passed away and he was diagnosed with cancer and diabetes. Like many pioneers, Sonya sought

to raise her daughter in an integrated environment, which she equates with better schools. Even though Sonya originally lived very close by in a black segregated
community, Parkmont once seemed a world away to her:

> I thought it would be a little better than my old neighborhood. I have
> one daughter, and I thought the school system would be better. As far
> as raising her up, I thought it would be better to just bring her up in
> a racial [integrated] neighborhood, instead of just all black....Every-
> thing seemed so far 'cause I had never been up here, and I was like, "Oh,
> this looks like a nice neighborhood." My friend said, "It's out of the way.
> I think you need to move up there." And when she moved, that's when
> I seen like a couple of blacks, and I said, "Okay."

On the topic of white flight, all of the pioneers I interviewed said they were
disturbed by Parkmont's rapid loss of white population. However, for some,
like Erma Williams, the older nurse mentioned in the beginning of this chapter,
race was more incidental. Like so many pioneers, Erma knew very few facts about
the attractive, integrated neighborhood. She was bothered by the racial change,
but reported that her advanced age and lack of school-aged children made it less
of a concern than was true for other pioneer families. Much of the research on
black housing in cities emphasizes the role of institutional discrimination as a
cause of segregated housing outcomes, but the findings in Parkmont add to our
knowledge by pointing to the importance of the dual processes of white flight and
pioneers' conscious but constrained decision making. Many pioneers have jobs
that force them to live in the city, and to the best of their knowledge they have
selected a neighborhood that meets their criteria as far as convenience to family
and work, safety, schools, and affordability. Those who have jobs that allow them
to live in the suburbs either believe that they cannot afford such a move, find the
commute to the city to be too cumbersome, or in many cases they simply prefer
to be closer to their social networks in the city. The importance of social networks is notable for working-class blacks and striving blacks in general, who are
more likely than similar whites to have low-income family members and elderly
parents needing their assistance on a regular basis.[40] With their work constraints,
family obligations, and greater sense of collectivism, pioneers often make decisions that are distinct from those that whites with similar incomes might make.

Like the pioneers, the whites who remained in Parkmont have their own story
to tell. Within their social circles, the choice to stay in an integrating neighborhood was not a popular one. In this way, pioneers and stayers share a common

---

40. Heflin and Pattillo (2006).

experience: they selected Parkmont with purpose, watched it change, and then adapted.

Stayers Overcoming the Pressure to Move and Dealing with Racialized Crime Concerns

The United States Department of Housing and Urban Development (1999) has reported that, on average, elderly Americans are "among the best housed citizens." The report noted that most live in good homes that are affordable and in their preferred neighborhood, and it stated that most elderly people in the United States have the financial means to address housing problems as they arise. When asked why they chose to stay when so many of their neighbors were moving, some of Parkmont's stayers mentioned concerns about finances. However, a closer look at their responses showed that money was only one reason underlying the decision to remain in Parkmont, and it was not necessarily the most important one.

Aaron and Roberta Schneider, two "originals," provided me with a detailed list of explanations for their decision to stay in Parkmont. Both are concerned about their finances, but they also listed many other reasons for staying. Age presents a barrier. Like most stayers, Roberta and Aaron are more than eighty years old, and having lived in Parkmont for their entire adult lives, they feel too old to move. Their particular housing preferences also play a role in the decision to stay. They dislike the idea of apartment living, citing their use of the outdoor space in front of their home as antithetical to life in a condo. Many stayers demonstrated great pride in the rooms in their homes, the upkeep of their yards and patio spaces, and the treasured elements of décor that they would have to abandon were they to move to a small space. As with most stayers, the fact that the Schneiders viewed their housing situation in Parkmont as optimal is an important consideration in their decision to stay. Stayers' satisfaction with Parkmont also stemmed from their observing the outcomes of their friends and former neighbors. Many stayers reported that even now, years after the start of white flight, they continue to hear horror stories of regret from elderly movers who were living miserable lives of dependence and loss of control in retirement communities. Stayers often believed that the elderly people who left the neighborhood were filled with regret, and they boasted that many "leavers" have continued to visit, finding that Parkmont has remained a viable community for errands and shopping. These nonfinancial considerations have all validated the stayers' decisions to age in place.

Muffy Nussbaum described the pressure on her to move, but said that she has stayed because she loves her home and wants to maintain continuity in her lifestyle. Though financial affairs are often on her mind, she claimed that she really could afford to leave Parkmont. The problem is that any move from Parkmont would not be on her own terms:

> It's mine, and I am living within my means, and I like my little house. At this moment, I'm not thinking about moving because I don't know what the future is gonna bring with my job at the synagogue. My family kept asking me [about moving], and I finally got the courage to say, "This is where I can afford to live." If I could afford to live downtown, I would. Of course, I really *could* afford it, but then I would have to change my lifestyle—theater, dinner out.

According to Sadie Underwood, aged ninety, stayers often have the financial means to move, but simply prefer not to. Though she mentioned her own budget concerns as a hindrance to moving, Sadie said that she is planning to make the move soon because of her desire to be near extended family:

> I was thinking I would go to the [local retirement home]. They give you one meal, a dinner. But if I go there, I have nobody. I would be alone because my family lives an hour from here. If I move near them, I'll have my family. They feel that if I'm closer to them, I'll get out more because they'll see that I get out.

Sadie went on to identify some elderly neighbors who have not moved and some who have, explaining the complexities of their reasoning:

> Joanne isn't doing so good, but she said she's gonna die over here. She could—in all due respect—be in a nice retirement home. She has the means. I couldn't go to a facility like she could afford, but hopefully I will go to one, and probably it will be nearby. Leo and Gladys, I think they could afford to go, but I think they *want* to stay....Mrs. Brody, she just moved around a month ago to an apartment house not far from here. When her neighbor moved, I don't think she wanted to stay. And her sons didn't want her to stay here, especially if her neighbor wasn't there because she lived by herself. And she wasn't in the best of health either.

Some elderly stayers on fixed incomes have been priced out of the housing and neighborhood options that might have been appealing enough to draw them away from their homes and community. Even so, many stayers had housing choices outside of Parkmont within their reach, but instead chose to remain at home. In sum, the role of finances should not be minimized, but economic constraints are only a small part of the story for stayers, most of whom have the means to live in a "whiter" place. In fact, for many staying in Parkmont was not a sad fate, but a hard-won victory. Nearly all of the stayers in Parkmont have overcome enormous amounts of pressure to move. In general, the stayers' adult children were the key source of this pressure. On many occasions, I informally talked to the stayers' children; usually, they would interrogate me for a while, fearful that I was an intruder, salesperson, or scam artist seeking to take advantage of their elderly parents. Many adult children seemed to feel guilty or embarrassed about their white elderly parents living alone in a black neighborhood. The adult children who live out of state are less able to easily check up on their frail, elderly parents and were especially vocal about wanting them to move out of Parkmont. In addition to fears about their parents falling down or becoming ill, they worried about vulnerability to scams and criminal victimization. For instance, on several occasions protective adult children would initially try to intervene during my interview sessions. In such instances, they would interrogate me about my motives, and many times they would attempt to silence their parents in some way, editing, interrupting, correcting, and censoring the stayers' responses to my questions.

Rose Berger used the word "it" to refer to the coded language she uses when she guardedly discusses the familiar topic of moving from Parkmont:

> My sons said, "Let's talk about 'it.'" I said, "Well, what do you have to say to us?" And that's when they said, "You should think about it." So I said to them, "What is it that you're going to tell us?" And the older son said he wants to get some information for us. And I said, "That's all right. You can get information." But I said, "Just bear in mind, my checkbook is locked away, and I'm not signing anything."

Despite urgings from loved ones, nearly all of the stayers I met told me several stories about how they have actively resisted the pressure to move. Rena Grubman was not one to sugarcoat the challenges of aging in Parkmont, but she told me that her sons' nagging has only made aging in place worse. Although she appreciates their good intentions, she said that staving off her sons is an additional and unnecessary burden when she simply wants to maintain the routines of her life: "I'm lucky that I have friends that don't mind picking me up to play bridge and shop.... Both sons wanted me to move because they were afraid of the steps and want me to be in an apartment and with other people my age to socialize more."

Some stayers have not experienced a great deal of family pressure yet, but that does not stop them from fearing that their children will involuntarily extract them from Parkmont. To avoid potential confrontations about moving, many stayers have devised defensive strategies for interacting with their adult children. These often involve maintaining a veil of secrecy about anything that might cause their children to question their ability to live alone, such as problems with their home or their health. When asked if her son has ever pressured her to move, one stayer described how she dodges her son's potential imposition: "I'm very independent. I never complain to him. I just had a cataract operation. I didn't even tell him until it was over with. 'Cause a lot of my friends, they call their children, kvetching [the Yiddish word for complaining] or whatever. I would never do that."

However powerful their children's pressure to move has been, the insistence that Parkmont has become an inappropriate home for white elderly people extends far beyond concerned family members. Friends and former neighbors have been actively interested in stayers' residential choices and are extremely vocal in their disapproval of stayers' decisions to remain in Parkmont, often citing crime and race-based reasons.

Nobel laureate Gunnar Myrdal (1944, 622–23) argued that "informal social pressure from whites" plays a key role in residential segregation. When I asked about the decision to stay, elderly residents typically framed their answers in terms of their personal feelings of safety from crime. Since so many of their friends and family members have repeatedly expressed race-based and crime-related fears to them, stayers often assumed that I was concerned about these issues as well. In fact, stayers' comments intertwined the topics of race and crime so much that the two were analytically inextricable. According to stayers, friends, neighbors, and relatives rarely discussed race in an open manner when trying to convince them to move. Instead, they would try to persuade stayers to move by raising the issue in terms of concerns about health, loneliness, and crime. As evidence of the duplicity of their loved ones, stayers often cited the timing of their loved ones' sudden interest. Why had they become concerned just as blacks started moving in? Why had they started pressuring them to move away when stayers were still in good health and their spouses remained alive? With the population change so visible in the complexions of the residents, stayers had many discussions about race over the years, and they insisted that the pressure to move was anchored to racialized views about crime.

Dolores Duskin is seventy-two, and like many stayers she described friends who tried to convince her and her eighty-nine-year-old husband, Warren, to move. She detailed her friends' remarks, which she believes connect Parkmont's racial change to a fear of crime:

> I hear them saying, "You should not be there." They don't like us living here. My old neighbor said something about that. I don't even think he likes to come to Parkmont because he never comes now, and he will not go downtown. It annoys me because there's nothing wrong with the neighborhood that I see. If the conditions were terrible over here,

I wouldn't be here. We hear about crime occasionally in the neighborhood. Occasionally. Chitter chatter.

Parkmont's elderly stayers frequently reported that they found the disapproving comments about their longtime community to be insulting. They believe that their friends' concerns are unfounded and racially motivated. Many stayers acknowledged that they had altered their lifestyles in response to stories they had heard about crimes in the neighborhood, but very few reported that serious violence was a source of worry. Gerri Holtzman described her friends' fears as irrational, and offered a typical view that illustrates stayers' determination to adapt to the changes in the neighborhood environment while dealing with the increased feelings of vulnerability that have accompanied aging:

> There's a lot of people that moved away that won't come to Parkmont. They're afraid. It's amazing. There *is* some crime. In the row of stores where the strip is, a woman from the condos went to a cleaning establishment there, and she was knocked down, and her bag was stolen. So, my friend that lives at the condos is afraid to use it. I said, "There's crimes all over. Why should you feel afraid to come here?" Well, I live differently, too. When I come home, if I'm going out at night, I take my charge card and any checks in my pocketbook. I feel that if anything happens—because there are times—it happens. It happens everywhere. My car was stolen twice, too. My friend's car was stolen from here. She wouldn't come back after that.

Similarly, eighty-two-year-old "original" resident Aaron Schneider emphasized that as he aged and the city's crime problems worsened, he began to place reasonable limits on his behavior to guard against victimization. However, Aaron also maintained that he is not fearful because the crime in other parts of the city is far more serious, and even then, the crime tends to be intraracial and thus not a threat to whites: "Most of these killings are fights. It's all between themselves."

Thus, stayers have not naively buried their heads in the sand, but nor do they live a carefree life in Parkmont. They have adjusted their lifestyles to deal with being older in a changing city neighborhood. Because of the social changes that have occurred in their lifetimes, they perceive crime to be a society-wide problem that is especially severe in cities, but is relatively minor in Parkmont.

A common reaction to their friends' fears is that "crime is everywhere" and the commission of criminal acts is not restricted to black people and urban neighborhoods. Susan Waxman, whose deceased husband was the cantor (a musical prayer leader during religious services) at the local synagogue, recognized the racial changes in Parkmont, but insisted that the influx of black residents did not translate into danger. She defended Parkmont in a fashion similar to many stayers:

> Of course, we are the minority here now. It's still not a bad neighbor-hood. There are people that think it's a bad neighborhood. I understand people don't frequent the restaurants. I am not comfortable going out late at night by myself, but my street is fine. Look, if your intent is to do bad, it's just part of your personality. Anyone can hop into a car and go anywhere. You can do bad in the suburbs, too.

Leo Katz's reaction to the issue of crime in Parkmont was similar to many other stayers: urban crime is inescapable. He has struggled to explain this to his daughter, who has been urging him to move. According to Leo, his desire to stay in his home has persisted despite the fact that his daughter has been "starting in" on him:

> My daughter lives in Florida. She wants us there. She started in a couple years ago. She's worried about us. We have no other family here. We have absolutely nobody. She's afraid we can get stuck, and there's just nobody here for us if we fall or whatever, but I like the house, the area. It's okay. You know, like everywhere, crime's getting greater.

Why They Stay: Independence, Sentimental Attachment, and Livability

Given the barrage of people who pressure them to move, Parkmont's stayers have obviously had to carefully consider their decision to stay. Stayers easily articulated a range of "pull" factors that led them to value their life in Parkmont. Perhaps the simplest of these factors is the hassle involved in moving at an advanced age. As Leo Katz explained, moving is "too much trouble," and staying is "just easier":

> Inertia. The whole prospect of moving is scary. We talk to people who move, and they say if you survive the move, you're lucky. We ought to be moving someplace. It's getting difficult to take care of. There's not much to take care of, but then you begin to neglect things. The house doesn't look terrible, but it doesn't look like it should.

Many other elderly whites stay because they enjoy the independence and free-dom to come and go. This is especially true for those who drive, as one widowed stayer explained:

> I drive. That's my independence. I go to the supermarket. I take them, too—the ones that live around here. I didn't always have a car. I had a

terrific husband. He would have to take me shopping all the time, and he hated it. He bought me a used car, which was very nice, and he says, "Now, you can go shopping." And I had my license to drive, and he left the car there, and I was afraid to drive it. It was sitting there for two weeks, and I didn't use it. I thought, "He means business." So, I got in it, went around the corner, and I loved it.

For stayers who are still able to drive, Parkmont's proximity to stores means that they can comfortably limit their driving to short distances during the day and still do errands and be social. As Leo Katz noted: "It's convenient. We can drive in town. Also, it's close to stores and shopping. Actually, they closed the supermarket. I used to go there all the time, but they closed that. We're close to the near suburbs. I am driving, but driving gets more limited." Several stayers who have remained involved in cultural activities find that Parkmont's central location makes driving to events more manageable. Leo and Gladys told me the details of their activities:

> GLADYS: We keep busy. We go to the JCC (Jewish Community Center). There are different programs: opera, art, current affairs, a variety. And the teachers are very good. They're professors.
> LEO: We're big moviegoers. We like to go in town to the theaters. We drive downtown. We have subscriptions to a couple of theater companies in town and one in the suburbs.

However, for some of the widows who do not drive, Parkmont offers less and less, especially with fewer friends around. As Sadie Underwood said:

> At least I can walk around, because I don't use buses anymore. If I'm okay, I go up to the shopping center, but I can't always do it. Once in a while, when I'm up to it, I do it. I used to walk it three or four times a day, and it was nothing. And when the supermarket was there? I used to push the cart. It was nothing. The library, that's my godsend. I never drove because my husband took me everywhere. And my sister, she drove, and my friends all drove, so I never had any problems. But now?

Those who do not drive and have no children are more dependent on what is available in Parkmont, and many have been forced to use the new neighborhood businesses that seem foreign to them. For instance, Joanne explained that her local hair salon closed its doors, and she now has to have her hair done at the only beauty salon in walking distance. As we sat outside on the patio, she whispered: "I get my hair done at a black hair salon. I was afraid to go there, and I told them that when I went in. The girl asked why, and I said, "Because I'm white." You know what? The girl said they never wanted to hear me say that again. They give me free cuts sometimes and won't take my money."

At eighty-nine and eighty-seven, Lorna and Abe Rothman were the oldest stayers I interviewed, and they vehemently announced that they had no plans to move. Their home was decorated with family photos, Jewish artifacts, and with teddy bears wearing Jewish symbols, such as the Star of David. Lorna and Abe explained in detail that their home holds many fond memories of marriage, raising children, and activities at the synagogue located a few doors down the block. They discussed the practicality of keeping their beloved home, as well as the ways in which they have adapted their lives in order to extend their remaining time in Parkmont and maintain a sense of independence:

> ABE: As the children got older, people moved to apartments. That's why they're in condos. They don't need a house anymore.
>
> LORNA: Basically, we need a house. Our younger son's in Israel, and his family are in Israel. Our granddaughters come here, and his wife comes here. My older son enjoys coming here with his family. They love coming here because for our boys, this was their home.
>
> ABE: Over the years, for the synagogue, the cantors came to stay here.
>
> LORNA: For holidays. We're religious. And I love my home. I put a lot into it. The steps did bother me because I had a hip replacement, but now I walk. And if I feel I'm tired, I crawl like a pussycat up and down the steps. I do my own laundry. Sometimes, the cleaning girl will do it, but she'll always bring it up because I can't carry a heavy basket with my hip.
>
> ABE: And I've learned to do the laundry [laughs].
>
> LORNA: He's not supposed to carry anything either. I wash it myself. I do my own cooking.
>
> ABE: Yeah. It's terrific. We'll invite you over for dinner some night.
>
> R. W.: Any challenges to living alone here?
>
> LORNA: No. Not really. I have a very good neighbor. She's here forty years. She helps if we need a favor, like for her to take me [to see him] when he's in the hospital. She took me, but other than that I don't drive. And we have nice friendships here, and even our Italian woman neighbor is friendly. Yeah, because we're the old-timers.

Even though stayers have had to adjust their lifestyles both within their homes and within Parkmont, their sentimental attachment to their homes remains strong. For instance, although Sadie Underwood told me that she has scaled back her lifestyle to the point that it is hardly comparable to her younger years in Parkmont, she repeatedly emphasized how much her home has meant to her: "I never wanted to move. Never. I love my home. No matter where I went. We took nice vacations, and when I would come back from a vacation and open my door, I would say to my husband, 'Home, sweet home.' I loved my home. I loved it."

Compared to many other communities, Parkmont has several advantages for those who have decided to age in place. Though many older residents mentioned that they have friends and relatives who drive them places when needed, shop for them, and run their errands, the fact that Parkmont is centrally located and adjacent to the strip makes it ideal for people who have limited transportation options. In general, stayers find that this urban neighborhood meets their needs and makes them feel more empowered and less dependent. Staying in their original homes and neighborhood also accommodates stayers' need for stability. In addition, their location is close enough to family and friends that they get basic needs met, while minimizing their burden on others and ensuring a continued social life in a setting that is less artificial than a retirement community. Thus, Parkmont is a neighborhood that has *allowed* these residents to age in place and extend the period of time that they live independently with privacy and control over their personal and home lives.

As Joe mentioned, he frequently walks to the park to play golf. He also strolls to the strip to make purchases from the pharmacy and have breakfast. Rena reported that she enjoys her trips downtown to the theater with friends and participating in a theater group and travel club, but she also attends synagogue functions in the community, eats at the Grapevine diner, and enjoys visits from her son, who teaches at the local school and frequently checks on her. Joanne also spoke of her Parkmont rituals of eating at the Grapevine, shopping at local stores, getting her hair done, and awaiting visits from her younger friend who helps her shop. Both Joanne and Joe especially appreciate the simple pleasure of sitting outside on their patios in warm weather, which gives them opportunities to socialize with neighbors, both old and new. For instance, Joanne, a retired professional dancer and dance instructor, told me how much she looks forward to interacting with the new children who have moved onto the block: "They have boom boxes. I love the music and excitement. I can't dance anymore, but I tell them what to do, and they dance for me."

The Two Groups' Reactions to the Changes

Both the stayers and pioneers actively chose Parkmont to be their home and both seemed pleased that they were able to realize their goals, whether those goals were a continued period of familiar independent living or a better neighborhood that is relatively safe and orderly. However, over time, as Parkmont's racial change became more complete, resegregation became a source of disappointment for both groups. Since white flight occurred rather quickly, the stayers and the pioneers found themselves trying to make sense of what happened and struggling to understand the ways that racial prejudice has affected their lives and residential aspirations.

Stayers, many of whom have faced continuous criticism for the decision to remain in a black neighborhood, have taken comfort in their experiential knowledge of the truth about the pioneers, which is that they are decent people and good neighbors. Yet they also expressed a sense of loss regarding the close-knit community that had characterized Parkmont for so long. The pioneers' feelings about Parkmont partially reflect gratitude about being safe from the violence in their old neighborhoods, but they also feel resentful and agitated by white flight, which continues to serve as a very real reminder that both individual and institutional acts of racial discrimination continue to directly impact the most important decisions in their lives. Additionally, as younger people with children, the pioneers could be said to be more future-oriented than the white stayers, who are at the end of their lives. Pioneers know that they have many decades ahead of them in Parkmont, so any threat to their financial investment, personal safety, and quality of life is not taken lightly.

Stayers Recognizing "Nice Blacks"

Speaking about moving caused intense discomfort for many stayers, who often became defensive about their own capabilities and lifestyles, and especially about the character of their new black neighbors. The sensitive nature of the topic of moving was most strongly manifested when I brought up the subject of Parkmont's racial change during interviews. It was not uncommon in these situations for stayers to outline the numerous ways that pioneers have defied negative stereotypes of black people and residents of black neighborhoods.

Stayers' positive views about Parkmont's black residents have bolstered their decisions to stay in the neighborhood. Elderly whites often described their black neighbors as "nice," and elaborated by providing me with social class indicators of their neighbors' decency, such as details about their cars, their employment status, their marital status, and where their children attend school. As Aaron Schneider told me:

> They're all working class. And they're not poor people. I mean, I don't know what they buy or what they save. They really all have good cars. They're all working. During the week, it's plenty of space to park....And a lot of these kids don't go to Lombard. I see a lot of school buses. On the other side, next door, she goes to private school.

Lorna and Abe Rothman concurred and mentioned that most black residents have respectable jobs and own well-maintained homes. As Abe said, "Some of them look nicer than the homes when the white people left. New doors, new windows, the lawns are well kept. The blacks are very nice. Professionals, government workers." Dolores Duskin admitted she has noticed some signs of decline in the appearance of the neighborhood and some blocks seem to be in better condition than others, but she did not attribute these changes to the fact that blacks had moved into the neighborhood. In fact, she expressed an extremely favorable opinion of the pioneers as neighbors: "Those that I know are extremely nice. You should see the lawns! They're incredible. It's still nice. The people are so nice. Everybody who walks by you says 'hello.' You know them, or you don't know them, but you say 'hello.'"

Stayers do not possess a self-conscious pride in their racial tolerance,[41] but take a more pragmatic approach to neighborhood change. They believe that those who disapprove of Parkmont are ignorant about the profile of the black population residing there. In their way, stayers do not fit stereotypes of elderly whites, with static, ignorant, and simplistic opinions of blacks. Forced to justify the decision to remain in their homes in a black neighborhood, stayers have given a great deal of thought to race relations in modern urban neighborhoods. Also, stayers' increased contact with black residents in Parkmont has resulted in an evolving and more nuanced set of views about race. Thus, white elderly stayers view themselves as far more sophisticated and less racist than those who left. This is not to say that they have always promoted racial integration or have not struggled with their own preexisting negative stereotypes of blacks. However, despite intimidation and pressure, stayers rejected the idea that racial change was reason enough to leave their homes.

In general, stayers consider Parkmont's pioneers to be very respectable citizens. Several researchers have studied the ways that social interaction affects one's views about respectability.[42] Elijah Anderson (1999, 38), referring to the many moral, hardworking blacks in extremely poor communities, framed this kind of labeling of residents as a distinction between families who are "street" (e.g., uneducated and alienated people who embrace a less mainstream set of values about legitimate work, abiding by the law, and moral decision making) and those who are "decent":

> Decent families tend to accept mainstream values more fully than street families, and they attempt to instill them in their children. Probably the

---

41. See Anderson (1999, 19) for a discussion of white middle-class people who take great pride in their identity as residents of an integrated community where racial harmony is the norm.

42. See, for example, Anderson (1978, 1999) and Duneier (1992).

most meaningful description of the mission of the decent family, as seen by members and outsiders alike, is to instill "backbone" and a sense of responsibility in its younger members. In their efforts toward this goal, decent parents are much more able and willing to ally themselves with outside institutions such as schools and churches. They value hard work and self-reliance and are willing to sacrifice for their children.

It might seem as if a street/decent distinction about black residents should have been even easier to make in Parkmont because it is not a poor community. However, Leo and Gladys Katz insisted that white outsiders (i.e., friends, relatives, and former neighbors) have great difficulty recognizing the decent nature of the pioneers. As Leo explained:

> The racial aspect is there. A lot of people who move, and at the JCC, their attitude is that "I'm not coming over there," because of the racial situation, because of the fear. I've discussed this with people. The fear is people who *live* here are not going to bother you, but they provide cover for others. In other words, when it was a white neighborhood, if some black hoodlums came wandering down the street, everybody would recognize them. Now, since it's a black neighborhood, they blend in. You can't differentiate between the respectable residents and the undesirables. You get that attitude.

Many stayers, like Joe Cassidy, pride themselves on having the savvy and open-mindedness to recognize the social class and cultural diversity within the city's black population. He explained to me that the more successful blacks are the ones who have moved to Parkmont: "All the whites moved when black people started coming. In the last ten years. There was a scarcity of houses for them, a successful black person. If they make 25 or 30K, they can move out of the ghetto and into a white area."

At the time of my interview with Lorna and Abe Rothman, Parkmont's synagogue had not yet closed its doors. Like most stayers, the Rothmans often had to listen to former neighbors' negative comments about the black presence in Parkmont. In their case, at synagogue or "shul" fellow congregants often expressed their concerns, both publicly and in private. According to the Rothmans, the disapproving comments were usually tied to fears about crime and were rooted in a generalized fear of black people, but these generalizations about black neighborhoods do not match the lived experience of stayers: "People have prejudice from years back. They say it's gonna become dangerous. I feel safe. In fact, all of the black people that moved in across the street are very friendly."

The efforts of friends, former neighbors, and family members to persuade stayers to move away tend to fail because they do not see white outsiders as credible or knowledgeable about Parkmont's pioneers nor about the current day-to-day life in Parkmont. Stayers have continued to live autonomous lives in their own homes and have negotiated relationships with their black neighbors. Theirs is not a stagnant or naïve perspective on race, crime, and social class, so they tend to be dismissive of the worries expressed by their friends and relatives. Rather, stayers' discussions of their experiences with black residents and their lack of alarm is offered as evidence to outsiders whom they believe have an ignorant, unsophisticated perception of black neighborhoods, Parkmont, and their new black neighbors. Leo Katz elaborated:

> You can't escape the racial aspect. If anybody thinks that racism is disappearing in America, they're delusional. Jews have been much more genteel. When the blacks moved into the Italian neighborhood down the hill, there were repercussions. One black family moved there and had police protection for six months. I don't think that Jews are any less racist than Italians. They're just not likely to be confrontational. They just quietly packed up and left. That's all.

Indeed, stayers' satisfaction with their homes and residential experiences necessitates an ability to engage in "urban learning"[43] wherein residents acquire and use clues about their neighbors' appearance, location, and behavior to define situations. Senior citizens, on average, have less tolerant views about a variety of race-related issues,[44] but for Parkmont's stayers, residential integration has encouraged more refined understandings of blacks. Older populations who choose to stay in integrating communities cannot live in peace while simultaneously succumbing to the fears and suspicions of their families and former neighbors.

As retirees, stayers spend more time at home than their younger white counterparts and have had ample opportunity to observe the new neighbors. The appearance of pioneers' families, homes, clothing, cars, their respectable professions, and the simple fact that pioneers now live in Parkmont were all factors that set the stage for stayers to categorize their black neighbors as good, decent people.

Pioneers Dealing with Racism in Their Own Backyards
I expected people to move out, but not that fast.

—Ken Wilkinson, aged forty-seven

---

43. Lyn Lofland (1973, 96) used this term.
44. Taylor, Funk, and Craighill (2006).

It's changed as far as being a white neighborhood to being a black neighborhood. It changed. And this is something that I've said. I hope this doesn't hurt your feelings. It was just like the plague, like the plague was coming. Once the blacks started buying here, it's like the plague. I mean, when we came up here, it was nothing to have ten or twelve "for sale" signs on a block.

—Anne Jackson, aged fifty-five

On a macro-level, suburban development, taxes, suburbanization of jobs, and aging housing stock in the city are all factors that contribute to white flight.[45] However, the pioneers are suspicious of people who try to argue that nonracial factors were the main source of Parkmont's white flight. In general, the pioneers are very sensitive to racial issues and reject the idea that race played a trivial role in white residents' decisions to flee. As Joy Parker said, the whites "probably think that too much black people moving in. They probably think that it will be a problem." This is not to say that the pioneers believe that race was the only trigger of white flight, but they suspect that nonracial factors only became critically important to whites when black families began to arrive. As Erma Williams said:

> There were "for sale" signs all over the place. You couldn't go a half a block without "for sale" signs. On this block, there wasn't that many "for sale" signs, but after I moved here, it was all up and down the block. I knew the neighborhood was in a process of changing, and I knew that it was changing over to African American because the stereotypically white families moved out because they are afraid to live with black families. They think crime will go up and property values will go down. If they would stay and support the neighborhood, I don't think it would be true. It won't turn over.

Like Erma, many pioneers blame racial prejudice for white flight, and they report that this is a topic that pioneers frequently discussed as they watched their white neighbors sell their homes.

Sonya McCall mentioned earlier that race was very much on her mind when she arrived in Parkmont. In addition to seeking an integrated environment for her child, she also decided to move here because her old neighborhood was "getting bad," and she wanted to transition out of her parents' home. However, after describing the white flight that had taken hold since her arrival, she told me that she now wants to leave Parkmont: "I was the second black on the block here and both my neighbors had 'for sale' signs as soon as I moved in. Both neighbors

---

45. Blakeslee (1978).

put the 'for sale' signs up, but she [gestures to one side] took hers down, and we became friends. So, it has changed. I've seen a lot of 'for sale' signs now."

Anne Jackson also asserted that race was the main reason that whites left Parkmont. She told me that other blacks she knows have mentioned Parkmont's white flight to her in a self-satisfied manner as if to say "I told you so." Anne said that fear of blacks was the dominant factor in whites' mobility decisions, but acknowledged that negative perceptions of blacks are associated with whites believing in a slippery slope of "nonracial" neighborhood concerns: "First, there's race. Then, after race, then the crime comes in. Then, after that, the decaying and destroying of the neighborhood comes in. So rather than stay, they leave." However, both Anne and her daughter, Carla, view white residents' fear of blacks as part of the large-scale discrimination that blacks routinely face in public places:[46]

> CARLA: I kind of figured it was going to happen. As more blacks came in, the more whites were going to move out. That's how it is all of our life. If you go on vacation, and there's a white family in the pool, as soon as a black person steps in, all at a time, they all get out.
>
> ANNE: We had a day or something at a spa, and she got in the water and everybody got out. I was like, "Don't worry about it because now we got the whole pool to ourselves."

The Persisting Presence of Stayers and Involuntary Moving

It is common for stayers' ultimate or final relocations away from Parkmont to be involuntary, often preceded by the death of a spouse, a debilitating fall down the steps, or a serious health problem that has limited their driving and physical mobility. For elderly stayers, these are the critical events that prompt a departure from Parkmont, not the presence of black residents. For the many stayers who have not died at home yet, the eventual move will be to a retirement community where most residents are extremely old, are at advanced stages of illness, need mobility assistance and walkers, and where many suffer from compromised cognitive function. Thus, a very common theme among the elderly white stayers' narratives is their preference to live in their homes in Parkmont rather than the age-segregated institutional settings that await them as they become part of the subgroup of the elderly population that is eighty-five and older.

---

46. See Feagin (1991) for a description of everyday racial discrimination that blacks experience in restaurants, stores, classrooms, and on public streets.

It is easy to see why stayers prefer aging in place and why they avoid spending their final years in what they view to be an unfamiliar, depressing, decrepit person's setting. Although many gerontologists view age-segregated communities as a positive form of housing that promotes sociability and feelings of security, this type of residential situation interferes with cross-age social interaction and may actually work to intensify ageist views of older people. Some have even suggested that retirement communities can be seen as an extreme form of residential age segregation.[47] In Parkmont, stayers clearly view these kinds of settings as a last resort. To them, retirement communities translate into a disruption of daily life and a loss of connection to the outside world. Rose Berger, a seventy-five-year-old stayer who lives in Parkmont with her husband, described her children's pressuring her to move out of Parkmont. She explained the rather mundane reasons for her preference for Parkmont over a retirement community:

> Our children say, "It's not safe for you. We want you out of there." They say, "You shouldn't be here." They want us to live in an apartment complex that has what they call "services." Some of the places have nurses that are on duty if you have an emergency, and they give you bus transportation, or they have cleaning services. And what our sons don't understand is—and I've tried to tell them—as long as we're happy in our house and we're living the way we enjoy....If one day we have a heavy lunch, maybe we just want cornflakes for dinner. Why should we have to go down to a dining room and eat what they tell us? This is just our personal feeling because we don't really adhere to a schedule. That's my objection at this present time.

Often, the impetus to move is the loss of a spouse, which is usually very devastating to elderly people who have married young and spent a lifetime together. In Parkmont, as friends and neighbors moved out in the midst of white flight, many older couples carried on, further settling into their home routine and taking comfort in the privileges of marital companionship at an advanced age. Many stayers, like Gerri Holtzman, who moved away from Parkmont during the course of the study, described how a spouse's illness was the main reason she considered moving:

> My husband and I had thought of moving when he got sick. We thought we'd move to an apartment. I felt it was time for us to be in an apartment. In fact, I still tell married couples that reach our age, "Move while there's two of you." If one dies, you're in a place that you have more security, less problems. Things are taken care of for you.

---

47. Hagestad and Uhlenberg (2005).

Many stayers reminisced about their recently deceased spouses and the effect of the loss on their home life. Sadie Underwood cried as she showed me photos of her husband and explained the difficulties that she experienced when she became his caretaker:

> I had so many things, but then when my husband got sick, I couldn't take care of a lot of things, so I just got rid of them. I couldn't take care of them because I had to devote time to my husband. [Begins to cry.] Look, he wasn't young when it happened, but things break down. And then he ended up with a little dementia, which was rough, but I kept him home. I took care of him. He was good, and I have wonderful memories.

Those stayers who have been able to continue to live in Parkmont with their spouses consider themselves to be part of the fortunate few. However, even they were plagued with worries about the future death of their spouse, failing health, and stresses associated with becoming a primary caregiver. To many stayers, losing a spouse translates into a sense that their days in Parkmont are numbered. Leo Katz discussed the way he thinks his wife's death would affect his residential stability:

> As long as there's the two of us, we're all right. But ultimately there's gonna be one of us. At that point, the move will become harder, but also more mandatory. One lady down the block, Rena, lives by herself, but she's much younger than we are. We're lucky. We've been married sixty-five years.

In the three years during which I conducted interviews, most of the stayers who moved away from Parkmont did so because of their deteriorating health and inability to climb stairs or drive. Morris Barsky, aged ninety, had recently left Parkmont for a nearby retirement community. He discussed the pressures to move from his adult children, his resistance to leaving the neighborhood, and his eventual acquiescence:

> I was thinking about coming here for years. I knew this was where I was going to end up. Then my leg gave out. Even though I had an electric chair, they said, "Daddy, you cannot drive the car." I said, "Well, we'll see." And within a couple of weeks, I says, "Okay, come here, and make arrangements." And before you knew it, I was here. And I've been here only about six, seven weeks.

When his family eliminated the car from his life, Morris said, "That was the end." However, when I summarized his story and said that losing his car made him want to leave Parkmont, he emphatically corrected me. He emphasized that moving was not his preference, but a matter of necessity: "It's not that I didn't 'want.' I couldn't. I couldn't do the shopping. I couldn't do anything."

Many stayers provided me with lengthy inventories of their numerous health problems. Even in this community with its accessible stores and extensive public transportation, age has taken a toll on the stayers' physical mobility. In fact, the ability to get around was more of a concern than crime for most stayers. Dolores Duskin explained: "Steps are hard. My husband doesn't have a problem, but I have a horrible back. I have every problem imaginable. I have high blood pressure. I'm diabetic." As Dolores listed her ever-growing physical limitations, she said that she walks far less in the neighborhood now. Notably, crime was never the reason she gave for cutting back on her regular walks to the strip. Rather, she lamented that she can no longer manage the journey up the steep hill that takes her from her home to the business district. Muffy Nussbaum, aged eighty-five, agreed that the difficulties of aging in place take precedence over other factors when trying to understand why older people find themselves leaving Parkmont:

> My generation found the same problems I have. As we get older, it's more difficult to walk steps, and it's not just a two-story house. We have to go to the basement to do laundry. I think all of them who moved have moved for that reason. As far as race, I am going to be honest and say probably it mattered, but the physical maintenance and walking steps is just as much a reason.

Clearly, my interviews with Parkmont's stayers reveal that the decision to depart from their beloved community is not a simple matter of individual preference. Rather, the cause of a move is often part of a far sadder story about losing one's life companion and coping with declining health. These tragedies result in the long-dreaded move, which brings with it a loss of independence that is both sudden and extreme in its impact on stayers' quality of life.

Decline Watch: The Primacy of Disorder over Crime

The stayers and pioneers both expressed concerns about a process of decline taking place in Parkmont. These worries typically focused on disorder problems, which the residents perceived to be indicative of a larger breakdown in neighborhood social norms. However, with the elderly stayers' time in Parkmont soon coming to an end, their anxieties about decline especially concentrated on immediate problems of physical and social disorder that they observed. Also, despite a generally positive view of their black neighbors, stayers' narratives about social disorder revealed that many have experienced strained interactions with blacks when out in the larger community.

Despite the differences in age and ethnicity, the pioneers strongly identify with the stayers in many ways, empathizing with their plight and sharing their distress about the spread of social and physical disorder in Parkmont. At the same time, the pioneers made it clear to me that they resented Parkmont's white flight, which they viewed as the root of the neighborhood's recent decline. Pioneers shared a strong belief that the community's increasing problems are directly the result of earlier years of white flight and the city's lack of responsiveness to black communities, a category to which Parkmont now belongs. Notably, the pioneers demonstrated a far greater sense of urgency about the signs of decline in Parkmont than the stayers. This makes sense since given that the pioneers have long lives ahead of them and their children's futures to worry about. They feel that they must carefully monitor the neighborhood and consider both the immediate and long-term implications of community change for their families.

Stayers' Focus on Physical Disorder and Their Racialized Perceptions of Social Disorder

Urbanist Jane Jacobs (1961) asserted that vital neighborhoods have landmarks to which residents feel deeply attached. However, with such complete and constant population turnover in Parkmont, few meaningful landmarks remain. For instance, Parkmont's stayers spent a great deal of time with me lamenting the transformation of the shopping district and describing the way it had operated in its heyday. They described the loss of the markers of a strong Jewish community, and, like many pioneers, they complained that the strip has gained a reputation for being cheap or "downscale." When I specifically asked about what had changed in Parkmont since the onset of white flight, Sadie Underwood echoed the comments of most stayers:

> Everything changed. First, your stores. You have very few. You have a lot of take-out stores. You always have the cleaners and the butcher. There's still the produce place. It's an Orthodox set-up; the Orthodox buy there. Everything is kosher there. The shopping is different. You name it, you had it here. Now, you don't have it. Most of it is all take-out. There's no restaurant anymore. Before, on Saturday nights, a few of the neighbors, we'd all get together. We would go for waffles and ice cream. It was great.

Dolores Duskin agreed that the strip has seen better days. When I asked what it used to look like, she said, "Everything was upscale. Now, it's downscale. It's dirty up there. Just a couple of dollar stores compared to beautiful card and gift shops."

For business owners, white flight and the subsequent changes on the strip were more than distasteful: they had severe consequences for their livelihoods. Louie Romano, a first-generation Italian American and former Parkmont resident, recently closed his custom tailoring shop on the strip. When we first met, he was working on clothing alterations and telling about his plan to close the business. Not only did he mourn the loss of Parkmont's "upscale" Jewish business environment and the rise of "cheap Chinese stores and take-out places," but he provided a business owner's perspective on crime. He, personally, has had several run-ins with serious crime. One time, thieves broke his storefront window and stole his gun from the store. Another time, five men mugged him as he was closing the shop. In addition, he has had problems with trash and littering outside. However, he seemed most upset about social disorder and loitering on the strip (which included the discarded remains of cigar wrappers or "leaves" used to make marijuana "blunts"). To him, the problem had become so extreme that he felt compelled to remove his "sitting bench" that had long been located outside of his shop for the purpose of friendly socializing with customers, residents, and fellow merchants. Louie represents many of the concerned business owners who have fled the strip in that he was extremely focused on both crime and disorder, and was very pessimistic about Parkmont's future. As Louie spoke to me, Valerie Cross, a pioneer who recently retired from a career with the city's housing authority, entered the shop with her three grandchildren. They agreed with Louie that Parkmont has recently changed for the worse. Valerie told me she was disappointed that Louie was leaving, but said that she could not blame him since she also was ready to move out: "I wasn't thinking about what Parkmont would look like in twenty years when I decided to move here in 1998. I see a downward trend. I mean, drug dealing is openly happening on my block."

Muffy Nussbaum described the changes in the neighborhood's racial composition, the loss of important institutions, and the downscaling of the strip. Yet she emphasized that she still feels safe, and as Parkmont residents mentioned repeatedly, she takes comfort in the knowledge that crime is everywhere:

> It's all black now. The synagogue membership has gone down. There's no Hebrew school. The caliber of stores has changed, but we still have drugstores, banks, and a supermarket. You have to drive to the supermarket. It's five minutes away. We don't have the lovely shops we had back then. I miss the children's shop, the gift shop, the women's shop. Most shopping now is in the suburbs. I have no way to judge, but I would imagine it might go downhill. But I don't feel frightened as far as crime goes because there's crime in every area.

In general, the pioneers strongly argued that the increases in disorder go far beyond the business transitions on the strip, and some stayers agreed. Stayers provided examples of social disorder on their blocks that they believed were associated with the new second wave residents, not the pioneers. Janus Kaplan, a white stayer in her seventies, described symbols of disrespect that have interfered with the enjoyment of her home and that make her want to move:

> I'd much rather live in the suburbs. It's nicer, prettier. It's quieter, and people seem to have more culture and respect for others. Now, there are loud car radios going up and down the main street. They don't even have to be in their car. They'd just be standing near it and have their radio blasting. I don't mean just teenagers. Adults do it, too. I have a neighbor who's an adult, and she'll blast her radio so that everything in my house vibrates. You can't talk on the phone. You can't hear the TV. You just want to go away and not hear it. And this is a woman who has a grown son and a grandchild. That's how disrespctful. She doesn't care. There's no reason to have your car radio on so loud that the car itself was vibrating. Also, groups of teenage boys just sit around and sit on their patio late at night after 12:00. They don't care who has to sleep. They make noise, congregate, and loiter.

Very few stayers reported that they possess a general fear of crime and none said that they had personally been victims of violence, but some shared stories about "racial situations"[48] in which they felt disrespected and intimidated. For instance, Dolores Duskin found the students from Lombard to be "iffy" and described one negative interaction she had with a group of them:

> I was in the pharmacy one day, and there was a girl beside me with her friends. I have no problems with them. When you are standing next to someone to pay, and you're waiting to be next, where do you look? You look at the other person as to what they're doing or whatever. Well! Lookin' at that other person, they put eyes on me as if they were knives! It was scary. When they walked out, I said to the girl who was taking care of the customers, who was black, I said, "Boy, what a piece of crap." She didn't say a word. And then I thought, "I don't know why I said that."

Sadie Underwood also admitted to having race-based fears when black residents first arrived, but she said that she has become more open-minded over time.

---

48. See Hartigan (1999, 14) for a description of "racial situations," which often occur in the form of misunderstandings or "competing interpretations" during encounters in racially integrated environments.

Many white residents were reluctant to discuss their initial concerns about black neighbors, whether because of politeness or embarrassment. In fact, although we were alone in her house, Sadie actually whispered when she recalled her fears about the new black neighbors moving into the rental property next door:

> Well, *now* I have a nice neighbor next door, a very nice middle-aged couple. They're quiet. They're fine, *but* the two before that, after my friend moved out? The one wasn't too friendly, but she had a retarded son, which, look, it's unfortunate. But, he was like, six feet tall, black as coal. Black as coal. And it frightened me. It scared me. And probably, he wouldn't harm me, but I had that fear. She lived here around eight months, and I think she didn't pay her rent or whatever, and the landlord had to put her out.

Pioneers Identifying with Stayers and Blaming White Flight and the Second Wave

Even more than the elderly stayers who are nearing the end of their lives, many pioneers are extremely vigilant about monitoring any signs of neighborhood decline. Although their ability to exercise agency allowed the pioneers to move into Parkmont, they recognize that there are limits. For instance, the pioneers know that they are relatively powerless to stop further population change, to alter the policies and practices of the real estate industry, or to improve the city's economic and educational opportunities. The pioneers' uneasiness about signs of decline does not mean that they can instantaneously move at the first sign of problems; rather, there is a time lag. In the period of time between buying a new home and moving away again, they most closely observe the changes in the social environment and plan their next steps. For some, like Joy Parker, the fact of racial change alone is a sufficient cause of concern. She was now waiting for the other shoe to drop in terms of a downward spiral of disorder and crime:

> Most of the people are getting older now, so they are moving out. 'Cause that other lady over there moved out and went into a retirement home, and a black person bought it. So after a while, it's going to be an all black neighborhood. Then, there is always some problem.... There is always robberies, always mischief.... Not *yet* though. *So far,* everybody here is okay. Nobody bother anybody around here. Yeah, and people watch out for one another when they notice. *So far.*

Sonya McCall also associated black in-migration with neighborhood decline and expressed regrets about ever coming to Parkmont when she said, "Now, we only have maybe two or three whites on the block, where before there was only two blacks on the block. So, it *has* gotten bad, and I wish I didn't move around here." Beyond her concerns about segregation, Sonya said that she has become intimidated by some of the men and boys in Parkmont and said that they contribute to a downward trend in the community. Like many residents, men and women, white and black, young and old, she went so far as to say that she avoids groups of boys and men on the street and thinks that they deter the more desirable potential residents from moving to the neighborhood:

> It looks bad. Who wants to move into a neighborhood where you see five or six guys walking and standing out there? That looks really bad. You can't even go into the store without fifteen of them standing there. If I see three or more people in the store, I'm not taking the chance. Or if you see them walking up and down the street, just standing there, all in a huddle. Who wants to walk by? You would be really scared.

Other pioneers, such as Korrie Dawson, try to look beyond race, instead searching for more concrete signs of a downturn in the neighborhood's cultural norms of decency. Korrie, a realtor who moved to Parkmont nine years ago, was taking care of her young grandson while her daughter was serving in Iraq. She was also caring for two small girls, a foster child and an adopted child. On the day of the interview, two other grandchildren were at her house visiting, and Korrie was getting the girls ready for a swimming lesson at the local Jewish Community Center (JCC), where her foster child also attended preschool. Surprisingly, Korrie told me that all of the neighbors whom she knows on the block are white and elderly. Perhaps then it makes sense that Korrie expressed empathy with the aging whites and frustrated pioneers who have moved away. She explained that she identifies with residents who are afraid of the "street" style and behavior that are popular among black youth and have now become more visible in Parkmont:

> If you look at the news, young black boys with their pants falling all down is enough to make you a little bit nervous. That's what I try to tell my grandson. I think if they were "hood-acting" whites, they would have felt that way, too. These boys, I don't know what kind of direction they have.

Like Korrie, many of the pioneers who came to Parkmont when it was first integrating did so to escape the threatening aspects of life in ghetto neighborhoods. When they arrived, they brought with them a desire to fit in to the new community, connect with the longtime residents, and maintain the norms of the neighborhood to which they were first introduced. For many pioneers, adjusting to life in Parkmont was not difficult because moving to this neighborhood had been a major goal and served as a benchmark of success for them. Furthermore, it was obvious to pioneers that Parkmont was preferable to their old neighborhoods as an environment for raising children, and they believed that they had a more in common with the stayers in terms of community and life aspirations than with many of their old neighbors. Thus, when I would tell pioneers that some stayers believed that Parkmont was deteriorating in its appearance and social order, it was very common for them to defend the stayers' and their perceptions. At first, I interpreted the pioneers' support of the stayers as a form of general respect for the elderly or deference to specific white neighbors with whom the pioneers were acquainted. However, increasingly it became obvious that most pioneers were not just being charitable or patronizing to a naïve older generation, but actually shared the stayers' worries about neighborhood change.

As much as they identify with stayers' concerns about a decline in cultural norms, the pioneers are unwilling to drop the issue of white flight as a cause of decline. Pioneers believe that the loss of a white presence has translated to a decrease in accountability when it comes to local services. Margaret Meadows insisted that the timing of white flight coincided with a decline in the city's responsiveness to Parkmont residents:

> We noticed that as whites left, the services started to dwindle that they had up here. We had to fight with the city to keep our trash in the back. They wanted us to put our trash in the front, and we said "no." They wanted it so they didn't have to bring the trucks back there [in the driveway], but it was no problem when this was an all-white neighborhood for them to bring trash trucks back there. It was no problem when we first moved up here.

Anne Jackson also described the deterioration in the quality of a wide range of services. She too blamed white flight:

> When we first moved up here, we had a truck that goes past, and puts water down the street, to sweep it down. They don't do that no more. You should take care of the park because it is a part of the city parks. They used to take care of that. They don't do that no more. From the school and education part of it, to the upkeep of the neighborhood, all the things. Before, when it was all white, and there were Jews here, they did it. So why would you stop lettin' the water truck go around and sweep up the street? There's no reason.

Most pioneers also think that the police have stopped taking Parkmont's problems seriously. They suspect that police believe that crime, though higher now than when Parkmont was all white, is at an acceptable level for a black community. Anne reported that the police are not as responsive as they were when the community was mostly white. She said that the racial composition of the neighborhood is the main reason for the lack of attention that Parkmont now receives:

> I wish that the police in this neighborhood would address the new drug problem that has come into the neighborhood. This neighborhood is really not bad. It don't have a lot of problems here, so they don't focus on this neighborhood. They come over here—the drug dealers. The same way they did in my old neighborhood. They stood on the corners and sold drugs and all that. When we came up here it wasn't like that. When they first noticed those boys on the corner sellin' drugs, they should've stopped it.…If I know about it, I'm gonna report it. It's not only just the drugs, you know what I mean?

Nina Jones also said that white flight is what has led to poor police responsiveness. She considers herself a model citizen and takes pride in doing her part to call the police when problems arise in the neighborhood. She described her disappointment with the police department's responsiveness to Parkmont residents, citing a time when she reported a domestic violence incident on her block:

> If I hear something or if I see something, and I know it's not right, I'm calling because I want to be on the safe side. I save a life instead of feel sorry for one if I could have prevented something from happening, so I call. Not that the cops is coming any quicker. They come when they want to come. One day, that lady was over there screaming, and I called. And in like an hour, the screaming had stopped, and he [the woman's husband] had gone, and here they [the police] come. Like, she could have been dead by now.

Rhonda Hamilton, a sixty-five-year-old school nurse and pioneer who had just moved out of Parkmont, had this to say about the decline in police protection:

> It used to be, we had a police officer that patrolled the strip and the shop owners and all. As of last year, we never saw another one. It's like they don't care anymore. You know? The district doesn't do it, or they just can't afford to send someone out. But we once had an officer and the shop owners felt a little safer. We knew his face, and there was someone all the time.

Pioneers and stayers have the shared experience of actively choosing Parkmont, though for different reasons. Parkmont's pioneers have stretched their finances to move to an unfamiliar place surrounded by strangers. Many had the goal of living in an integrated community, and all sought to escape dangerous and stifling living environments. Like the pioneers, the stayers have also overcome obstacles to continue to live in Parkmont. As the stayers see it, their decision to continue to reside in Parkmont, even in the face of so much pressure to leave, ought to demonstrate to younger people that they are competent and independent. To stayers, there are trade-offs in moving away, and they are not yet ready to make those sacrifices. In their eyes, living in a retirement community is a threat to their independent identity and actual freedom, and they fear that such a move may strain their mental, physical, and emotional well-being. Given that the stayers respect the pioneers and believe that minor forms of crime and disorder are a standard part of modern urban life, they hope to stay in their beloved homes for as long as possible.

3

STELLA ZUK'S STORY
Choosing to Stay

By the fall of 2006, Parkmont had already become a predominantly black neighborhood, and the number of white stayers was dwindling. It was at this time that I met eighty-seven-year-old Stella Zuk, a resident of Parkmont since 1951. We were at Parkmont's synagogue for Saturday morning Shabbat (the Jewish Sabbath), sitting in the large ballroom located on the first floor above the sanctuary. We joined a table where a small group of elderly congregants was seated, snacking on cold cuts for the kiddush meal held on Friday nights and Saturday mornings to sanctify or celebrate Shabbat.

At its peak, the synagogue's morning kiddush meal provided for many congregants, including a large number of children; so back then, the ritual consisted of a simple snack of grape juice, cakes, and cookies after the morning service. However, with the synagogue's depleted membership, almost all of whom are elderly, the morning kiddush became more elaborate. Parkmont's elderly Jews eagerly looked forward to the recently introduced "sit-down lunch" kiddush, an incentive for attendance. In general, elderly members watch their pennies, have limited mobility, and look forward to a meal that they do not have to prepare themselves.

Few people were in attendance on this morning, a fact that was magnified by the setting of the kiddush in the synagogue's enormous ballroom. This grand space once accommodated hundreds for religious celebrations, bar and bat mitzvahs, Hebrew school functions, and organizational brotherhood and sisterhood meetings, but the small group gathered on this day barely filled one corner of the room.

Rabbi Kaplan introduced me to Stella and her son who, at the time, accompanied her to shul every week. As I broke off a piece of challah, the braided egg bread shared by congregants on Shabbat, the rabbi told me that next week's Shabbat would be the last in Parkmont's synagogue. The rabbi and several congregants explained that low membership and poor attendance made it impossible to hold a "minyan," a prayer service requiring a quorum of ten adults, usually men, at those synagogues that practice Conservative Judaism, such as Parkmont's.

After fifty-three years, the synagogue would be closing its doors. Soon, a black nondenominational Christian congregation, mostly consisting of congregants who commute in from outside of Parkmont, would be worshiping in the building. This poignant "changing of the guard" was symbolic, a sort of official end to Parkmont's era as a Jewish neighborhood that also signaled its rebirth as a black community.

Stella Zuk had had an image of what her senior years in her longtime neighborhood would be like, but the reality has been quite different. Stella's story is her own, but it also illustrates several important themes common to many stayers in Parkmont. Through an in-depth consideration of Stella's experiences, this chapter furthers an understanding of *why* white elderly people stay in racially changing neighborhoods by exploring their familial, residential, and lifestyle experiences, how they cope with loss and change, and what they most appreciate about aging in the place where they have spent most of their lives.

A Stayer's Journey to Parkmont

Stella Zuk invited me to her row house for a taped interview in the summer of 2007. We spent an afternoon together on her patio. Stella has lived alone in her three-bedroom house for the last four months because, as she explained, "Unfortunately, I just lost my husband in March. I'm not a happy camper. All those years." Stella showed me beautifully framed bar mitzvah and wedding photos of her three sons, all of whom were in their fifties at the time. She also told me that the son whom I had met months before at the synagogue actually lives in the nearby suburbs. She told me that she feels lucky that she can still drive and that her son visits her frequently.

Reflecting their strong preference for independent living, most elderly people in the United States live in conventional housing as opposed to housing situations that are specifically adopted to aid older people, such as assisted, shared, or supported housing or senior citizen communities.[1] Like the homes of most

---

1. Schafer (1999).

stayers, the interior of Stella's home was meticulously maintained and preserved in what looked to be its original style. The décor was what many younger people today would consider "retro," but in contrast to the trendy reproductions found in stores today, the furniture in Stella's home was clearly authentic and old. The rooms were filled with furnishings from the 1950s and 1960s, probably unchanged and unmoved for decades. The main updates were the cable box resting near the flat-screen television and the recent photos of her grandchildren. Stella keeps kosher, so in compliance with Jewish law her kitchen was stocked with Jewish foods and meats. I noticed that unlike many of her black neighbors, Stella's home had no burglar alarm system and no security doors for protection against intruders. When I asked about this, she told me that she does not feel a need to fortify her home in this kind of neighborhood.

With the dual losses of her husband and the synagogue, a day in Stella's life now involves waking up at 8:00 or 8:30 in the morning and retrieving the newspaper, which is delivered to her home. Then, she said, "I do a little something in the house, or I go shopping. I read. I go to the library. Nothing important." She told me that she was considering getting involved in some form of volunteer work because, as she said, "Really, I'm home alone too much."

Immediately after getting married, many stayers lived with their own parents or their in-laws in tight quarters. Eager to start a family and be on their own, these couples were excited when they heard that Parkmont was a new and affordable community. Stella told me that with so many friends moving to Parkmont in the late 1940s and early 1950s, word spread fast that the homes there were ideal for young Jewish families:

> When we were first married, my mother had a four-bedroom house, and we weren't making too much money. We lived with my mother for less than two years, and then everybody we knew seemed to be moving here. It was just being built at the time, so we came here. We liked this house, and we bought it. And we're here all these years. We bought the house from people who had lived here about two years, so it wasn't brand new. I had already had one child. After we came here, we had two more boys. If the people here today heard about what we paid, they'd drop dead. We paid $12,500 for the house. Across the street, recently, in the past year, I saw in the paper, $119,000. Of course, I'm sure the house was greatly enhanced.

When I first approached Stella for an interview, I could not help but notice that she felt the need to tell me that she was not an "original," meaning one of the stayers who were the very first to buy a home in Parkmont. Many stayers felt obligated to disclose this information to me, as if they feared that they would otherwise be misrepresenting their place in Parkmont's history. I also noticed Stella's enthusiasm about the rise in Parkmont's property values. By this time, I was beginning to recognize that many stayers had become keen observers of the way that homes in Parkmont were selling and of the improvements that black residents were making to their properties. Stayers would scour the newspapers and take note of any sales that occurred on their blocks. However, contrary to what one might suspect, the stayers' interest in home sale prices did not feed a desire to leave Parkmont or "cash out." In fact, they seemed comforted that local property values were holding up and often told me that the stable home prices served to further validate their decision to remain in Parkmont.

Fortunately for me, Stella was eager to share her memories of Parkmont, drawing a historical timeline. She said that when the stayers first arrived, Parkmont was almost entirely Jewish, but eventually Italian immigrants could be found scattered among the Jews. With the postwar baby boom, the typical household contained a working-class father, a stay-at-home mother, and one, two, or three children. When I asked Stella about "the feel" of Parkmont when she was younger, she almost glowed while recalling it:

> It was known as Rabbitville. Get it? A lot of children. There were all young couples having children. It was predominately a Jewish neighborhood. Also, many Italian families. I had an Italian lady here who didn't speak English, Mrs. Sparelli. And here, I have Jewish neighbors, and the next two houses were Jewish. It was very friendly. The school was excellent. We only had one public school, Lombard, and it was very highly rated. All three of my kids went there. When we moved in, every Friday night, we would go to my mother's for dinner.

Stella is similar to many stayers in her recollections of the baby boom, the memorable new presence of Italian immigrants, the prestige of the local school, and the important role of family and neighbors in her social life. Back then, community life for a young housewife was vibrant, and parents could send their children to Lombard, confident that they would learn and flourish.

Deciding to Age in Place

Financial considerations affect the spending and relocation decisions of elderly stayers, but I have argued that aging in place, even in integrating or black neighborhoods, gives white stayers an opportunity to maintain a sense of continuity, comfort, and power. Still, although neighborhoods like Parkmont offer an

opportunity for elderly residents to live a manageable and familiar life, challenges continually arise:

> I drive, fortunately. Otherwise, I'd really be stuck. I would take the bus
> occasionally when I was going to the hospital. If you have the bus sched-
> ule, it's very convenient. It takes you right there, and they have an air-
> conditioned room to wait for the bus. So occasionally, when I had to go
> there I would use the bus, but otherwise I would drive. There's only one
> supermarket here now....I do use a cane now because I had a very bad
> fall. And at the time, my husband was in the hospital, and I don't know
> if you're familiar, but the floors, many of the floors there are marble.
> They're so shiny that I was terrified to walk on them, so I bought a cane,
> and it helps a lot. I know a lot of women, the doctor told them to get
> canes, but they're so vain, they refuse.

Of course, as the stayers' narratives in chapter 2 have demonstrated, the loss
of a spouse also interferes with the happiness of stayers who are surrounded by a
lifetime of memories as they age in place. Stella explained:

> Lately, my life has been hard....My husband was in a nursing home
> for almost a year, and I used to go there every day. He had strokes, and
> he couldn't swallow, so they had to put a gadget in his abdomen. They
> said it would give nourishment. Just the way you put gas in your car.
> He would say to me, "I'm hungry. They don't give me anything to eat
> here." It would just kill me. Sometimes, he would say to our children,
> "Tell Mom to bring me a chicken sandwich or some cookies." Then
> sometimes, on a real hot day, you have a cold glass of orange juice or
> something good and cold, and it's so good and so refreshing. And he
> couldn't have that. He couldn't have nothing by mouth. It was just ter-
> rible to watch.

The pain, loneliness, helplessness, and frustration of caring for her husband
was made that much harder by the rapid changes occurring in Parkmont around
the same time. Yet Stella's need for some form of stability to help her manage
such challenging times only reinforced her decision to stay. Whereas some might
predict that declining health and the death of a spouse would lead an elderly
woman toward a greater inclination to move, for some stayers even the most
extreme personal stressors are not sufficient motivators to flee. Though Stella
admitted that she feels pressured to move by her children, she seems to take pride
in successfully realizing her preference to stay. She expressed a general satisfaction with life in Parkmont, though she does get lonely now that most of her old

neighbors are gone. Even so, Stella told me that she has not given any serious consideration to making a move:

> It was always a quiet, friendly, and convenient neighborhood. What more can you ask? My children don't like me to be here alone. They want me to sell the house. They've been telling me for a long time, even before my husband died. My son went around looking at different retirement places and took me to Shalom House and wanted me to go to Jacob's Run. I knew Jacob's Run because a friend from here had lived there for a while until she died. I have one friend at the other end of this block, but otherwise, I have no friends on this block. You know, friends that I can call all the time. But these people are lovely. Everything has changed. Nothing is like it was.

Stella's main reason for staying in Parkmont is that she wants to hold off on moving into a housing development designed for the elderly:

> Personally, I don't want a retirement community. It's funny, but I met someone that I knew when I was a kid. He's walking with a cane. He lives in this neighborhood, but I haven't run into him in a long time. He said his wife doesn't want to go to a retirement home because old people are using walkers! It's not a pleasant ambiance. You want to wait until you really have to. At Shalom House, they only give you dinner and breakfast. And lunch is on your own in your apartment. There are quite a few people there that I know who had belonged to the synagogue. They like it fairly well, some of them. And some didn't. Some people, you can never please. When I can't drive, I may have to go to a senior facility, too.

Stella has consciously adapted her lifestyle so that she can continue to live in her home in Parkmont. Even though she has had to endure the deterioration and loss of her husband, she said she prefers life in Parkmont to what she perceives as the far more unpleasant alternative of a retirement community. Although her children pressure her to move and fear for her well-being as an elderly white woman living on her own in a black neighborhood, Stella's firm understanding of her new black neighbors has allowed her to feel a sense of security and comfort that is difficult for white outsiders to see or comprehend.

Perceptions of White Flight and New Black Neighbors

In many white-flight neighborhoods, race is a subject that is avoided at all costs, especially by Jews who pride themselves on their liberal racial and ethnic tolerance.

However, like many stayers, Stella acknowledged the role of racism in Parkmont's white flight, though she only discussed it in relation to the non-Jews who left:

> There were people across the street that were antiblack, and they definitely moved. Not Jewish. They talked about it, how they didn't want to, you know, live near black people. You wouldn't hear people say too much "it's because of the blacks." It's not nice. But everybody knew. It so happened they were both firemen, the people who moved out *and* the blacks who came.

Although many Jewish and non-Jewish "leavers" wanted to move away from Parkmont's increasingly black population, the elderly stayers had more nuanced perceptions of blacks as a group to begin with, and these views became more sophisticated and sympathetic as black residents became more familiar to them in real life:

> I think the blacks just wanted to move up to a better place. They were earning good money, and they wanted to move up to a better neighborhood. Fortunately, my neighbors, they speak good English. They don't speak, you know, the black slang. They seem to be very refined and very nice. With the exception of one house, I think it's fairly respectable here. Hopefully, it won't worsen. You don't see anybody during the day. Everybody's working. Very quiet.

In the above account, Stella Zuk described her general perception of her black neighbors. Her assessment of them as *decent*[2] is similar to that of many stayers and closely matches the ways pioneers view themselves. Income, employment, speech patterns, appearance, dress codes, and etiquette are all sources of information that both groups use for making judgments. Although Stella said she has relationships with her black neighbors, many of her perceptions were also based on observing them from a distance. Parkmont is a public place, and residents use their observations on the streets to understand the people who live in the homes that are attached to their own. Like many residents, Stella watches the pioneers as they go about their lives, leaving for and coming from work, and interacting with their partners, children, and extended families. Along with these mundane behaviors, Stella takes great stock in the degree to which pioneers greet her and offer to help her. To the stayers, this information about the roles and statuses of blacks, combined with the place-based fact that "these blacks" were able to move into Parkmont, was all that stayers needed to know to feel a sense of safety and security around their new neighbors.

---

2. Anderson (1999).

Indeed, researchers have suggested that individuals' actions in public places are very much like "performances,"[3] and the first black newcomers to Parkmont were quite aware that white stayers were watching them. The pioneers' demonstrations have succeeded in convincing Stella of their civility and goodwill toward her and their investment in Parkmont's best interests. To be sure, black pioneers in a largely white community are strangers, but for these stayers, who have taken the time to observe, meet, and better understand the pioneers, black neighbors do not inspire fear and loathing. Thus, despite their age and the social rigidity that is assumed to accompany getting older, stayers' decisions to remain in Parkmont have evolved into an ability and commitment to judge their new neighbors more accurately.[4]

As the next two chapters will explain in detail, the neighborhood integration that occurs after white flight provides opportunities for a range of meaningful cross-racial contacts between elderly white stayers and younger black newcomers. However, for some stayers, relationships are less likely to form. Stayers' desire to appear independent and their visits from adult children who live nearby can function as a buffer that inhibits interracial contact in the neighborhood. Stella explained why she only periodically accepts help from her black neighbors: "My son, the one that lives nearby, always comes over and cleans my snow, cleans around my neighbor's car. And then one time, we had a lot of snow, and my neighbor's boyfriend came out and cleared my driveway. I'm a very independent person. I don't ask for help."

Yet even Stella, who greatly benefits from her son's help and who considers herself to be very self-sufficient, needs her black neighbors and routinely benefits from their daily acts of kindness. She was emphatic that Parkmont's black residents are vigilant and proactive in watching out for stayers in a range of settings, rather than just coming through in emergencies:

> After the trash guys take the trash, they just toss the can. There's a black man who lives in back who always puts mine back where it belongs. One day I forgot to put out my recycling. You have to put everything up front. The guy behind me took mine, and put it out, too. I think that's going the extra mile. I noticed it, too, when I get on the bus. I don't do it too often, but when I go on public transportation, black people will jump up and give me a seat. White people don't do that.

As I will detail in future chapters, stayers' potential for cross-racial contact is also shaped by the circumstances of the pioneers, especially their busy lives and

---

3. See Goffman (1963, 1971) and Lofland (1973) for detailed observations on this topic, especially as it relates to maintaining public order.
4. Lofland (1972).

lack of time for socializing and their eventual black flight from Parkmont. For those stayers who have only recently become needier because of advanced age or loss of a spouse, the time to become acquainted with new pioneers has come and gone. Many of the pioneers who were most involved in community life have left Parkmont, and the newer and less familiar second wave families are the now the most common cohort of black residents:

> Now, you hardly see anyone at night. Years ago, in the evening, sum-mer evenings, everybody would come out on the patio and socialize, even at night. I guess they come home from work, and they have things to do. You know, laundry and stuff. You don't see anybody. I know my immediate neighbors. This is a very long block. I don't think there are six white families here now. All black. I have very nice neighbors on both sides. We don't socialize, but I'm fortunate that I have very nice neighbors. This one lives there alone, and she has a boyfriend. She's an older woman. There's a young woman, and she has a son who goes to high school. Lovely. Next door is a young woman who's been here thirty-some years, not a Jewish woman, but she is still one of the old neighbors and she still calls me Mrs. Zuk. [Laughs.] I don't know the newest people. I only know my immediate neighbors. I don't know the people across the street even.

Like so many stayers in Parkmont, Stella's immersion into an elderly life cycle stage that involves aging in place coincided with white flight and the rather sud-den change of having daily neighborhood contact with blacks. Given that the living arrangements of the elderly are closely associated with the level of assis-tance they receive in their homes and communities, it makes sense that Stella's assessment of the pioneers played a role in her decision to stay. Stella was unfa-miliar with the pioneers when they first arrived, and family members, friends, and former neighbors subjected her to negative stereotypes about blacks that encouraged her to fear them and flee. However, Parkmont's integration provided positive interracial neighboring experiences and welcome assistance. As an el-derly woman coping with a myriad of difficulties related to her personal life and daily living, Stella feels grateful for the pioneers' help and friendship.

Recent Decline: The Strip, Crime, Losing the Synagogue

Many people appreciate living in a neighborhood with a pedestrian-friendly commercial district filled with retail and service establishments. In fact, real estate developers frequently design new master-planned housing developments with mixed-use components, and they market, sell, and promote the residential area's access to offices, retail, dining, and entertainment.[5] However, when neighborhood commerce zones become distressed, the success of nearby residential areas can become threatened.[6] This may be especially likely in white-flight neighborhoods, since population change and loss have been shown to negatively affect a community's commercial life,[7] sometimes having a lagged effect that takes time to appear.[8] Consequently, many of the original businesses in Parkmont may have failed, in part, because they could not or did not adapt to the tastes of the new black population. When businesses in a neighborhood shopping district have been catering to the locals, instability in the local population presents a major disadvantage to profitability. At the same time, racially biased business decisions, discrimination, and disinvestment also play a role in decline, as local business owners may flee communities that are in transition. The reasons for the downscaling and exodus of local retail and service establishments in white-flight neighborhoods include race-based fears among business owners, the tendency of many business owners to discriminate against black communities when considering location, and the possibility that less desirable businesses may attempt to capitalize on opportunities that emerge as vacancies appear.

Pioneers and stayers agree with researchers that such changes in business districts are a notable cause of concern. Although many stayers sentimentally miss the Jewishness that once dominated Parkmont's strip, Stella reported that she is more concerned about the fact that the business district is increasingly characterized by transience, low quality, and a lack of order that has negatively affected nearby local institutions, such as the school and library:

> Things have changed. The stores are all different. There's no kosher butcher, and there used to be a deli that was very popular. Now, sometimes it closes at night; Koreans own it. To tell you the truth, I really don't go in those stores, so I don't know. They're all different now. I mean, they're not Jewish stores, so it's a whole different ballgame. Antonio's Restaurant was so popular, and that's gone. The only thing, the Grapevine, that's still very popular. Very busy. That's about the only place today that's been here over the years and stayed the same. I may run into the ladies' stores there to see what's available, and there's usually isn't anything for me. I like to go to the library when school is in

---

5. Katz (1994).
6. See Downs (1981), Jacobs (1961), Koebel (2002), Kraus (2000), and McRoberts (2003).
7. Koebel (2002).
8. Immergluck (1999).

session. If you go there when school is out, it's like Grand Central Station. I complained a few times, but it is so noisy. The kids were never told, they were never taught that in the library, people want to read or study, and you have to be quiet. It's become their baby-sitting spot. Another thing about the library system now, every time you go in there, there are different librarians. At one time, you got to know them, and you were friends with the librarians. But now, every time I go in there, there's different ones.

Given that so many whites associate black neighborhoods with crime, and so many who fled Parkmont prophesied that it would become a high-crime ghetto, how did stayers assess the crime in Parkmont? Of course, stayers are not as likely as some of the younger blacks in the community to have their fingers on the pulse of the action when it comes to crime. Even so, Stella's assessment of Parkmont as relatively safe is a reflection of her personal feelings of security, satisfaction, and trust within her longtime neighborhood:

We had very little crime. Maybe now, more so, but I walk to the library, which is only a block away. I feel safe in this neighborhood. Occasionally—well, very often—I'll accidentally leave my garage door open, and nobody ever touches anything. My neighbor thinks some people play such loud music that she can't sleep, but *I* don't hear it.

Stella, like many Jewish stayers, also described the hard times faced by Parkmont's synagogue in recent years. She explained to me how her son, a chemist, came to be the cantor there. Typically, a synagogue's cantor is a specially trained leader whose main job is to lead the congregation in song and prayer. In some synagogues, like Parkmont's, the cantor is as important in status as the rabbi, acting as a key contact person and a major source of support to congregants. Parkmont's Jews have been mourning the downsizing and eventual closing of their synagogue, which marked the culmination of years of change. Stella described the reasons that this has been a particularly difficult transition for many stayers:

My son was very active in the synagogue. The past few years he was acting cantor! Every Saturday. We didn't have a cantor anymore. It's too expensive. Towards the end, not too many came to services. On Saturday, if we had twenty-five, it was a good one. During the week, on Friday night, at one time they had a minyan there every night and every morning. Recent years, there was a man that lived a couple doors away, Mort. He would always get the minyan together. Then he died, and my husband took over. They had about seven people that were regulars that they could count on, and then my husband would maybe make ten or fifteen calls just to get three more people. We could've stayed if they would be able to get minyans and have enough people to come in. We wouldn't have left. We wouldn't have closed shop, but all the young ones moved away and the older people, they're dying, and they don't go out at night, or they don't drive at night. So, some of the people are angry. They wanted us to use the money that was left to us and continue, but you can't.

Because Parkmont's synagogue received a large monetary gift after one of its members died, many leaders at suburban synagogues were eager to "merge" with the congregation. By the time of the last Shabbat service, a deal was reached, and Parkmont's synagogue was absorbed by another temple located in a very wealthy nearby Jewish suburb. Still, Stella told me that many of Parkmont's observant stayers refuse to attend the services at the new synagogue because they say that they do not approve of the "liberal" practices used at this younger, less conservative temple:

> Abe Rothman, he comes on Saturday, but his wife refuses because on high holidays the synagogue has a choir, and the people singing are not Jewish. That's Lorna's complaint, mainly. I said to her, "Lorna, sometimes even if you don't want to go, you have to go for your husband's sake, sometimes." But she doesn't want to go to the Orthodox one either. The Orthodox synagogue moved out. They just dedicated the new building last Sunday. So, I said, "Sometimes you have to do something that you're not too happy with." I begged her last Tuesday. This week, they had a program for seniors that was to talk about the neighborhood you grew up in, and they had a nice turnout—mostly people from our old synagogue. And I told her, I said, "Why don't you come?" I said to Abe, "Try to get Lorna to come." And he says, "You call her." So I did. She had an appointment that particular day, so that was her excuse. Her husband comes on Saturdays, but she hasn't set foot. On high holidays we're gonna have separate services: one with the choir and one without. Our old rabbi will lead the service without.

However, aside from the conflicts about adhering to Jewish traditions, the loss of the local synagogue has presented other challenges, as well. The leaders at the new synagogue promised to provide transportation to and from Parkmont, but so far, many stayers have had a difficult time finding a ride to the suburbs. Additionally, stayers reported that they have struggled in adjusting to the new people and strange environment at this late point in their lives. This is especially distressing, because for many Jewish stayers the synagogue has been the center of their social world and a constant in their lives. Stella explained the practical barriers to continuing her religious practice at the new synagogue and her sense of alienation there:

> I go on Saturdays, but I don't drive at night. It's difficult. It doesn't feel like my synagogue. It feels like I'm in a strange place. It's very beautiful. I'd never, in as many times as I'd been there, I'd never gone into the ladies' room. This lady said, "Stella, come on in. I want to show you the ladies' room." It was magnificent. Beautiful wallpaper and the sinks and everything was just state of the art. But I liked it when the synagogue was here and we could walk there. The new synagogue is very big. It's overwhelming. It's magnificent, but I mean, we were members here. We knew everybody. Everybody knew us.

The Problem on the Corner

Although Stella's home appeared perfectly preserved, and most of the homes and lawns on her block were maintained and attractive, there were some eyesores in Parkmont that would have been visible and offensive to even the most casual observers. The house located two doors down from Stella's was one of the most blighted I had seen during my fieldwork there. Several rusted appliances, including a large washing machine turned on its side, sat on the patio. A massive tangle of wires and hoses, broken and frayed, hung from the building.

In addition to these markers of physical disorder, social disorder plagued the residents of this once peaceful block. While I sat with Stella, a white male visitor arrived to the blighted house, left, and returned, each time screaming to an upstairs open window for a woman to let him inside. Stella told me that she now avoids going outside and that her neighbor, a pioneer, has become so fed up that she is planning to move away:

> We have a problem on the corner. That's a duplex right there on the corner. See all that junk there? They have that side boarded up, and every board is a different color and a different size. It makes this street look like a shantytown. They've had the electricity and the water shut off. They're renters, and it's a lot of people. They're related. The upstairs people are related to the downstairs. And this lady who has not been living here that long—she's black—and she's moving out 'cause they're so loud and so vulgar. She said she never heard such language in her life. She said she's gonna move from this house. She has a "for sale" sign. I'm not sure where. She's a very fine lady, very nice. Nice children, too.

I don't really dislike anything about the neighborhood. I've no complaints about the neighborhood, except neighbors like that. Our neighbors were respectable, always. These are the only trash.

Almost any observer would be saddened to watch Stella contend with such drastic problems right next door, especially at this stage of her life. Just as disappointing is the fact that incoming black residents have been forced to live with this level of disorder, and possibly crime, after believing that moving to Parkmont would be an escape from these kinds of disturbances. Stella told me that she often speaks with her black neighbors about this house, gathering information and strategizing about what to do. I asked Stella whether this house had always been a nuisance:

> Oh, no, no, no! It's just since late September. I've been living here fifty years, and it's the first time we ever had trouble with a neighbor. We've called the police. I have not noticed it, but my neighbor thinks they're selling drugs 'cause people come there all hours of the night. And she also thinks there's prostitution going on. She's seen one of the young ladies came out with nothing on. Outside, in nothing but a towel. My neighbors tell me, too. The blacks tell me. I have not seen or heard the things these people have seen or heard. Like, that a young lady that lives here was servicing men in their trucks, and didn't get paid. Stuff like that. I have no knowledge of that. And the one day, the man was chasing a young woman up the street and my [pioneer] neighbor, Marla, she called the police. And she said, "Hurry, hurry! He's gonna kill her." She was so upset, and she said she saw that he had his hands around her neck. By the time the police came, they disappeared so she doesn't know what happened.

Many stayers and pioneers have accepted the resegregation of Parkmont, but they have refused to tolerate the emergence of disorderly behaviors and signs of crime. For practical reasons, pioneers and stayers have put aside race and instead blame the problems on the far-reaching shortcomings of a substandard class of people that has recently entered the neighborhood. The stayers' and pioneers' estrangement from the second wave and their agreement that these newest residents are the main cause of local disorder leads them to cooperate with each other to deal with such problems. However, such efforts are not always effective. With so few stayers healthy anymore and a decreasing number of pioneers choosing to remain in Parkmont, the longer-term residents' levels of involvement and vigilance may be insufficient, especially in a black neighborhood where city officials have become unresponsive to residents' needs. Stella described the frustrations that she and her pioneer neighbors have experienced in reporting the nuisance house to city officials and their own failed initiatives at taking action:

> We reported the house to L and I [the city's Department of Licenses and Inspections]. We reported it to everybody we could think of. It takes time. L and I says, "We'll be there in between five to fifteen days." We reported it two weeks ago. These ladies have been calling every department. Marla, the neighbor over here, went and rang the bell there [at the blighted house] yesterday. I said, "You're very brave." You hear about these people who are dealing drugs—they have guns. I can't understand. If they're dealing drugs, why is the water shut off, the electricity is shut off? I can't understand. My son said maybe they're not selling enough. We read that when they have these drug busts, they find tons of money. They didn't have any water, so they hooked onto Marla's water spigot, so she shut her water off. Then, they came here. I came out one morning and the patio was soaked. The hose, we hadn't used that hose in ten years! It was not connected. It was laying here. [Laughs.] And they even took the nozzle off and had some kind of a fancy nozzle of their own. They left it here, so I kept it. I said, "It's evidence that they were here." I've even gotten to jotting down the license plate numbers.

Many researchers are interested in the social forces that bring residents of a community together.[9] As described above, in Parkmont the social integration between the stayers and pioneers has created productive forms of neighborhood social participation. Stella further elaborated on the role of social capital in helping her to deal with neighborhood problems:

> Only now, since we have this problem do I have my neighbor's phone number. I don't even know her last name, but one day I gave her my phone number, and I asked her what hers was....We exchanged phone numbers. In fact, my son was here last night, and it so happened when we drove up in the back of the house, this lady and that lady were outside, and I said, "Now that I'm here, we can have a meeting!" [Laughs.] And then her boyfriend came, and he and my son were examining the wires that were hanging in the back of the house, and they said, "That's really dangerous for your house." And Marla said the electric company has a phone number for hazards, and Marla said that she had it. So, my son called Marla and got the number. Then, he went home and called me back. He says, "Mom, I called the electric company, and I wasn't

---

9. See Putnam (1995) and Woldoff (2002).

satisfied with the woman that I spoke to." She says, "Oh, why are you worried if they're stealing electricity?" He said, "It has nothing to do with money. I don't care about their stealing electricity. I'm concerned about the fire hazard." So she says, "Well, I'll let you talk to a supervisor." So she says, "That's not a hazard."

Stella and her neighbors seemed to think that they had hit a dead end. I provided Stella with the telephone number of the civic association president, Sam Wilson, who was still holding his office at the time, although he had already joined the large group of pioneers who had moved away from Parkmont. The next time I visited Stella's block I observed the status of the nuisance house. Its patio was clear of appliances and debris, and the landlord had replaced the mismatched planks and boards with windows. After asking around, I learned that the disruptive tenants had been evicted.

Conclusion

At the ends of their lives, most elderly people find that their worlds are shrinking and their prospects for independent living are threatened, but for Parkmont's stayers the introduction of neighborhood racial change provided new, unexpected, and enriching social opportunities, along with challenges. Stayers like Stella appeared to possess little to no animosity toward black neighbors. Much to the contrary, they often relied on black residents for help, social contact, emotional support, neighborhood information, and trouble-shooting when problems would arise. Stayers' relationships with black residents developed over time, whether these contacts originated at the start of integration because of basic hospitality and sociability or whether such relationships formed at a later point in time out of practicality and need. Because stayers were invested in the community, they took the time to learn about the pioneers as individuals. The process of carefully watching new residents, interacting with them, and reserving judgment has been crucial for stayers' successful adaptation to white flight.

Although Stella Zuk's story is representative of the lives of many stayers, she is also a "negative case"[10] in some respects. Specifically, her delayed and subdued neighbor interactions with black residents contradict some patterns described in the next chapters. Stayers, such as Stella, who are fortunate enough to have healthy family members who reside in close proximity can be less enmeshed in the immediate community in some respects. Yet even for the stayers who

---

10. Lincoln and Guba (1985).

received substantial and frequent help from their adult children, black residents repeatedly materialized as a continued and regular source of assistance, social contact, and problem solving. These findings suggest that, at least while they are healthy, elderly whites who stay in changing neighborhoods have the potential to be leaders in efforts to improve race relations, educate their younger counterparts and peers, and share in community problem solving. In chapter 4, I focus on the cross-racial neighboring between stayers and pioneers that dominates black-white social relations in this white-flight community. These stories provide hope for the prospects of interracial relations in changing neighborhoods and for the ability of people to evolve and adapt over their life course.

4

CROSS-RACIAL CAREGIVING
Pioneers Helping Stayers to Age in Place

My neighbors are black on both sides. The ones on one side have two cars. They're very nice, and she is pregnant. He shovels for me and always asks if I need anything. He even gave me his phone number and told me to call him in case I need anything....On my street, people get up, go to work, get dressed, and their cars aren't there all day.

—Rena Grubman, stayer, aged ninety-two

They're wonderful people. They're somebody you can talk to and listen to. When I met this guy, they could tell me that the guy was crazy before I even knew. Sometimes, older people can give you something that you can't see. They could see he wasn't right for me, and they was right.

—Joy Parker, pioneer, aged forty-two

Laws do not require us to reach out to, befriend, or help our neighbors. We have the option of subscribing to the philosophy underlying Robert Frost's famous quotation, "Good fences make good neighbors." Many people choose to remain distant from their neighbors for various reasons, and one might imagine that those who lived through Parkmont's rapid population change would have been especially loath to build new relationships with incoming black residents.[1] Neighborhoods that experience white flight are vulnerable to their longtime residents feeling threatened, fearful of the unknown, resentful of unstoppable change, and prejudiced toward newcomers. Or perhaps more benignly, residents of such communities may simply anticipate a lack of common interests when it comes to fitting in and socializing with people who are different in terms of life-cycle stage and culture. Thus, in a neighborhood such as Parkmont, where elderly whites are

---

1. See Anderson (1990) for an interesting example of community conflict between white and black residents. In his study, whites were newcomers who attempted to gentrify an urban community, causing clashes with the residents of an adjacent low-income black neighborhood. Kennedy and Leonard (2001) also provide interesting insights into the differing viewpoints of gentrifiers and original residents and the challenges of neighborhood change even when it comes in the seemingly positive form of revitalization efforts.

increasingly outnumbered by younger blacks and where change has come about rather quickly, it might be expected that "birds of a feather will flock together" or that residents would tend to limit their relationships to people who are similar to them and with whom they would be more likely to feel a true connection.[2] Yet Parkmont's stayers and pioneers have built meaningful and useful relationships and have done so for a variety of unexpected reasons.

On a sunny afternoon in early 2007, a most exceptional story of such cross-racial relationships came from Linda Hopewell, a black Parkmont resident who purchased her home from an elderly Jewish man she called "Mr. Morris." Linda said that after careful searching, she chose Parkmont because she believed that it was a safe community where property values would continue to appreciate. After placing a bid on Mr. Morris's home, Linda had an unexpected encounter with him:

> After I accepted the bid, Mr. Morris called me a couple days later, and he asked me if I could help him pack. He said that he would leave me some things to help me. I said, "Well, you don't have to leave me anything." He's like ninety-one at the time. I said, "I will just come and help you." So, my mother and I, we came over. We helped him pack for about three weeks, and he told me that he was gonna leave me all this [gestures to the dining room]. He left me this cabinet. He left me the dishes. Actually, I'm trying to sell those dishes. I got it appraised, and it's something like $1,200. He got those dishes as a wedding gift. He left me his whole hope chest that they had for their wedding. He left me three TVs. Yeah, but I wasn't expecting anything. He was a Jewish man, and his wife died in March, I think. And he sold his house in May. They had been together for years, and he was so heartbroken. I still keep in contact with him. I still call him and talk to him. He lives in a home, a retirement home. He was very lonely because he was the only owner of this house, and they been around here for like forty-three years. He was the original owner.

One might think that it would be hard to conjure a more unique story of Parkmont's emerging cross-racial social interactions than Linda's. However, this was not the first time I had heard black residents tell me about the ways in which they had helped the elderly whites who were scattered on their block. In fact, both white stayers and black pioneers shared accounts of younger black residents coming to the aid of elderly whites. For instance, stayer Joanne Newcombe was sitting outside on the patio with me when she greeted her next-door neighbor,

---

2. See McPherson, Smith-Lovin, and Cook (2001) for a review of the literature on social network homophily.

Talia, a young black woman. As I chatted with Joanne, I watched Talia's sister carry a basket of clothing from her car into Talia's house to do laundry there. Talia said hello to us, followed her sister into the house, and closed the door. Then, Joanne leaned over to me and whispered, "See how nice they are? They'll do anything for you."

In Parkmont, cross-racial neighboring encounters take two major forms. The first is helping tasks, both routine and more intimate. Most commonly, blacks are helping whites, sometimes in basic, instrumental ways, and at other times in very personal and intensive ways, almost as if they are family members. A second form of cross-racial neighboring can be seen in the exchange of social support and companionship, which is more symmetrical in the sense that blacks also receive some tangible benefits. Using interviews from both blacks (mostly pioneers) and whites, this chapter explores the nature of these two types of cross-racial neighboring interactions to better understand their range, character, and origins.

Help and Neighboring

> My neighbors are black on both sides and very lovely people. I have no complaints. They are very congenial and helpful. They shovel [snow] for me. I have a neighbor two doors away. She called me and said, "Miss Muffy, take my name and phone number, and call if you need help. Any time of night."
>
> —Muffy Nussbaum, aged eighty

Routine Help

Meaningful neighboring is not as common as it once was in many U.S. communities,[3] but in Parkmont, whites' positive evaluations of black neighbors were significantly rooted in their personal experiences of cross-racial neighboring. Stayers are frequently on the receiving end of a core dimension of neighboring: routine help. Almost every stayer and pioneer in Parkmont eagerly shared a story about cross-racial helping behaviors, demonstrating that instrumental support can be an extremely common and important dimension of the culture of racially changing neighborhoods. This is especially true in the beginning stages

---

3. Putnam (2000) described the decline in neighboring, as well as other forms of civic engagement. Among the more interesting findings reported, data from the General Social Survey data (1974 to 1998) show that people in the United States experienced a decline in the social time that they spent with neighbors.

of white flight, when relations are just starting to form between white stayers and black pioneers.

Research has shown that "routine neighboring" is an important component of neighborhood attachment.[4] Routine forms of neighboring can be defined as ordinary, civil behaviors toward neighbors that represent tangible forms of aid.[5] Neighbors who know each others' names, greet each other frequently, have long talks, borrow small items, and "help out" may be seen as engaging in routine neighboring. I was curious about the extent of routine neighboring between whites and blacks in Parkmont.

In general, I suspected that the elderly whites were poor candidates for rolling out the red carpet to young blacks with whom they appeared to have little in common. However, the pervasiveness and the range of cross-racial neighboring in Parkmont violated my expectations that white stayers would be afraid of, or at least guarded toward, black newcomers. In fact, many elderly whites told me that they were quick to reach out and welcome their new black neighbors. When I asked about their cross-racial interactions, many whites recalled stories about the memorable period of time when their very first black next-door neighbor moved in. For instance, Rena Grubman said: "When my neighbor, who is black, moved in, I brought her a Jewish apple cake. You know what she said? She said, 'When are *you* moving?' It wasn't meant in a mean way. She really wanted to know. I told her, 'I have no intention of moving.'" Rena's interpretation of the early connections between stayers and pioneers was that some black pioneers treaded lightly when they first moved in, anticipating that whites might not be welcoming and suspecting that all whites were eager to depart from the rapidly integrating community.

After the excitement of moving settles down, it is common for new residents to experience a period of adjustment to a community, during which time newcomers may feel disconnected, disoriented, or uncomfortable. One might expect these feelings to be even more exaggerated for blacks moving into a white neighborhood, anticipating the watchful "white gaze" of elderly residents.[6] But many of the pioneers, though hesitant at first, decided that they wanted to be the first to initiate contact with the stayers and make a good impression. For instance, stayer Gerri Holtzman told me about the time that she received a gift from Dana, her new pioneer neighbor:

> Dana came. She was a single woman. Now, her mother lives with her. Her mother's not well. But one day she brought a cake over and said, "I

---

4. See Woldoff (2002). See also Lee, Campbell, and Miller (1991).

5. See Sherman, Ward, and LaGory (1988) for a discussion of the differences between instrumental and expressive forms of support among caregivers of the elderly.

6. See discussions of Fanon's (1967) "white gaze" and DuBois's (1903) "double consciousness," concepts that are used to analyze the objectification of blacks by whites.

didn't know if I should bring it or not—whether you would eat this or not—but my mother said it's the thought that counts." She said, "Your husband was so nice to me and treated me so nice when I moved in."

Elderly women were not the only ones receiving help from pioneers. Male stayers also formed useful neighbor relationships with pioneers. When I interviewed Morris Barsky, he had just moved into a retirement home after losing his wife. At the time that he moved out, his neighbors on both sides were black. Morris told me that when it came to relying on neighbors for help, the pioneers were model citizens.

> The other neighbor was a very nice man, and he took care of my car. He took the snow off of it. One time, he said, "Morris, you need a tune-up." I says, "Okay, Stanley." And he took it apart, and he left everything on the cement in the back of the garage. And I said to myself, "Morris, you fouled up. That man will never put it together again." And he did. And he did such a wonderful job. I never had a tune-up like it. He wasn't even an automobile mechanic. He was a medic in the fire department.

By far, the most common form of cross-racial neighboring in Parkmont consisted of black households providing routine forms of instrumental help with the stayers' household chores. A typical example of this was explained in Leo and Gladys Katz's account of their pioneer neighbor watching out for them as they struggled to attend to basic home upkeep:

> LEO: The guy across the street, his name is Gervis. He came over one day and changed my light bulb.
> GLADYS: He ran across the street. He's a real nice guy.
> LEO: I had Gladys standing on a ladder out there to change a lightbulb, and he came across the street, and he said, "Get down off there." And he got her off of there, and he changed the lightbulb. It's somebody, you know, you wave to. There's a guy in the back. We frequently walk out, and he waves. [Laughs] I'm not too pleased he calls me "Pop."

On the patio at the home of Dolores Duskin, I could hear the sound of the loud bass thumping from speakers at a nearby block party. Dolores told me that she stays inside to avoid the noise, most of which she attributes to the second wave of newer blacks who are now coming into Parkmont. Dolores told me about her pioneer neighbor, Ken Wilkinson (see profile in chapter 5), who strongly disapproves of the recent spate of block parties near his home. Ken handles all of Dolores's lawn maintenance and much more:

> Ken, he's all over the place. He works for the city. Ken cannot stand dirt, and he walks up and down this street picking up pieces of paper. You

probably could eat off of our street, and he's training his sons how to run a business. He's gotten this lawn business, and he's got quite a few customers in the area. And he's just, sometimes, if you need something done, you can call Ken. I had a problem with the door, and he came over and fixed the door lock....And his sons are very bright. His wife has her master's degree in education, and they're just a wonderful family.

Stayers report that since the whites fled from Parkmont, their casual contacts with black neighbors have become more regular. Sybil Cutler, a widowed stayer who moved to Parkmont in 1948, described this new dynamic:

> I have wonderful neighbors. As my husband used to say, "My neighbors *now* are better than the ones that were here before." I can't reach anything. I'm not allowed to get up on a ladder. If I need the batteries changed in the smoke alarms, I call somebody. Anybody. Oh sure, I have their phone numbers. They gave them to me. They *asked* me to call, and they gave me their phone number in case I needed them at night. Yeah, one lives behind me. I gave him all of my husband's weightlifting equipment....My next-door neighbors here—her nephew came to live with her from Jamaica, and he's a doll. If I need a lightbulb, he'll get up there and change it....I needed a new window shade, and when I got it, I called Ronnie [a pioneer], and he put it up for me. Upstairs, I don't have drapes; I have mini-blinds. I noticed that one wasn't working too good, and Ronnie came up. I knew what was wrong with it, and I knew how to do it, but I couldn't do it myself because I am not allowed to get up on even a step stool.

For many stayers, the fact that the pioneers can be counted on is crucial to their independence in Parkmont. Included among the benefits of helpful pioneer neighbors is the fact that they mitigate the need to move. When I asked Gerri Holtzman whether her children are comfortable with the fact that she wants to continue to live in Parkmont, she told me about her daughter, who lives in Indiana but who briefly returned to Parkmont after Gerri's husband died. "My daughter says, 'I was always worried about you there until I met the very nice woman next door.' In fact, my neighbor and I call each other every morning to make sure we're all right." Clearly, Gerri thinks that her neighbor's support helped to convince her daughter that her mother is well cared for in Parkmont. As will be discussed later in the chapter, it is also notable that Gerri believes that this relationship is reciprocal, and that her neighbor also benefits from their connection. For Gerri and others, living next to pioneer families has allowed them to prolong an independent lifestyle in their own homes.

For older residents, the freedom to live independently is so valuable that many stayers are afraid to ask for help from their adult children. In some cases, the fear of being sent away to a retirement home translates into stayers becoming more guarded and secretive about problems they are having, which further places them at risk. Vera Goffman, an eighty-year-old widow, talked with me as we waited for her son to visit from out of state. With no relatives nearby to help her, Vera often feels helpless to deal on her own with household problems that have compromised her safety. She confided to me about the much-needed routine help that she receives from pioneers such as her neighbor, Douglas, a divorced father of three who works as a city bus driver:

> I've got one next door here, and he'll do whatever I want. Well, of course, I pay him for it, but he's very nice. One day, I couldn't open up my backdoor. I finally opened it, and then I couldn't close it. So I put a lot of things against the door so no one would know that it was not locked. So he knocked on my door, and he said, "Vera, did you know your door was open?" I said, "Yes. I couldn't close it." He says, "Well, why didn't you let me know?" So he fixed it for me. So we became friends. I needed the bathroom painted, and he says, "Anytime you want anything, please let me know." So, he didn't want money, and I said, "I insist." And he shovels my walk when it snows and all that. And that's worth more than anything really....I think they're wonderful. They're very respectful....It's just that they always say, "Hello. How are you?" Which is all I want. Look, I wasn't a busybody before. I certainly am not one now, so I always say, "Hello. How are you? How are the children?"

Because many of the neighborhood's black families must be away at work all day and the elderly whites spend most of their time at home, stayers who are able to sometimes reciprocate in providing help to black families. Margaret Meadows, a pioneer and nurse, told me that at first she helped the elderly whites more than they helped her. However, she soon began to call on them to help her manage her own household:

> My neighbor next door, she passed away but my son used to go to the store for her because she couldn't get out. Just to the regular store. Rite Aid. Milk and ice cream and things like that. Then, she moved with her daughter. She was getting sick anyway. We would always come out and talk....When we got our sewer done, the guy—I think he's Greek or Italian—was a retired plumber. He stayed right here, even though me and my husband had to go to work. He watched them to make sure they did what they were supposed to do.

Thus, for a time the social world of Parkmont became a far more racially diverse place than ever before; it was not just a neighborhood for exchanging pleasantries and welcomes, but it was also for extending real help to people in need on a regular basis. While becoming established in their new homes and community, the pioneers often found themselves reaching out and coming to the aid of their elderly neighbors. However, in many cases the relationships extended beyond the expected small, polite gestures or the routine forms of household help. Over time, neighbor relationships between stayers and pioneers in Parkmont evolved, matured, and deepened to become far more.

Intimate and Intense Social Neighboring: Anything but Routine

The stayers' needs for more intense forms of support have grown with age. In response, Parkmont's blacks have increasingly helped in ways that are more intimate and expressive, as well as more labor-intensive and crisis-oriented. Many stayers who have become sick do not have the benefit of a healthy spouse or adult children who live nearby to help them. In particular, many Jewish stayers have children who are successful professionals who have left the region in pursuit of better job opportunities. Some stayers never had children and only have infrequent visits from extended family members. Pioneers often fill these voids for stayers, as revealed by residents' own stories about their surprisingly intense levels of neighboring. These cross-racial encounters between neighbors involve forms of support such as caregiving during an emergency or illness. Typically, in black families these more private matters are reserved for family members and friends. In providing this special kind of help, the pioneers have taken the role of neighbor far beyond what most people would consider "routine," obligatory, or expected.

Parkmont's cross-racial neighbor relationships often transcend routine helping in times of emergency. Joe Cassidy explained how one of his pioneer neighbors greatly surpassed his rather low initial expectations:

> I have a black on each side. One side talks to me, and the other doesn't. This one time, one [pioneer] neighbor lost her power. Her name's Lisa Williams. She calls me "Mr. Joe." Anyway, she asked me if I had any candles. Then, guess what? *She* gave them to *me*. And I used them. I thought she was asking, but she was really offering.

Similarly, Sadie Underwood, a widow with no children, gushed with praise when I asked about her black neighbors. She elaborated on how much she has missed

Jodi, a pioneer from across the street who was like a daughter to her when she became ill:

> She was a policewoman. She was the first one to move in here. She came with one child. Her mother lived with her, too. Her name was Rosa. Very nice. Light-skinned. And the kids were great. She moved away. See, she didn't send her kids to Lombard. She had two more children here. They were the nicest kids. If it snowed, they would come over and shovel the pavement. They were great. And then, I had come home from the hospital. I had a stint implant, and the little girl came over, and she says, "I'll do your laundry. I'll do your cleaning. You tell me, and I'll do anything for you." They were great. They were wonderful, wonderful children.

Joe's comment about his suspicion that the pioneers were going to be needy or pestering and Sadie's fixation on skin tone reveal that some stayers had less than enlightened views of black people. However, like so many stayers, both Joe and Sadie developed strong feelings of fondness, appreciation, and respect for their pioneer neighbors who have provided so much support during difficult times.

For some elderly stayers, pioneers' involvement and interest in their lives can mean the difference between life and death. Although stayers could, in theory, contact professional human services workers, they are often hesitant to do so, especially when dealing with relatively minor concerns. Additionally, professionals do not offer the more natural, sincere, and preventative support of close neighbors who are familiar with their elderly neighbors and are watching and checking in on a regular basis. When the pioneers opt to intervene in the lives of stayers, what they give in terms of comfort, support, and a sense of security is profound. Leo Katz spoke of the extraordinary bond that he and his wife, Gladys, have formed with Joy Parker, a Jamaican hospital worker who is a pioneer neighbor:

> I met Joy. She was buying the house next door. She's not always easy to understand; she's got this Jamaican accent that when she talks fast, it's tough.... She moved in. We went to see her, to welcome her. She appreciated the way we made her feel so much at home, and so we became friendly. Anyway, I had an incident one night. I wound up going to the hospital at 12:00 at night. Joy took me—with Gladys. Joy had been sleeping and [had] gotten out of bed. We get to the hospital, and I thanked her. And I told her, "We'll take a cab home when they're finished with me." And she looks at me, and she said, "You think I'm gonna let Gladys sit here by herself?" Joy sat there until 2:00 in the morning and brought us home.... Just a few months ago Gladys had an incident and was in the hospital for a couple of nights.... Later, I came home and we left

Gladys there, still in the ER. Joy heard this, and she took me back to the hospital just to make sure that she would see Gladys, and nothing was gonna happen to her. And then Joy brought me back. So, she's there, you know, if we need her.

When eighty-six-year-old Edda DeLuca's pioneer neighbors moved away from Parkmont, she felt an acute sense of loss that epitomizes the bond that some stayers feel with pioneers. A widow with no children, Edda is originally from Italy, and she spoke to me with a thick accent. Even in the heat of summer, she wore heavy support stockings, and her head was covered with a blue lace scarf. I noticed that a wheeled walker was parked in the corner of the living room, and the mail on her coffee table included literature about retirement homes along with an English language magazine titled *Catholic Digest*. In her broken and heavily accented English, she excitedly told me about how close she had been with the black pioneer family who once lived next door. They were the first blacks on the block, but a couple of years ago they decided to move to the suburbs in an adjacent state:

> They shoveled. When they were moving, the sign stayed up a long time. I wanted them to stay, but they left. They used to put salt down and clean the street and the sidewalk. When he did his lawn, he did my lawn. He said, "I have to do like someone else would do for my mother." When I lost my husband, my neighbor gave me a lot of encouragement. He said, "In case you're afraid or see something or hear something, knock on the wall. If you just notice some noise or thing that make you upset, just you knock on the wall. You no have to call us on the telephone."

Edda went on to tell me that her neighbor insisted that they exchange phone numbers, and when his family moved away, he gave her their new address and told her to stay in touch. Edda proudly said that the family still sends her Christmas and Easter cards every year. To emphasize the continued strength of their bond, she told me that they come to her home every year to bring her a poinsettia at Christmas. Then, with a sigh, Edda lamented that her new black neighbors do not seem interested in having a more familiar relationship with her. She said the new people often shovel the snow for her, but then she shook her head and said, "But, that's it."

The Reasons That Black Neighbors Support the Stayers

Black Caregiving Culture

Many cultures treat older people with heightened levels of respect, but reverence for the elderly is especially pronounced in African American culture. Though blacks are a heterogeneous group, research has shown that there is a distinct black caregiving culture grounded in core religious and spiritual beliefs, family orientation, and a distrust of the health care system. Some Afrocentric theorists have highlighted the topic of respect for the elderly in their efforts to tell a more balanced story of the U.S. black family,[7] arguing that many dimensions of black Americans' cultural respect for the elderly originate from or share similarities to African values.

Thus, African Americans' reverence for the elderly stems, in part, from the intergenerational transmission of cultural values from ancestors who also passed on other cultural values that are seen in U.S. black culture such as "collectivity, sharing, affiliation, obedience to authority, belief in spirituality, the importance of the past."[8] In Parkmont, I observed that black residents rarely called elderly people by their first names, and even with permission to do so they preferred to use the word "Miss" or "Mr." before addressing them by their first names. One pioneer explained her almost unconditional reverence for Parkmont's elderly in this way:

> I think it's because of the way you're raised. I wouldn't dare disrespect an old person. I was raised that you don't disrespect old people. Because they're old. And out of bad, comes good, you know? Like the neighbor that used to live here. She was all right, but you know, she was strange. We still did for her, though. I would rake her leaves up. And she would come out and say "hi" when she was there.

Because the relationships between stayers and pioneers seemed to benefit the whites so much, I wanted to get a sense of whether black residents felt used or taken advantage of by the older whites or whether the stayers seemed like a burden in any way. In general, the pioneers did not report feelings of resentment or bother, but rather a sense of duty. When asked if the stayers had ever done anything to help them out, one pioneer seemed to think that I was missing the point, saying that for blacks, respect for the elderly takes primacy over reciprocity or a shared cultural background:

> Nah. They never did anything for us. They really don't bother us that much, I don't think. Actually, they really never asked us to do anything for them. We just did it. If it needs to be done, we'll do it. You know, black people aren't as prejudiced as whites, I don't think.

Blacks are more likely to be the main caregivers for their aging family members or "to take care of their own people" than to place them in assisted living,

---

7. See Durodoye and Coker (2007), Hill (2001), and Nobles (1985).
8. This quotation is from Lee (2001, 171). See also Nobles (1985).

and often take great pride in this aspect of black culture.[9] Many blacks are distrustful and even disapproving of the practice of placing elderly kin in nursing homes and hospital-like settings.[10] Frequently, black families work together to care for elderly parents and grandparents by taking them into their own homes or taking on specialized roles (e.g., finances, transportation, shopping, meals). In Parkmont, some pioneers expressed moral indignation about the way that they believe white elderly people are treated by their families. In general, many pioneers felt sorry for their elderly white neighbors because they have noticed that many stayers' families live far away and visit infrequently, leaving the elderly in need of help and companionship. Part of this opinion stemmed from pioneers' experiences in Parkmont, but part was based on what they have witnessed at their jobs in helping professions.

Occupational Socialization

Reflecting national trends among African American workers,[11] Parkmont's black residents primarily held human services and city jobs with most working as nurses, social workers, police officers, corrections officers, street cleaners, EMTs, loan officers, postal workers, teachers, public transit workers, and "direct care" hospital workers. Following the housing frenzy of the times, many were also breaking into real estate. In general, Parkmont's black women were more likely than the men to be professionals or employed in private industry, but the relatively generous pay scales and benefits associated with city jobs and the human service professions have enabled working-class families to afford the move to Parkmont. These jobs have also provided black residents with the socialization, experience, and sensitivity that are conducive to helping elderly neighbors. Furthermore, though few residents were regular churchgoers, spirituality is likely to have played a role in pioneers' neighborliness as many mentioned being "with god" and strongly identified as Christians (with the exception of one newly converted Muslim family).

White stayers Jerry and Sally Dubrow strongly preferred their black neighbors, whom they viewed as compassionate and nonjudgmental, to their old white neighbors. They believed that they had been treated as outcasts by Parkmont's whites because Jerry worked the night shift as a janitor and because Sally is obese and physically disabled. Jerry reported that they regularly receive help from black

---

9. See Hill (1997), Turner et al. (2004), and White-Means (1993) for explanations of racial and ethnic differences in the "ethic of caring."

10. Turner et al. (2004).

11. Katz, Stern, and Fader (2005).

neighbors and this kind of aid increased greatly when Sally's disability forced her to rely on a wheelchair:

> The neighbors, there's a gentleman across the street—there's two brothers and two sisters, they work for 9–1–1. All four of them. They would run out—even in the middle of the night—they would run out and pick her up if she fell. One time she fell, and she sprained her bad foot. She had to go to the hospital. They called the other shift workers to take her over to the hospital. That's why I say we got wonderful neighbors now.

Anne Jackson, a pioneer who works as a nurse, elaborated on her special relationships with stayers and her family's significant efforts to support them when times got tough. She said that she and her husband, an EMT, continue to offer stayers plenty of unsolicited help, always refusing payments that are offered. Anne and her husband, perhaps due their lines of work, keep on top of the health status of their elderly neighbors. They also seemed protective of the stayers' reputations, as Anne made a point of telling me that when her next-door neighbors had to move away recently, it was due to health reasons and not because of racial antipathy or discomfort. She emphasized that she and her family have fostered special relationships with many stayers that go beyond simple helping gestures, often having them over to socialize and share celebrations:

> My next-door neighbor, she was older. She had a heart attack, a triple bypass. She couldn't cut her grass. She couldn't keep her yard up. So, my husband would cut her grass, and I would mess with [tend] her flowers, even in the back. I would just do it. If it was snow, my husband would shovel....And the Jewish couple? They were really old. She went to the senior hangout here all the time, the Jewish, what do you call it? [JCC?] Yeah. She went there all the time, and they were nice. They'd talk, play with the grandkids. We swept up for them. We just helped out. They were nice. Really sweet. They would come over at Christmastime. They loved my husband 'cause he did all the work. [Laughs.] He got the Jewish cookies. He got presents because he did a lot for them. The Jewish couple had to move because they were getting old, and Al was on dialysis, and he just couldn't do it. He couldn't do the stairs anymore. They honestly moved because of a health reason.

The intensive support from pioneers became more important as stayers' family members and friends moved away from Parkmont. In general, elderly stayers cannot turn to one another for support because the remaining elderly whites are burdened by their own problems. Additionally, as the neighborhood turned over, fewer stayers lived directly next door to each other. Thus, when in need, stayers turn to those who are accessible and offer them help. White stayers consistently made it a point to relate to me that pioneers usually offered support to them without even being asked.

Symmetrical Social Support: What Blacks Get Out of It

Reciprocity is an important component of neighboring. A shared feeling of reward can strengthen the bonds between residents and build a sense of community morale. Many of the examples of cross-racial neighboring mentioned so far could be seen as asymmetrical or nonreciprocal exchanges between elderly white stayers and younger black pioneers. However, those who provide support to older people often reap rewards that are less obvious or tangible. One can infer that, as with all altruistic behaviors, one incentive for helping other people is that it adds meaning and satisfaction to our own lives. Parkmont's residents explicitly stated that cross-racial neighboring in the form of asymmetrical helping often flourished into deeper relationships that the residents viewed as mutually beneficial.

Emotional Support and Companionship

Heterogeneous groups are often seen as having little in common, whereas people of a similar race, culture, age, and family structure are assumed to feel more comfortable with one another, and thus are likely to be more social. Social similarities are thought to increase individuals' motivation to spend time together and heighten the potential for meaningful interactions. Yet in Parkmont, residents reported intimate cross-racial relationships that seemed to transcend rigid social categories. Both groups reported that these kinds of relationships involved an exchange of support and friendship, rather than a mere one-sided civic duty to help the aged.

The relationship between Leo and Gladys Katz and Joy Parker provided some insight into the multidimensional and mutually beneficial nature of Parkmont's cross-racial neighboring. The couple told me that Joy loves to go to their house to chat with Gladys and they even have the keys to each other's home. They explained that Joy makes them feel as though they "have somebody," which gives them great comfort in a neighborhood where longtime friends are no longer easy to find. At the same time, Leo and Gladys stressed that they have also "been there for her" when "she has her problems." They specifically mentioned that they have been a shoulder for Joy to cry on when she has been hurt by past boyfriends, some of whom they described as "disasters." Leo and Gladys also emphasized that their relationship with Joy has not been based on her pity for them as elderly shut-ins. Joy corroborated this, and went so far as to say that she actually envies the old couple's social life:

> I never felt sorry for Gladys and Leo 'cause there ain't nothin' wrong with them. They go out more often than me. And they'll have to ask me, "Come on, let's go out to dinner." And I'll be like, "Look, I'm too tired." They go out New Year's! They be coming in late that night. I be in bed sleeping, sound asleep, and they be gone. After ten, they be coming in, and I be sleeping. They be havin' more fun than me. They go to shows. They go to the movies. Ain't nothin' wrong with them to be sorry for them. They can do stuff. They can go shopping. I wanted them to stay here forever.

But after many health problems, Leo and Gladys had recently moved into a retirement community in a high-rise apartment building. A few weeks after the move, I visited them; they seemed sad and regretful. They no longer own their car and told me that they long for their old life. They were especially depressed about being surrounded by elderly people in extremely poor health. After my visit, I stopped by Joy's house. She asked me all about her former neighbors and told me how much she misses them. She confided that she had a hard time sleeping on the first night that her "best friends" were gone:

> They're wonderful people. They're my best friends. We call each other every night and make sure each other is okay. They came over here and ate my food. They enjoyed it. Jerk chicken, salad. They ate dessert. They eat everything. They had a good time. They be my good friends of eight years. When I just came here, they welcomed me with cake....The first night they moved, they called just to make sure that I was okay....Anyone can call first. Sometimes they call and leave me a message when I'm not here. I'll call Gladys right back. We talk on the phone. And if she ain't got nothin' to talk about, then she just callin' to make sure I'm okay. They make good friends.

Skeptics might consider the cross-racial relationships in Parkmont to be parasitic in that one party seems to benefit far more than the other. However, when I proposed that some might find it hard to believe that a healthy woman of her age gets very much out of a relationship with older people who have been in poor health, Joy became annoyed. She quickly responded with disbelief and outrage, saying people who believe that are "crazy" and stressed to me that her life has been greatly improved because of the bonds she has formed with some of the stayers:

> Older people's far more important to me right now. I don't have many young friends. I talk to people, but I try not to get close to them. That's the same thing the pastor preached in church today. The people you laugh and talk with? They're not your friends, but Gladys is my friend. I can tell Gladys anything, and I'm okay. 'Cause my younger friends tell me I'm too secretive. Things I tell Gladys and Leo, I'm not gonna tell them. The older people and the younger people are friends. No, I could never lose them. We talk every night. There is not a night we go to bed and not talk. Just call and say "hi." They call me and tell me how was their dinner. I went up there to make sure they was serving them good dinner. They gonna be my friends forever. I'm just a normal person. I'm young and talking to old people as friends.

Rena Grubman told me a story that revealed the more intimate and balanced nature of her relationship with her pioneer neighbors. When I ran into her on her block one day, Rena told me that her neighbors, Nina and Daryl Jones, had a small kitchen fire. Nina and their newborn stayed in Rena's spare room until the fumes dissipated. Later, Nina told me more about the mutual exchange that characterizes her family's relationship with Rena and with Joe Cassidy, another stayer on the block. Like many pioneers, Nina told me that as Parkmont has continued to change and the population of blacks has continued to churn, the only neighbors to whom she feels close are the stayers:

> Miss Rena's really nice; she's older, so we look out for her. But other than that? That's really all that I talk to on the block. Mr. Joe, we look out for him. If I don't see him in a couple days, I'll ring the bell 'cause I know he's alone, too. So, we look out for those two. You ring the bell. "You okay, Mr. Joe? Haven't seen you in a couple days. Need anything?" My husband doesn't even ask Miss Rena if she need him to shovel; he just shovels. If we see her going out, like she walks on a cane, so we'll go over help her walk down to whoever's picking her up, things like that. If I'm going to the store, I'll ask her if she need anything. I'll call her. We talk. She called me to ask me if my husband and I had shoveled for her. I said, "Yeah." She said, "Oh, I'm coming over." And she came over; she said, "I would bake you a cake, but I bought you one." She comes over on my son's birthday. When I had him, she came over and during the summertime when I was home with him on maternity leave. We would sit outside and talk and stuff. She was just over here the week before

last—brought him an Easter present. A duck. She's Jewish, so it touched me that she bought him an Easter present, and she doesn't celebrate Easter. She gives us gifts at Christmastime. Mr. Joe gives us cookies every Christmas.

Morris Barsky also provided examples of the ways in which he and his black neighbors both reaped benefits from their relationship, whether it was watching over each other or celebrating important milestones in their families' lives:

> My neighbors were black and very, very nice. Oh, I knew them well. I knew them enough to go to birthday parties, graduation parties, and all that. I always gave a check and card. They were very nice to me. They did my lawn, you know. Reciprocated. We were nice to each other. And they made calls. If they didn't see me in a day or two: "Mr. Barsky, are you okay?" They had my phone number, and I had theirs. And when they went away and left the house, they gave me the key to the house. I liked them as neighbors. Best neighbors I ever had.

Sense of Stability and Institutional Memory

When a neighborhood rapidly loses long-term residents, the incoming residents are also deprived of something important: an institutional memory of the community. Parkmont's institutional memory takes the form of the collective memory of long-time residents who have a body of knowledge gained through various resources and experiences that they can share and pass on to future generations of residents. In order for stayers to effectively pass on their historical wisdom about all they have witnessed and learned, they need opportunities to connect with an audience who cares. Though the elderly stayers have faith in the pioneers, they also know that the pioneers are being replaced by a second wave of black residents who seem less invested in neighborhood leadership and participation, making it unlikely that the stayers' collective memories of Parkmont will be retained. This new group, the second wave, is different from the pioneers in that its members have no memory of Parkmont in better times, have minimal contact with the white old-timers, and only rarely do they have positive, meaningful interactions with pioneers.

Residents' acquisition of and socialization into community norms are ecological in that they are a response to the population and environmental conditions that are specific to Parkmont at a point in time. Because of their long tenure in Parkmont, stayers believed that they have the power, authority, and institutional memory to serve as "sponsors" and teach new residents the norms of life in Parkmont.[12] In general, this was true in the past when new white people would move in to Parkmont, and it was especially true when integration began to take hold. One stayer described her husband's longtime habit of reaching out to socialize all newcomers into neighborhood norms, emphasizing that her husband did not discriminate by race in this practice: "My husband was very outgoing. The first black people, my husband taught all of them. He would get out the first snow and clear the whole path and both pavements. He taught them and the white ones that moved in after the 'originals.'" Like many communities, Parkmont's social structure placed the older residents at the top of the hierarchy. At the start of integration, stayers could still effectively perform this role because they remained relatively healthy and active, but they were eager to pass the baton to Parkmont's pioneers, who had young families and who seemed eager to fit in to the social fabric of the community.

In general, the pioneers were not only accepting but enthusiastic about the stayers' sense of ownership over the community; it demonstrated to them that they had made a good decision in choosing Parkmont and had entered a neighborhood where residents remained invested in quality of life even after the onset of integration. Though the stayers' desire to spend time with pioneers sometimes felt overwhelming to the newcomers, pioneer Korrie Dawson appreciated their proactive efforts to maintain the neighborhood. She asserted that the stayers made genuine efforts to get to know her and share with her their love of Parkmont:

> Mr. Goldberg would walk up and down the street and pick up the trash. You would never have believed his age. Wonderful man. And he loved my daughter, the one in the military. He always came over to ask how she's doing. And when he just saw her car parked, he'd see her, and come running out. Oh, I really, really hated to see him leave. The funny thing is that all of the Jewish couples that lived here, it was a ritual for them in the evening to sit out. I'm not a sitter-outer, and sometimes I used to feel bad, like I might be offending. Because they would say, "Oh, if you're not doin' anything, come and sit out with me." I'm like, "I don't really have that kind of time".... When I came here nine years ago, my neighbors on both sides were Jewish and older. The one on this side, really nice lady, would come out and talk to us all the time, bring little things over for us. Her daughter took her to the nursing home. And on this side, they were

---

12. See Linde (2009) for a discussion of the role of places in establishing institutional memories and for an explanation of the ways in which hierarchies, such as age, determine which people have the "right to speak" for an institution.

> a really nice couple, always together, and when he passed, the kids, you
> know, took her away [from her home and the neighborhood].

Parkmont presented an unusual opportunity for younger black and older white residents to have intimate social contact, which in such a segregated city, seemed almost exotic.

Perhaps because interacting with older people often involves listening to their stories and recollections of memories, many pioneers found themselves fascinated by stayers' cultural backgrounds. Anne Jackson was awed when she learned about the details of her elderly neighbors' early lives: "We had a Jewish couple, and they were in the Holocaust. They were Holocaust survivors. You could see the numbers. They were sweet. They were really good." Anne credited the fact that she chose to move to an integrated neighborhood with exposing her family to a group of older people who have unique knowledge and valuable lessons to share. Similarly, Sam Wilson, a pioneer who was serving as the first black president of the Parkmont civic association at the time of my fieldwork, told me that he made it a priority to know the names and life histories of all of the white stayers on his block. He urged me to interview some of the stayers on his street so I could appreciate their community knowledge and hear the interesting stories of long-time residents as well as better understand the bonds that stayers had formed with pioneers in the midst of racial change: "You'd like to talk to my next door neighbor, too. She's Russian. She's lived there since the '60s and '70s. Another guy on my block's been living here since the '60s, and he's Italian, and I mean, he speaks Italian. He's from Italy, and he's seen the neighborhood grow and all."

Stayer Sybil Cutler believed that pioneers may actually prefer to have the elderly whites as neighbors because they are informed, predictable, and quiet. She told me this anecdote about her neighbor, a pioneer whose family took the time to visit with Sybil after her husband died:

> He had only lived here maybe not quite a year, and him and his wife
> came in to give their condolences. The first thing he said to me was, "Are
> you going to move?" I said, "No, Sir. I'm not going to move. Don't worry
> about it." He says, "We were worried." In other words, they don't want
> it. They don't know who they'll get as a neighbor. They're black people.
> They're not new; they've been here about six years. Yeah, that's the first
> thing he said to me. "Are you going to move?" I said, "No, Sir."

Ken Wilkinson's family fondly remembers the two elderly Jewish sisters who were their next-door neighbors when they first moved to Parkmont. He and his sons, Ken Jr. and Marc, told me about how distraught they were when one of the sisters died. Marc, the fifteen-year-old, shared the following story about his relationship with them:

> If we were to get locked out after school, we would usually go over their house 'cause they were usually home after school. When we'd get our report cards, we'd go over there and show them. And they'd give us candy and stuff like that for our birthdays. And we'd go over there for dinner or something like that. That's what we did with them.

Ken Jr., the sixteen-year-old who plans to become an engineer, shared similar stories about the good times he shared with these elderly sisters. In fact, he choked up during his interview with me while confiding that he felt especially "emotional" when his neighbor died:

> In the morning, my mom and dad would leave early and they would take care of us. I was upset when she passed. Also, for forty-five minutes between school and when my parents would come home, we stayed with them. We liked the Steelers and they liked the Cowboys. Recently, we had a "Cowboys versus Steelers" game. You could hear us cheering in our house, and then you could hear them cheering in their house. They came up to the window when they scored! When I would be there, they would ask me how school was going. You have a nice conversation. When she passed, I was really upset. I was crying.

While it may seem that elderly whites would have very little to offer young black residents, both pioneers and stayers told stories about the ways in which they find cross-racial relationships in Parkmont to be mutually fulfilling. The pioneers' gifts are routine as well as intense forms of instrumental help and social support that allow stayers to age in place for a longer period of time. Stayers provide what little they have to give at their advanced age: emotional support and companionship, as well as a sense of community stability and institutional memory that is needed to foster an attachment to Parkmont.

Conclusion

In the process of investigating the cross-racial neighboring context of white flight, I uncovered a surprising story. Many pioneers and stayers have made a special connection. This happened even though the pioneers had not known the stayers for long, had every reason to suspect that these elderly whites would hold racist attitudes toward them, and even though pioneers had very little in common with stayers in terms of age, family structure, and cultural background. It is ironic that so many of the whites who left Parkmont were threatened by the idea of blacks moving in, when in fact, the pioneers' arrival turned out to be fortuitous for those who stayed and benefited from the support of younger black neighbors. Many stayers rest better at night knowing that they can call their pioneer neighbors in case of an emergency, and their families have peace of mind because they know that their elderly loved ones have people who watch over them. Much of the pioneers' willingness to help stayers stems from their cultural values about the elderly and their socialization in helping professions, but they are also on the receiving end of social benefits from their access to older, long-term neighbors.

In navigating Parkmont's interracial relationships, the importance of the cultural intersections of race and class emerged as an important theme. I had expected that stayers would have great difficulty adjusting to the rapid influx of blacks. After all, Parkmont's elderly whites reported minimal meaningful exposure to black families in the past. In addition, stayers' openness to integration was likely to be contaminated by the unanimous fears expressed by stayers' friends, family members, and former neighbors, who ominously warned them about the supposedly inevitable decline and danger that would follow the arrival of black residents. Yet many stayers kept an open mind, whether because of their unique religious or cultural backgrounds, more tolerant individual personalities, or simply because of their resolve to stay in their homes. Most stayers reported that they were relieved to see that the pioneers "belonged" in Parkmont. In other words, they were pleased that the new black residents were homeowners, held working-class occupations in helping professions, and held respectable cultural orientations toward family and community. The stayers especially did not anticipate the extraordinary efforts of so many pioneers to reach out to them and make their remaining years in Parkmont feel so much easier and more secure. To many stayers, the pioneers' respect for the elderly represented a commitment to a personal morality code that seemed to extend to the community as a whole.

From the perspective of the pioneers, the elderly stayers were allies in their aspiration to maintain the status of their neighborhood as a safe and calm place, despite the reality that their hopes for stable integration were fading away. Overall, the pioneers reported positive feelings toward the elderly whites. Despite their advanced age and limited ability to offer equivalent types of help, stayers' life experience, knowledge of Parkmont, and sense of community ownership was a welcome change for pioneers seeking a better quality of life. In many ways, pioneers considered their own values about family and community to be more similar to those of the stayers than to the people they had left behind in their old neighborhoods. Despite differences in race and age, both pioneers and stayers share a value system that places their home and community as a top priority. In part, this can be seen as part of a shared working-class value system. But social class similarities alone are an insufficient explanation for the cross-racial bond. As I discuss in chapters 5 and 6, pioneers differ from the incoming second wave of black residents in their assimilationist cultural orientation, timing of arrival, and family structures.

Although the topic of neighboring is not new, this chapter shows that in white-flight communities, pioneering black residents can play an important role in the lives of those who remain. In places like Parkmont, what starts as cross-racial intergenerational neighboring based on asymmetrical forms of support can develop into something more symbiotic and satisfying for both stayers and pioneers. The next chapter's vignette is about Ken Wilkinson, a pioneer who took a leadership role in maintaining community values in the midst of Parkmont's rapid population change. His story represents the aspirational journey that many pioneers made when they integrated Parkmont, and it demonstrates how the community has transformed now that the era of white flight is over and the new phase of black flight has been set in motion.

5

KEN WILKINSON
Striving for the Next Generation

Ken Wilkinson, a forty-seven-year-old pioneer, represents a linkage between Parkmont's two major stages of change. His narrative provides insights into the community's transition from white to black by illuminating the pioneers' reasons for selecting Parkmont as a destination, their perceptions of white flight, and their relationships with elderly stayers. Ken's story explores black flight by portraying pioneers' discussions of sources of dissatisfaction with the school and neighborhood environment as black flight began to set in, their conflicts with the second wave residents, and their hopes and plans for the future. As one of the first pioneers to arrive, and as an especially informed and active community member, Ken's framing and detailed interpretations of events add to the voices of other pioneers and provide access to an insider's perspective on the specific cultural dimensions of neighborhood change that have troubled so many of Parkmont's pioneers.

Ken and his family invited me to spend some time with them on Halloween to observe the neighborhood on a busy night when children and parents were on the streets and neighbors were expected to open their doors and participate in the festivities. As Ken sat on his patio giving out candy in the evening, it was clear that he viewed this time as an important opportunity to build community and reinforce high standards of behavior for the families in Parkmont. At one point, a little boy who was trick-or-treating unaccompanied by parents, siblings, or friends came up to ask Ken for candy. He told us that he was dressed up in a costume called "dead gangsta." Ken grimaced, but took this episode as an opportunity to teach the child a lesson. He said to the boy, "Dead is right. That's how gangstas end up—dead." The child just stared uncomfortably at Ken, politely thanked him for the candy, and solemnly moved on to the next house. A few minutes later, as we talked outside, I asked Ken why his patio was so dark when other residents left a light on to signal that they were hosting trick-or-treaters. He told me that he had unscrewed the lightbulb to improve his supervision of the people on his block:

> I can just sit out here, and nobody will see me. I pretty much see what's going on. Who goes in when, what time they come in. I know who lives where. I know what car belongs on the block and which one don't. I recognize everybody. I'm pretty much familiar, but sitting up on the porch, people walk by and they don't even see me. It's convenient. Plus, I'm out, constantly watching.

Ever since Ken and his wife, Jill, moved to Parkmont with the goal of improving their quality of life, they have been model citizens. Residents commend them for their parenting and many neighbors praise the couple's two teenage sons, who are unusually mature, polite, and smart for their age. Several neighbors called Ken "the mayor," referring to his vigilant efforts to keep his property, as well as the entire block, in order. Ken did have a few critics who expressed the belief that he could sometimes go overboard in his efforts to monitor the block. For instance, one resident told me about a time when his car was towed after Ken reported it to the police's abandoned vehicle unit. But on the whole, it was plain to see that Ken exemplifies the goals and values of Parkmont's pioneers and that his fundamental roles as a father, spouse, homeowner, neighbor, and community organizer contribute very much to his little corner of Parkmont.

Ken and Jill live with their sons, Ken Jr. and Marc, in a Parkmont row house. Ken was recently promoted in his municipal job doing waste and snow removal, and Jill is teacher who has been taking night classes to earn a graduate degree in education administration with the ultimate goal of becoming a school principal. In addition to his regular job, Ken is an entrepreneur. He designs and sews window and patio awnings for people in Parkmont and is an equal partner with his sons in a lawn care business that serves the neighborhood. The boys attend science-focused magnet schools across town and both have plans to study engineering in college. Although Ken and Jill are in their forties and are known for their strict parenting style, they somehow manage not to come off as nerdy or square. They both wear contemporary clothing styles and enjoy popular music, movies, and dining out, and have come to enjoy annual cruise vacations.

On the night of one of our taped interviews, Jill was dressed in a velour tracksuit as she made hot dogs for dinner before heading off to one of her graduate school classes. She has a fun and light-hearted temperament, which helps to balance Ken's more intense and serious demeanor. Wearing a Tupac Shakur T-shirt, baseball hat, and gold chain with a cross, Ken is a tall and imposing figure. He speaks in a low, deep voice, and though he has a tendency to drop one-liners and burst out laughing, these more carefree episodes take you by surprise. As one child on the block observed, "Mr. Ken don't play."

Before Parkmont

After serving in the U.S. Air Force, Ken returned home to live with his parents in a low-income neighborhood in the city. When he obtained a highly sought-after civil service job with the city's Department of Streets and Sanitation, he decided to move to a neighborhood that was located closer to his assigned work area. His new job, which involved long hours, including overtime and emergency snow removal in the winter, also carried with it the status of "emergency worker" and the associated requirement that he reside within the city limits. However, because the job paid well, was relatively secure, and offered a generous pension, Ken was willing to contend with the fact that it would limit his freedom in choosing where to live.

Soon, Ken met and fell in love with Jill. It happened in a way that many people dream about: "A guy I worked with in the city, I was in his wedding. We were both in the wedding party." After a brief courtship, they moved together to a densely populated neighborhood on the south side of the city. According to Ken, money was tight, "times was tough," and they lived there "more for convenience," since the community was close to both of their city jobs. In fact, Ken said that Jill's teaching job "was right around the corner."

Time passed, and Ken and Jill felt fortunate, grateful for their recent engagement, their secure jobs, and the birth of their two sons. However, the neighborhood in which they lived was another story. Their two-bedroom rented row house was all they could afford at the time, but it was located in a drug-infested area. Ken became alarmed when he noticed an increase in violent crime and drugs in the community. Yet the serious crimes were not the only problems that drove him and his family away; the more minor problems of disorder plaguing the area also contributed to the couple's dissatisfaction. Ken explained the mix of crime and disorder that motivated the decision to move:

> To move to a better neighborhood, and basically, to own my own home. My old neighborhood, it's a little closer in to the city. It had a lot of crime, people breaking in cars a lot, and it was pretty much a drug area—people selling on the corners. Every couple months I was putting

a new mirror on my car, or I'd get up and my car wasn't there. My car was stolen twice. Right off the block. And then you have to park on the pavement because another car would come in and take your mirror off. It was awful.

As a sanitation worker, Ken is extremely sensitive to the way a neighborhood is maintained, and he found the physical appearance of the last place he lived to be revolting. He never planned on making it his long-term home. Although now he prides himself on his leadership role in improving Parkmont, Ken was not one for calling the police when problems would arise in his previous neighborhood. In fact, Ken told me that he felt completely unsentimental about leaving his old neighborhood to come to Parkmont. So, without a single regret, Ken, Jill, and the boys packed their bags.

Moving to a White Neighborhood

In 1996, when their sons were turning ages five and seven, Ken and Jill embarked on a house search. Ken had grown up in a different region of the city, so he had never even heard of Parkmont at the time that they started to house hunt. In contrast, Jill was more typical of pioneers in that she had been raised in a black neighborhood near Parkmont and had a strong preference to limit the scope of their home search in order to relocate near her family. Ken told me that that if not for their city jobs, he would have moved the family into a detached house in the first-ring suburbs, which are located close to work and family. Still, Ken retained a sense of humor about his situation, joking about the bright side of his job: "There are no problems with snow removal here because I *am* snow removal."

Ken and Jill began to look for housing in and around Parkmont. They briefly considered a row house in a middle-class neighborhood located very close to Jill's family, but they felt discriminated against by the realtor, who was black:

> I went to Century 21 on the other side, where Jill's family lives. I guess it was because I was black, but the house they were showing me was tore up. It had some structural problems. They were row houses, but they seemed like they needed too much work. I wasn't willing to settle. I think the realtor was just trying to unload it.

After this negative experience with subpar housing, Ken and Jill decided to constrain the search for their first home to the boundaries of Parkmont: "We got in the car and drove around here and looked for signs." They fell in love with their block after seeing the backyards of the homes, which face a wooded park area. As

Ken said, "Right here, the back of our house is to the woods. Step out back there, and it takes us away from all that stuff in the city." With white flight beginning to take hold, it was not difficult to find a house on their favorite block, where several homes were for sale. The family was excited by the move, and soon after settling in, Ken and Jill got married.

Although many of Parkmont's second wave black residents, as well as a non-trivial number of pioneers, financed their homes through subprime mortgages, family loans, or low-income housing programs, Ken and Jill purchased their home in a more traditional way: "We saved up. I checked out the house, and I came by from time to time. And 'cause I'm a veteran, they approved it. I have a guaranteed amount of money with the VA." Even so, Ken believes that they would have been able to afford the home without his veteran status: "I probably would. I still had a good job. They guaranteed the mortgage. They just wanted to make sure that I wasn't paying too much or making the wrong decision."

When they selected their house, Ken and Joan knew that Parkmont was a predominantly white neighborhood, but unlike many pioneers, Ken said that he mostly chose it for the amenities that he associates with white communities. Ken attributed his generally positive views about white neighborhoods to his very memorable childhood experience of moving from a segregated public housing complex into a white community. However, he told me that soon after his family moved, his white childhood neighborhood resegregated and became all black. Decades later with a family of his own, Ken feels disappointed that Ken Jr. and Marc are now having the same experience that he did.

Regardless of whether it was mostly white or mostly black, Ken chose Park-mont because he wanted to move to a place where residents possess a strong sense of ownership about community life. In his opinion, neighborhoods like this are more often found in white parts of the city. He elaborated on the non-racial nature of his neighborhood research process, which focused on a sense of order and pride in the appearance of homes:

> It was not necessarily that it was white. It's that it was clean and relatively quiet. I took the time to come around and sit during the day and come by during the evening and check it out and make sure it was what I was looking for. You can go to certain areas where it is predominantly black, and you can see—like a certain block in my old neighborhood—every place around it is in chaos. But there's this one particular block that has this attitude. Everybody has plants on the porch, and everybody has an awning. Attitude.

Still, given his previous experiences with white flight and neighborhood de-cline, Ken is not naïve. He has remained sensitive to racial change and its causes and costs and told me that racism was the driving force behind the rapid population change that occurred in Parkmont shortly after the pioneers arrived. To provide an example, Ken told me that they purchased their home from a middle-aged Irish American couple whom they believed were typical of the kinds of whites who were eager to sell: "She was a crossing guard and her husband was a cop. I got a good idea why they moved. Because of the neighbors' being black. The other neighbors told me that he kind of reminded them of Archie Bunker." Even though he thinks the leavers fit this profile, Ken said that the older white neighbors who stayed in Parkmont were different; they made special efforts to reach out and get to know his family: "When I first arrived, they were nice. Especially next door. They were really welcoming and had us over to dinner and stuff like that."

Trouble Brewing: Problems with the School

In their old neighborhood, Ken Jr. and Marc attended the school where Jill worked as a teacher, and which Ken rated as "pretty good." However, Ken and Jill place education as an extremely high priority and wanted more for their sons. They arrived in Parkmont thinking that Lombard was superior to many city schools, and they expected an improved learning experience for their children. Perhaps that is why I was so surprised to learn that even though Jill is a teacher, neither she nor Ken had formally researched the quality of Lombard in recent years. Instead, they based their evaluations of the school on word of mouth and on personal experiences. When I asked for more details about this, Ken admitted that Jill handles school-related affairs in their family. Jill told me that she largely relied on information from her brother, who graduated from Lombard back when the integration busing program was in effect. Knowing the area was white and that Jill's brother had a positive experience at Lombard, they decided the school would be suitable for their children.

However, by the time of the family's arrival, Lombard had long been a black segregated school, and it was struggling in terms of students' academic success and safety. Ken explained the couple's realization that the information gleaned from Jill's brother was out of date and not accurate:

> Back at that time, I don't think that Lombard was that bad, because I think her brother was recently graduated from there. In '96, it was still relatively on its way. But lately, you know, with the uncooperation [lack of cooperation] with the parents and the kids, it's declined. It's out of control.

After a brief time at Lombard, Ken and Jill transferred their sons to magnet schools. I asked Ken whether the boys feel socially separated from the other neighborhood children because they attend school all the way across the city:

> No. They're pretty much grounded. A lot of the parents want to get their kids out of Lombard 'cause of the things that've been going on. I've talked to a couple of parents. Right now, Ricky, down the street, his kids aren't going to Lombard because of the lack of control. That's in Lombard, but that's in other schools, too. But the thing with the way the system is set up, there's not too much they can really do.

Ken and Jill have come to understand that they made a difficult trade-off when they chose to relocate to a safer community. In order to gain access to relative safety from crime and a better quality of community life, the family actually left behind a neighborhood school that was better than Lombard. Feeling hopeless about the future of Lombard and eager to protect their children, Ken and Jill believed their only option was to send the boys away from Parkmont for their education.

Signs of Decline on the Strip

In discussing his perceptions of Parkmont as a living environment, Ken seemed especially critical of changes in the quality of businesses on the strip, such as the increase in "Chinese" stores, which he and many other pioneers resent and view as low class, unattractive, and exploitative of black neighborhoods. Ken told me that he actively works to prevent further decline in the retail district:

> It's changed.... The beauty supply place? That used to be a restaurant, and after that, they tried to make it a "Stop and Go" where they would sell malt liquor or whatever, but we weren't having that. It ended up being a Chinese hair place. But overall, I mean, how many Chinese stores can you have? It's just these little shops that's on the strip now. They tried a lot of restaurants. Any new restaurants that come in don't survive.

Parkmont's pioneers take the neighborhood's appearance very seriously and fear that the influx of downscale businesses are a form of "broken windows" or a slippery slope of neighborhood decline.[1] To make the owners of businesses more

---

1. See Wilson and Kelling (1982) for a full explanation of "broken windows" theory, which asserts that a community must target small problems (i.e., disorder) in order to prevent further deterioration and to deter more serious or violent forms of crime. In Parkmont, disorderly behavior

accountable for maintaining their properties, Ken has worked with the civic association to pressure business owners on the strip to address the graffiti problems that he has observed. However, Ken told me that this so-called minor problem is very difficult to eradicate and is an uphill battle that requires great persistence from residents:

> We had somebody that wrote graffiti on the bank, and we talked to the bank, and the bank had it removed. 'Cause in Parkmont, we try to have a zero tolerance for that. They said that they had to go through corporate. They had to go through a certain chain. It's not like they can just go ahead, and somebody in the bank is going to come out. They have to get people to do that, but they took care of it *after* we kept complaining about it.

Ken's concerns about Parkmont's physical appearance and beautification also extend to forms of social disorder that current residents, visitors, and potential buyers are likely to find threatening. For instance, Ken is distressed by the drug dealers whom he sees hanging out on the strip. He believes that it is up to the residents to stay on top of this problem:

> The dealers still have their crowd here. I guess they're doing their thing, selling their wares or whatever. Selling something that they shouldn't be selling. You can tell. They're standing there, and they're watching the cars go by, and they're meeting the cars and all that kind of stuff, so we pretty much know. At one time, they had the police came up and put them all up against the ground, it was probably about a year ago. They had 'em, and that's when people were calling. I would call, and Ricky would call, and someone else would call. But then it stopped, but they're not quite as flagrant as they used to be. So I pretty much know where they are. They're teenagers into their early twenties.

Like most pioneers, Ken places an extremely high value on two dimensions of community life that are tied to the attitudes and behaviors of residents: a sense of ownership and an orderly environment. When asked what he likes most about Parkmont, Ken talked about the simple, often taken for granted, pleasures of living in a neighborhood where residents adhere to basic standards of respect for each other and where they maintain the appearance of the properties. Ken still

---

has primarily triggered pioneers' mobility thoughts and behaviors not because it leads to violence, but because disorder interferes with pioneers' quality of life, symbolizes degradation in the values of incoming residents, and represents a decline in neighborhood's status.

acknowledges many of Parkmont's virtues, but he has grown increasingly tired of feeling alone in his efforts to maintain and improve the community:

> What do I like most about the neighborhood? At this point in time? When I *do* have my peace and quiet. The other morning, I was out, and I was like, "Wow! This is really, really nice. Just being able to sit out. Me and my wife were sitting out front until everybody got up....Most of the time it's okay, but I used to like to go back into the woods. I don't go back there anymore, 'cause I was overwhelming myself with keeping it clean. I'd come out with two or three bags of trash. Trash drives me nuts, so I had to, for my own self. I used to walk. I had the fisherman's boots, like wader boots, and I would start at the very beginning, and I would walk all the way down to the falls. And I would pick up the trash and stuff like that, but then it got too much. And I used to have help, and then after a while, it wasn't like that.

Sources of Cultural Conflict between the Pioneers and the Second Wave

Ken told me that it has been impossible to ignore the fact that a large number of the pioneers have either moved away or are planning to move. He discussed the changes that have taken place in Parkmont since he first arrived, complaining about the constant population shifts that have affected the neighborhood's age, race, and family structure profiles. Ken clearly disapproves of the second wave of black residents and said that if he had to do it all over again today, he would never have chosen to move to Parkmont:

> When I first moved here, there wasn't as many kids. The new people are younger, and they're coming with a lot more kids. If I came now? And I seen across the street? There is usually about eight to ten kids. I'd rather it's all old people.

Differences in Parenting

Ken explained that part of the decline in Parkmont's quality of life is caused by the second wave residents' divergent values about raising children. Ken believes that parenting differences between pioneers and new residents cause conflict between the two groups, which also contributes to a milieu of social disorder. To illustrate his point, Ken described what happened when a very young group of rowdy boys decided to use his patio as a hangout on a weekday evening:

> I confronted them. There were a few kids that were hanging out. It was about 11:30, 12:00 at night. They couldn't have been no more than about ten. I told 'em, "If you're going to stay out, go out in front of your house, and make all that noise." And then the parent wanted to confront me on it. I was pretty much like, "You're supposed to be watching. I shouldn't have to watch your kids." They should be down there in front of their own house. Plus, I gave out the fliers as far as the curfews and concerns. What it is, on Friday and Saturday and stuff like that. They told the mother that I hollered at them. The mother came here and said that I shouldn't talk to her kids like that. That I shouldn't tell them nothing. That if I have anything to say, I should come down and tell her. I disagree with that. I should be able to say, "Why don't you go home? Go down to where you livin' at." I *was* hollering, but just: "Why don't you go down the street?" You know, "You making all that noise. Why don't you go down the street and make all that noise?" Who's raising who? You know? The kids were ten or twelve, but I guess the mom might have been twenty-seven. Who's raising who?

Ken's views about the negative effects of poor parenting also address the issue of physical disorder in the neighborhood, which he directly links to weak family values. He complained about neighboring children's habit of littering in their own community: "I would think that if the parents would make them clean it up, then they wouldn't throw it down. Just make them come out on Saturdays, and clean it up."

Ken's parenting philosophy is far more strict than most modern parents, a partial reflection of his military background. However, he is also a loving and supportive father, encouraging his sons to be independent and responsible citizens. Ken takes a preventive approach to both the community and his children, which shapes his definition of what constitutes a bad influence or a sign of larger problems. He feels his strategy for parenting in Parkmont is effective, and he is proud to say that, unlike many of the newer residents, he has never received a single complaint about his sons: "People pretty much say good things about them. They seem to be making pretty good decisions. Plus, for a long time I wouldn't let them go anywhere. I wouldn't let them go past the strip."

Thus, in contrast to many of the second wave residents, Ken sees the roles of proactive parent and resident to be inextricably linked. He reported that he takes many precautionary measures to keep his sons on track, which often means insulating them from too much unsupervised contact with neighborhood children.

For instance, Ken prefers that his sons stay home and have friends over in their basement family room, rather than go to other people's homes or spend time outside in the neighborhood at night where "things happen." Ken thinks that his sons' friends actually prefer to be at their house, especially the ones with family problems and fewer resources: "They come here. I think they may be a little more comfortable here. Plus, they may have a couple of things going on. The kids they hang around—I like them. They're pretty much good kids. They hang out, play their games. So far so good."

As Ken spoke to me about how much time he puts into teaching his children the values of respect and discipline, I recalled an early evening in late November when Ken was sitting on the couch listening to a what I thought was a fairly common request from teenagers: to order pizza for dinner. In a calm tone but with a bit of exasperation, he explained why ordering out was not an option on a weeknight: "Mom made dinner and that's what I'm having." He told them pizza was for weekends, and that if they wanted to have it on a weeknight, they would need to pay for it themselves. They complained that they did not have enough money between them; plus, they could not finish a whole pizza by themselves. Ken just said, "Oh well, then." Ken told me that he adheres to set rules, even for small matters, in order to help his sons understand how they are different from the other children around them. All of this is part of Ken's strategy to meet his larger goals of keeping his sons safe, successful, and respectable as they navigate the problems that have arisen in Parkmont:

> I think it's being consistent and trying to give them good values. I try to make them be the best people they can be as far as being honest, being helpful, and not looking at race. It's just being helpful and caring about the community. 'Cause they go out, and they have to clean up outside, and all the other kids may be out there. Having them see the differences. 'Cause they see the kids that are walking down the street without an adult, showing their underwear, and being disrespectful. It's nothing but disrespect.

I asked if his sons would like to dress in those styles if they could, since they are a popular trend, but Ken thinks that his children have come to accept his values, some of which come from being an "older" parent:

> I don't think it would be comfortable for them at this point in time, and before, we wouldn't have it. I think a lot of that goes with me being older. We were thirty-one and thirty-six when we had them. A lot of the other kids, their parents are almost as young as they are, and they're wearing their pants like that, too.

Although Ken is extremely tired after work and does not have the educational background to help his sons with some of their homework from advanced placement science classes, he prides himself on "being there" for them when it comes to school: "Some days I don't get a chance to check their homework, but if they're having a problem at the school, I'm definitely there for them. If it's either a problem with a student, a problem with a teacher, or a problem with their grades. That's what's important."

Clashes over Block Parties

Ken's ambivalence about Parkmont stems from his knowledge that it is relatively safe, yet he emphasized that he strongly disapproves of the way the second wave residents conduct themselves in the neighborhood:

> Overall, I'm still pretty much satisfied with the neighborhood, but it has changed. There are a lot of things that I don't like, like the attitudes of uncaring. My new neighbors may play the music a little bit too loud or they may pull up in their car and it's still blaring. And I'm sitting there on the porch, and they're not paying a bit of attention. They're just sitting there in the car, and they are just blaring with the music. It interferes with my peace.

Ken clearly views the second wave residents' attitudes about disorder to be a serious matter and believes that their nonchalance sends a strong message about how different their core values are:

> It's the change in attitude. You meet people, nice people, but you don't find a lot of people that's willing to do what you're willing to do. They just want to live. I think the neighborhood's more than that. I like to be comfortable. I can't sit back and watch that paper flow down the street. [Laughs] I just can't do it. I say, "Hey, pick that paper up."

Ken pointed out the recent appearance of block parties near his home as the type of conflict in values that epitomizes contentions between pioneers and the second wave. These parties symbolize a way of life that Ken was trying to escape when he chose to move to Parkmont. He told me that he would prefer that the new residents were more mindful of the elderly stayers and the ways that noise and blocking off main streets affect all residents. In contrast, Ken said that the pioneers' "get togethers" on the block tend to be more inclusive of the older people and more respectful of all residents:

> I don't like their attitude. I'm not one for a block party. We have a driveway for that. We may have a barbeque. Every Labor Day, we just block

off the driveway and choose to come out. It's all well and good, but it's not no big DJ. And it's real disrespectful to the neighbors. Certain neighbors don't want to. They might be ill or like that. Like what we did, we blocked the driveway off and had a little peace here and there. Even Dolores [a stayer] came out and had a couple of snow crabs.

I was familiar with the specific DJ event to which Ken was referring, a loud block party that took place on the street perpendicular to his. Loud rap and hip-hop with a heavy bass blared from large speakers, while a huge crowd gathered. Ken said that his block's driveway party is more of a planned event. While one goal of Ken's party is to have fun for families, there is also a clean-up component, a lunch, and an emphasis on community organization. Residents on the other block did not clean up after their party, leaving food, empty plastic bottles of "Little Hugs" brand fruit drink, and other trash scattered on the streets and sidewalks for weeks. To Ken, this is evidence that the other type of block party fails to adhere to, let alone teach, the community values of order, civility, and respect.

I noticed that Ken especially disapproves of holding block parties on streets rather than in the driveways that face the back of homes. His fear is that the traditional block parties held out in the open, which are common to many urban black neighborhoods, would attract the wrong types of people to Parkmont:

> Oh, out front? Then it wouldn't necessarily be a block party; it would be a people-party. 'Cause a majority of the time, when people come up here, it's people that we don't even know. People from all the other places. They come when they hear the noise. They're inviting family, friends, cousins, and people from the other side. It's nice and quiet up here, and those people may want to come back. I just don't agree with the block party.

Ken told me that he realizes that some people think a block party is "like, unity and all that stuff," but he strongly disagrees that the typical city block party is a productive avenue for community building: "I think it's just a time to 'show out.' Just get loose or whatever. Have a little bit too much fun." Ken elaborated and said that the emergence of block parties is the result of some of the newer people bringing the "hood" mentality with them to Parkmont: "They bring it right with them. That's what they do." Ken believes that the main difference between pioneers and second wave residents is cultural. He described a fundamental divergence in attitudes between the two groups:

> It's just a way of thinking. I enjoy the neighborhood. I enjoy where I live at a lot. A lot of the people that are moving here, they're here just for the moment. Stepping stone, starter home, no matter where it is, you

still have to do what you have to do to live here. They think 'We'll just go ahead and throw our trash and destroy whatever's here and keep on moving.'"

Differences in Personal Commitment to Dealing with Disorder: Formal and Informal Social Control

Ken is the "block captain" of his street. This title is an official neighborhood activist designation that is part of a citywide program to encourage leadership in civic tasks, such as monitoring one's block, welcoming new residents, circulating information about rules and meetings, and involving neighbors in beautification efforts. However, Ken views his activity in the neighborhood as emblematic of his sense of personal responsibility, not a by-product of his official title.

Because of his role as block captain and his visibility as a local landscaper, many whites and blacks recognize Ken and know him by name. Ken keeps tabs on his elderly white neighbors and talks to other residents about how the older people are doing. Almost every white resident on his block mentioned him by name to me, but Ken held a special place in his heart for Dolores and Warren Duskin, the stayers who live two doors down from him. One day, from inside of his house, Ken peered out his window, and told me that he is often on the lookout for Dolores to come home:

> I talked to Mary [a pioneer neighbor] 'cause I was wondering where Dolores was. Dolores had a problem and went to the hospital. She hurt her back, and then her husband, Warren, went to the rehabilitation center by himself 'cause he couldn't stay here by himself. I talked to her daughter, and she told us to keep taking care of the property, and she'd let us know when Dolores got back, but they'll have home caregivers staying with them now.

Personal Acts of Informal and Formal Social Control

Ken's attitude about getting involved in maintaining Parkmont's standards of decency can be summed up in this sentence: "If I see something that is uncomfortable for me, I pretty much am going to say something." Ken described a time when he organized residents on his block to purchase speed bumps after he noticed that dune buggies, all-terrain vehicles (ATVs), and motorcycles were speeding down the driveway that runs along the back of the block of row houses where children play. He seemed extremely fed up with newcomers bringing undesirable values and behaviors with them to Parkmont:

> They're desensitized. It's just like the people who ride the motorcycles around. That drives me nuts. If you want to ride that thing, take it out to the park. But they don't feel that they're bothering anybody. I ended up putting speed bumps down there to slow them down. I purchased them. I paid for mine and the other neighbors paid for theirs down the street in driveways. The driveway is our common driveway, but if anything goes wrong we have to pay the repairs. I talked to the neighbors and they agreed to pay for theirs. I purchased my own, and I put it out there. $146. It slowed things tremendously. Before, a lot of people would use the driveways to get around the lights. But after that, people got tired of going over the speed bumps, so now the people that really come through the driveway are the people who live here. It deterred them.

On many occasions, Ken has directly confronted people who are responsible for problem behavior in Parkmont, as when some boys were riding ATVs down his one-way street, in the wrong direction:

> They come from wherever they come from and decide that they'll keep doing that. That's what they did before they got here, and they come here and do the same thing. I have went out there and said, "I'd appreciate if you stop riding that thing up and down here 'cause I'll just have to call the police." And it has worked, but then you have those ones that zoom right past you, and if you don't get out of their way, they might run you over.

Ken thinks the general attitude among the second wave is "hands off" when it comes to personally intervening or taking a proactive role in preventing community problems. I asked what he has seen other adults do to intervene in such cases: "Nothing, pretty much. They let 'em do what they're going to do. They're afraid of confronting the parents. I think that I'd be afraid of the kids. Pretty much, when I say something, they listen."

However, at this point in the interview, Ken's son, Marc, interjected and provided an example of the kinds of problems that have occurred in the past when neighbors have confronted each other. Marc told us that he had recently witnessed two residents on a nearby block who were loudly arguing outside about their children's cell phones. He said the argument almost escalated into a physical fight but a neighbor phoned the police. When Marc finished his story, Ken made a gesture of incredulousness as if to suggest that people like the ones Marc mentioned are clearly not whom he had in mind for neighbors when he moved to Parkmont.

Still, Ken insisted that people like these should not deter residents from getting involved, especially where children are concerned. He provided an example of a time when he watched his neighbor ignoring a group of kids who were playing baseball in the street across from his home, an activity that he viewed as a realistic threat to property in dense and narrow row house communities like Parkmont:

> They were out here playing baseball. And the lady just walked into her house. I had to explain to them that you don't play baseball out there. You break the windows, and who's going to pay for it? They stopped for a minute. I came in the house, and I came back out, and they were doing it again. So I explained it to them again. They live down the street, which is where they were probably chased from. They just moved down to the middle section, so that they could play. I notice they respect *me*.

Ken takes the appearance of the neighborhood very seriously and believes that many second wave residents are not malicious but simply ignorant, having no idea how to live in a decent community. He wishes that all residents would behave as he does and speak up when even minor norm violations about neighborhood appearance are displayed:

> Some people just walk down the street, just throwing things. A guy just moved in. He pulls his car up, starts vacuuming out his car and throwing the garbage on the street. Taking the papers and stuff and just throwing them on the ground. So, I walk over to him with a trash bag, and I said, "You're cleaning out your car? I would appreciate if you just put it in a bag, and don't throw it on the ground." And he was like, "Well, all right." I guess he didn't recognize or realize what he was doing, but he hasn't done it since.

I asked Ken whether he ever felt afraid to walk up to strangers and have confrontations like this. He replied, "I think I kind of said it in a loving and caring way. I don't think he realized what he was doing. They think it doesn't matter. I did make a difference."

Though Ken is comfortable handling local problems informally by speaking to neighbors about their behaviors, he recognizes that many people are not willing to do this. As an alternative, he strongly urges residents to take on a sense of community ownership by reporting any suspicious behaviors to the police, no matter how minor. Ken told me that he, personally, has called the police at least five times about a range of nonviolent crimes and disorderly events. When it comes to contacting the police, he said, "I don't hesitate":

> I call them. People were sitting out there smoking weed. I guess they were adults. A guy down the street? Basically, the same thing. Somebody broke into a car. Somebody sitting here in the back that didn't belong. They just drove back there and parked, like they were going to do something. And back there by the park? I think the local prostitute was back there. I guess everyone expects me to solve the problems, but it's not necessarily like that. Somebody was breaking into somebody's car, and they come and tell me. Why tell me? Call the police. They're not willing to participate. I like a safe neighborhood. I enjoy peace. And I believe that if you're doing something, I'm going to turn you in.

Unfortunately, Ken's has developed a sense of despair about his new neighbors, finding them to be desensitized to all but the most violent crimes. His low opinion of them is not only tied to his belief about their lower standards for community behavior, but to his observation that they are only willing to get involved when their own personal property is damaged or when they are directly victimized. Ken has concluded that people in Parkmont have become far too dependent on block captains to handle their problems and conflicts regarding crime and disorder.

I noticed that Ken seems especially frustrated with residents who fail to share his views about contacting the authorities and with those who dismiss the importance of so-called quality of life crimes, also known as "nuisance crimes" or "livability crimes." These are relatively minor illegal acts that involve no violence and have no direct victim, but interfere with a community's sense of public safety and well-being (e.g., crimes against property, public use of drugs and alcohol, noise violations, and loitering to buy and sell drugs).[2] I asked Ken about the validity of some residents' assessments that Parkmont's quality of life problems are minor, but his opinion on this topic was unwavering and absolute. For instance, when I mentioned that several newer residents told me that they disagree with Ken's sentiment that smoking marijuana around the neighborhood is a big deal, he rolled his eyes and said: "It breeds crime. No matter what it is. It breeds crime. The person might run out or might be under the influence and might decide to go over and knock Dolores in the head. Things like that. They aren't thinking straight as it is. I've heard of home invasions."

---

2. These examples are only a subset of behaviors that are considered to be "broken windows," but they are the ones that are most relevant to Parkmont.

Ken explained that Parkmont's reputation as a relatively safe community actually places residents at a disadvantage in terms of crime control because the police refuse to take their concerns seriously. Ken said that the neighborhood's low levels of violent crime combined with the failure of the police to prioritize Parkmont means that residents need to take on an especially active and organized role in preventing the escalation of both disorder and serious crime. He described tactics that he and others use to get the police to take their concerns seriously:

> There's not really that much [serious crime] going on up here. It's a few things that may not be conducive, but overall this neighborhood is pretty safe. Just pay attention....It's frustrating, but if anything does go on, I have Reverend Jones who I can call. He's on Town Watch. They say that if you call the police, if one person calls, then they don't necessarily respond. But the more people that call....If they're having a problem over there, he'll call me, and I'll call the police. That way we get the response. The police have the fliers, and I have all the information. But the police don't come as far as that's concerned 'cause that's not, quote-unquote, a high priority. They may send one car here, and they send four cars over to worse places. The only way you can get the car over here is if you have five or six calls. You have to call. That's where someone else calls me, and I call them. And you can't call from the same number 'cause they have caller ID. Otherwise, they'll say, "We'll be out as soon as we can." They not going to tell you they're not going to come out.

When residents call Ken "the mayor," they are referring to his special efforts to observe and watch out for people's homes and safety. Ken is always on the lookout for suspicious behaviors and wants to let people know that Parkmont is an area where people like him are watching:

> One time, there was a couple who was sitting on the steps, and I was wondering, "Why are you sitting out here?" They were like, "We're waiting for somebody." And I was like, "Why you waiting for the people out here?" I find out that what they were doing was watching the mailman. And they were looking at certain doors that have mailboxes, and they were sitting there and stealing the mail. But I know that they finally did catch them.

In the same manner that he talked to the man who was cleaning out his car, Ken takes the initiative to socialize new residents into the norms of the community:

> It's more about attraction. I go out there and do what I do and hope that someone else will say "I can do that too." In years past, at the beginning

of the summer, I would put out a flier. "It's going to be a hot summer. We have a nice neighborhood. You see a paper on the ground? Pick it up. Don't just walk over it." I haven't done it this year, but in the past, I made that flier, because I, personally, was the block captain, and I still am. And it would give them some sort of insight. A lot of people get the house and don't know how to take care of the house. Maybe it's a learning process.

Organizational Participation in Social Control

According to Ken, Parkmont's white flight and subsequent black flight have resulted in a critical loss of residents who took an active role in the community. On several occasions, Ken raised the topic of the neighborhood civic association when describing his frustration with the lack of involvement among the second wave residents and the remainder of the pioneers. Ken explained that the timing of arrival to Parkmont had an impact on second wave residents' desire to get involved in the community. In contrast, he believes that the pioneers arrived at a time when neighborhood activism was on the rise:

> It was in the paper. It was in the *Parkmont Press,* and they talked about the Parkmont Civic Association, and there were a lot of people who were involved. Back then. And it was something to do every second Wednesday of the month. And we pretty much joined, and I joined beautification. And the guy Sy Bender, he passed about a month ago, he had skin cancer. Him and his wife, Jenny, moved to Maine to get closer to the grandkids, because they didn't think he would be around too much longer. So, he and I pretty much headed up beautification, cleaning up. He was head, and all he had to do was tell me when to show up. And that was fine. We scheduled cleanups all throughout Parkmont, and we had a locker where we kept brooms and trash bags. The civic association would sponsor trash bags and anything that we needed. At every meeting, we would tell people about it. We gave out a flyer that had the schedule of the places where we would meet, like a cleanup on the strip.

According to Ken and other residents, the civic association was once quite active, with involvement from whites, blacks, men, and women from almost every block in the neighborhood. Ken reported that this period of time stands in stark contrast to more recent years when the organization's efforts have been more limited, intermittent, and scattered:

> Before, what it would be is the Parkmont Civic Association, a collective effort of people all over. As far as beautification, about maybe thirty were

in it, but the association had much more than that. Maybe more than one hundred. They still have a lot of people who just pay dues, but who just don't show up. They're not active, but they still send their dues.

But to Ken, dues are not enough to keep the neighborhood orderly and safe: "People have to come out and do some things. That's the thing. That's the key."

Ken told me that participation in the civic association is now at a low point. For instance, he mentioned that only twenty residents attended the last meeting. Ken was incredulous when he told me that the president of the association at the time, Sam Wilson, was not even a resident anymore, but was a former pioneer who had left Parkmont as part of the black-flight exodus. Ken also complained about the limited male presence at civic association meetings: "A majority are women because the majority of people who live in Parkmont are women. The majority of people who live here are women 'cause I find that to be true when I landscape. There's a lot of people, and it's a lot of women." Ken asserted that Parkmont's male residents, although small in number, have been a disappointment. He thinks that if the men showed a greater presence, then community efforts would be more effective: "It would work. 'Cause it's more people who don't take the active role than the ones who do. There are a lot more men here than you see. They just choose to stay in the house and watch the satellite picture."

These days, even Ken has scaled back his involvement in the civic association because he has become demoralized by his neighbors' apathy. He admitted that he resigned from the beautification committee a year and a half ago, refocusing his attention away from the larger neighborhood to the smaller world of his own block. Once a leader within the civic association, Ken has since lost the motivation and incentive to expend energy on the anonymous residents who reside on other blocks. Yet Ken still considers himself to be far more involved than most people:

> I still go to the meetings. I still get into the organizational Town Watch. They still call me. Town Watch is where they patrol Parkmont. I don't do it any more 'cause I have my own Town Watch right here. My involvement, it's way down because I'm still interested in the neighborhood, but it's a limit to everything. I go to the Town Watch meetings, and there are only three or four people there, and they expect you to patrol all of Parkmont. And that, I'm not necessarily willing to do. Everyone knows that the Town Watch is right here. They know not to sit on my walk.

When Ken first moved to Parkmont, white flight had already been set in motion and stayers and pioneers were actively working together to maintain a sense of community stability. Since then, the organizational structure of the neighborhood has fallen apart, and the reasons for this are threefold. First, the long-term white residents moved, became ill, or died. Second, pioneers have become disillusioned and dissatisfied, and many of them have also moved. Third, second wave residents have either been too busy or too complacent to take on a leadership role. Indicators of the loss of organizational activity in Parkmont are numerous. For instance, by 2004 the *Parkmont Press* had ceased publication because of the loss of advertising from businesses in the neighborhood and surrounding suburbs. Important public sites and services in the community, such as playgrounds, parks, and ambulance stations, have become blighted. As Ken mentioned, the civic association meetings are now poorly attended, and he believes that eventually the organization will become defunct:

> I can see the lack of participation. I think that everybody wants the association to exist, but they don't want to participate. They think that the civic association is here to police the neighborhood for everybody else, when in reality it's all volunteers. It's a struggle. Everybody around is like, "When's there a meeting, remind me when the meeting is." It's not my job.

The Future: Stay or Go?

Like many pioneers, Jill and Ken have had numerous debates about the pros and cons of moving away from Parkmont to another neighborhood. Ken explained the reasons to leave, his misgivings about saying good-bye to Parkmont, and his desire to stand his ground and fight off the undesirable elements:

> Because of the change, Jill wants to move now. I've talked to my wife, and I said, "We can continue to keep running away from them, and eventually they'll have as much money as we do. And then they'll come, and they'll do the same thing there." Eventually, you have to go ahead and stay and say, "Okay, this is the way it's going to be here." Everyone can get on the same page. And, "If you come here and think you are going to do this here in this neighborhood, then we're not going to tolerate it, and *you* have to leave."

Yet Ken finds that his resolve to stay is often undermined by his aggravation over the lack of neighbor participation and the rapid population change that has left people like him in the minority. Like many city employees, he is eagerly awaiting the pension and relaxation that he hopes will accompany retirement. Ken looks forward to the time when he can finally have the option of living in his ideal location, the place he has aspired to since his youth: the suburbs. He told me that he dreams of retiring in seven years and living in a detached home in a sub-urban area named Arbor Hills, a borough that happens to be 93 percent white:

> Me and Jill were talking about that the other day. I was over there look-ing at a couple of properties for when I retire. It won't be long. I'm not sure exactly where, but I'll probably be able to move where I want to move then. If I could move outside the city now, I would. I *could* afford it now, but my job keeps me here, and for a matter of convenience.

Again, Ken considered whether he would have moved to Parkmont years ago if it had been in its current state, and he did not hesitate for a moment when he said:

> No. Maybe because I'm more set in my ways. I don't want to be going through a whole bunch of crap. I want to be around people that want the same things as I want—peace, safety for my kids. I don't mind some-body telling 'em that they are doing wrong. Today, it seems like they don't want you saying anything to 'em.

Ken's views about community have changed along with Parkmont's transfor-mation. His experience buying his first home and moving to a safe neighbor-hood once brought him joy and a sense of accomplishment. However, Ken has also learned some harsh lessons about the ways in which population change can leave neighborhoods vulnerable. He can only think of one solution for gaining access to a home that is acceptably distant from the kinds of people who do not seem to share his values:

> I pretty much want a detached house. I can put my fence up. More privacy, less noise. Like now, when they decide to play their music, you can hear it. My neighbor here, he's pretty much coming in the morning, coming in from work, and he might sit out there in the car for like five minutes, listening to his favorite record or whatever really loud. "Look, I'm trying to get my sleep." You know what I mean? Be mindful.

Conclusion

Ken Wilkinson represents a bridge between Parkmont's past and future. On one hand, he symbolizes the continuity between stayers and pioneers in terms of beliefs, values, and behaviors in the community. In this sense, he has tried to be optimistic in the face of rapid population transition, believing that the rising levels of disorder in Parkmont could be contained if only the residents would demonstrate an interest in keeping up the neighborhood. However, Ken also

personifies a harbinger of further change, as he and his family contemplate join-
ing the pioneers who have left in a wave of black flight.

As a husband and father, Ken perceives the gap in values and behaviors between Parkmont's two groups of black residents as real and threatening to his
family. He feels a social distance from the second wave because of their attitudes
about parenting, their norms about what constitutes community order, and their
lack of personal commitment to informal, formal, and organizational forms of
intervention in neighborhood problems. These differences are a source of conflict, as well as dissatisfaction with community life for pioneers such as Ken. In
general, Ken empathizes with Parkmont's black families and their struggles to
balance community with work, family, and finances, but he does not excuse their
apathy. As a result, Ken is nagged by ambivalence about how much more he can
invest in the neighborhood:

> In the long run, I know involvement has benefits. It lets you know what's
> going on and what we can do to keep it as nice as it is. But I'm just as
> busy as everyone. So, it's all about how much they're willing to go ahead
> and do. 'Cause I know the little bit of effort I go ahead and put forth
> around here, it pays off. Because the minute it gets too trashy or too
> overwhelming, then it's really time to move.

Ken pointed out a banner that was prominent on Parkmont's strip when he
had first arrived. He told me that now the banner serves as a painful reminder
of the loss of community that he has witnessed as white and black flight have
taken hold:

> I know that on the banner, it said, "Parkmont, the Neighborhood That
> Cares." Right? But now they don't necessarily care, as far as keeping it up.
> They're not willing to put forth the work. They think that maybe they
> purchase a house, and that's it. But you purchase a house, and you have
> to do work at it. You have to keep it clean. Then, when something goes
> wrong in it, you have to fix it.

Finding a community that is close to both work and family, safe from crime,
peaceful, and orderly is a goal of most American families, but for black pioneers
in the city it is one that is almost impossible to achieve. As if it had not been
enough of a challenge to watch rapid white flight descend on Parkmont, pioneers
have had to deal with adjusting to new neighbors who seem to hold vastly different values about community life. Many pioneers have chosen to leave, but for
others moving is not an option. For pioneers who must remain in Parkmont, the
search for ways to maintain an enriching environment for raising children continues. Chapter 6 explains in detail the ways in which black flight has transformed

Parkmont. It distinguishes between the pioneers and second wave residents and the distinct circumstances of each group's arrival in Parkmont. Chapter 6 also highlights the nature of the cultural conflicts that have emerged between the two groups, and shows the ways in which strained neighbor relations over daily disturbances can translate into neighborhood dissatisfaction and mobility thoughts among even the most dedicated residents.

6

BLACK FLIGHT
Consequences of Neighborhood Cultural Conflict

The neighbor that lived here before [a pioneer] was a woman. She told me she was moving because she felt uncomfortable that the neighborhood was going down.

—Lara Bianco, second wave, aged thirty-seven

I have to say that within the last two or three years, there have been at least five to six families who have moved out and new people have moved in. So it's definitely a revolving door.

—Linda Hopewell, second wave, aged thirty-nine

Before, you really didn't have to go outside your home and sweep up trash. You just had to go and do your leaves and a little litter, but now it's McDonald's papers. It's cups. It's whatever. Now, we have Popeye's coming.

—Clarice Nellis, pioneer, aged thirty-seven

Race, gender, social class, and neighborhood are all social structural factors that shape the complex web that sociologists refer to as "culture." Culture can be seen as a collective-level construct that describes a group's shared set of values, norms, and attitudes toward life. These values and norms are codified, whether formally or informally, into rules and sets of behaviors that group members use to meet their goals.[1] Such cultural codes can include rules that pertain to relatively mundane, everyday topics (e.g., how a family should maintain their property), as well as deeply held convictions (e.g., what constitutes a moral life).[2] Further complicating matters, people may or may not be conscious of their collective values and codes of behavior. In addition, a group's codes may be highly complex and multilayered, or they may be very simple and binary, or what some call "black and white."[3] Historically, social scientists and black intellectuals have embraced

---

1. See DiMaggio (1997), Geertz (1973), and Giddens (1984) for various definitions, underst⁺ ings, and applications of the term "culture."
2. Sewell (1992).
3. Griswold (2005).

cultural explanations of racial differences as a welcome alternative to biological essentialism.[4] Indeed, ethnographic research provides evidence that cultural
hierarchies are a characteristic of many communities.[5] Yet the topic of cultural
hierarchies, especially as they pertain to nonwhites, remains a taboo subject. Researchers often prefer to avoid, or even to rename, culture, arguing that the very
concept has been contaminated beyond utility by researchers and theorists who
have failed to balance discussions of culture with adequate analyses of structural
or macro-level causal mechanisms.[6]

People make decisions about where to live, how to spend their time, whether
to maintain their homes, how loud to play their music, and what their responsibilities as neighbors are. Social structures and constraints (e.g., factors related
to racial disparities in opportunities for wealth building, desirable housing, and
access to quality schools) influence these decisions, but so too does culture.
A neighborhood's culture is shaped by who it attracts, who stays, and who leaves.
In other words, "the people make the place."[7] Parkmont's pioneers frequently
pointed specifically to intraracial cultural differences as a main cause of their
dissatisfaction with their community.[8]

---

4. See Bay (1998) and Boaz (1894).

5. The ethnographic practice of providing contextualized "thick descriptions" of cultural codes
is crucial to understanding relations within neighborhoods. Geertz's (1973) term "thick description"
describes a practice by which ethnographers must not only observe, record, and analyze culture, but
attempt to understand the meanings within the specific context.

6. See Pattillo (2007) for a critique of the use of culture in sociological research. Arguably, one
of the most cited examples of the use of flawed cultural explanations is Oscar Lewis's (1959, 1966)
work, which argued that the conditions of poverty can lead people to form an adaptive subculture
with attitudes and behaviors that further perpetuate poverty. He described two subgroups of poor
people: one with "mainstream" aspirations that reflect the national culture, such as improved educational and occupational outcomes, and the other with values contrary to the mainstream. Lewis
argued that poverty has affected the latter group in such as way that they have formed a subculture
with a low sense of control over life and a sense of helplessness about getting ahead. These feelings
create a need to cope, so those who participate in the subculture of poverty adopt values that reflect
a more short-term outlook and take on behaviors that demonstrate a greater dependency on others.
To this day, scholars who are critical or suspicious of any kind of cultural explanation often point to
Lewis's research and ideas, which they interpret as scapegoating or "blaming the victim." These cri-
tiques are not limited to cultural explanations of the poor, but extend to studies that focus on the role
of culture for other subgroups. Specifically, Patterson (2003) has noted that research and theory exploring the role of culture in black communities has been known to create a backlash of sorts, while
explanations and studies that are strictly structural or political in nature are far more welcomed.
However, in recent years a handful of scholars has argued that research on racial inequality must
attempt to incorporate culture, especially when examining disparities among the poor (Lamont and
Small 2008, Wilson 2009).

7. This quote is from the title of a paper by Schneider (1987). See also Fischer (1975) and Gans
(1962) for explanations of the relationship between population and culture.

8. See Osofsky (1996) for an elaboration of the ways in which the Great Migration triggered
cultural conflict between two groups of black residents in Harlem.

Pioneers strongly believe that intraracial differences in residents' values and behaviors have become fatal to their neighborhood satisfaction and quality of life and are causing Parkmont to experience what one pioneer called a "downward trend." On the streets where black pioneers first found white families with long-standing ties to the community, there now lives a distinct and later arriving group of blacks: the second wave of blacks who are replacing the population of pioneers who have been moving out. This group has come to represent Parkmont's first episode of black flight and its second recent demographic shift. Black flight is a less recognized concept than white flight and is easy to overlook when scanning demographic data, but the process of black flight has been described in this way:

> At the "tipping point" the nonwhite pioneers join their earlier antagonists in contemplating, or actualizing, flight from the area....The delayed flight process from contested areas is one of the complicated social and psychological phenomena that are likely to be obscured by urban studies based on decennial census data.[9]

An analysis of Parkmont's black flight sheds light on this complicated and hidden phenomenon. On many conventionally studied characteristics and outcomes, pioneers and second wave residents appear to have a great deal in common. Both groups are black and are able to afford homes in Parkmont. Both have families that reside in nearby low-income black neighborhoods, and in general they both have moved to Parkmont from far worse communities. Both groups, to various degrees, but especially in terms of occupational prestige, are in the working class. However, pioneers and second wave residents each perceive differences between themselves and the other group. These differences are related to structural factors such as the timing of arrival in Parkmont and subtle compositional differences in the two groups' economic standing and family structures. The contrast between the two also extends to cultural factors, such as values and behaviors related to child-rearing and community.

In many ways a cultural study of Parkmont is consistent with an increasingly visible stream of research that provides evidence of significant intraracial differences within black neighborhoods. However, Parkmont is also a unique context in that it is a newly settled black area filled with working-class families who are striving for better lives. This is important because, even though blacks are more likely than whites to be members of the working class, researchers have called working-class blacks "the forgotten category" in contemporary race and

---

9. This quotation is from Krase (1982, 13).

class research.[10] Yet Parkmont's divisions in the aftermath of white flight are not about severe social class separations and fundamental commitments to different ways of life; nor are they about local politics or the rise of gangs. Parkmont's cultural clashes are over values and behaviors related to home and family life, and they show how changes in neighborhood population have consequences, both structural and cultural, that lead to black flight. These changes have splintered Parkmont's population, creating a quiet milieu of resentment and a continuing period of black population churning.

Structural Factors: Timing of Arrival and Compositional Differences

Effects of Timing of Arrival on Experiences with Housing and Neighbors

Timing is everything when it comes to one's experience of a neighborhood. People often have divergent experiences of places, and these differences are frequently determined by *when* they first arrived.[11] Even in racially homogenous communities, population "churning" or turnover can significantly shape the character of a neighborhood. In Parkmont, whites continued to trickle out of the community when they would die or move into assisted living facilities. Pioneers continued to depart in search of neighborhoods that were similar to the one that Parkmont had once represented to them. When the second wave of blacks arrived, they were filling these housing vacancies and keeping the population churning long after most whites were gone.

Timing has had important implications for both the housing market and the socialization process of Parkmont residents. Parkmont's white flight began before the housing boom of the early 2000s, but the fallout from subprime mortgages and predatory lending has shaped subsequent patterns of neighborhood change. Data from the Department of Housing and Urban Development (HUD) show that patterns of lending changed at the very same time that large numbers of second wave residents began moving into Parkmont. The city released a report using HUD data that shows that 25 percent to 49.99 percent of all mortgages made between 2004 and 2006 were "high cost" subprime mortgages (with interest rates that were more than 3% above standard rates), a status that is a strong predictor of foreclosure. The city also reported that Parkmont had a predicted

---

10. Horton et al. (2000).
11. Lieberson (1981).

foreclosure rate of 7 percent to 9.99 percent for the eighteen months following November 2008. Furthermore, the zip code in which Parkmont is located is one of twelve in the city that had more than 250 pre-foreclosure actions filed in the year 2007 and the first nine months of 2008. The city concluded in the report that Parkmont deserves a relatively high "foreclosure abandonment and risk score" (a score of seven to eight with ten being the highest), an especially troubling fact given that the community had a relatively low vacancy rate. Parkmont's foreclosure risk scores are especially convincing because they have not been inflated by the long history of vacancy and abandonment (caused by the loss of manufacturing and population) that is typical of many neighborhoods with high-risk scores. Indeed, Parkmont has seen many foreclosures, and many houses there have been turned into rentals. Subprime mortgages and programs aimed toward assisting financially vulnerable groups, such as first-time and low-income homeowners, were attractive to many black buyers because they required very small down payments, but eventually some Parkmont families could not afford their housing expenses and were forced to give up their homes.

Timing of arrival also differently affected blacks' experiences in Parkmont in that affordable housing was more widely available for second wave residents than for pioneers. It was often the case that when elderly white stayers died or became too ill to live alone, their adult children felt burdened by their parents' homes, and they were eager to unload these outdated properties. Many preferred to expedite the process and sell low rather than take the time and incur the costs of making home improvements or waiting for better offers. Thus, less expensive homes in Parkmont were easier to find for second wave residents, as were rentals, since it was not uncommon for stayers' children to sell their parents' homes to real estate agents who soon began to rent them out.

Pioneers' and second wave residents' relationships to stayers were also different from each other because of timing of arrival effects. The pioneers were engaged in episodes of intense community socialization by their white neighbors, but the second wave blacks arrived in Parkmont when opportunities to interact with stayers were scarce. At the time of the second wave's arrival, elderly white stayers were in far worse health. In addition, the idea of having a black neighbor was less of a novelty to these white residents who had already grown accustomed to black neighbors after experiencing the initial period of integration and were now well acquainted with the pioneers.

The character of Parkmont's *intraracial* relationships was also shaped by the timing of arrival of the two waves of black residents. As might be expected because of their conspicuousness in a white neighborhood or their status as outsiders when white flight first took hold, many pioneers formed positive, if not close, relationships with other pioneers. However, for a variety of reasons, the second wave residents' interactions with the pioneers have been minimal at best and strained at worst. Another factor making it difficult to form bonds across cohorts of black residents is that many pioneers had grown to identify with white stayers, while simultaneously taking on an air of cautiousness and apprehension about the incoming second wave blacks. Exacerbating the social distance between the two groups of blacks was the fact that with busy schedules and shorter lengths of residence in Parkmont, many pioneers did not feel entitled or inclined to play an explicit, active socializing role in the community. Thus, many pioneers were poor candidates to take on a leadership role with other young black families because of the fear that they would be perceived as pushy or snobby to newcomers whom they neither knew, identified with, nor trusted.

Intraracial Compositional Differences

In white-flight neighborhoods, black pioneers often do not differ much from long-term white residents in terms of socioeconomic status, but they are soon followed by less affluent blacks.[12] Still, it is important to note that pioneer and second wave residents do share many of the same characteristics. With the exception of retirees and single, childless women, the members of both groups often juggle several jobs with irregular and long hours, busily coordinate their children's lives and schooling, tend to their romantic relationships, and deal with their obligations to their extended family members who live nearby. In general, both groups have very little free time, and their lives are focused on family, work, and the struggle for balance in day-to-day life. However, Parkmont's second wave residents appear to be less economically stable than the pioneers. Residents repeatedly mentioned that they perceive this subtle difference in the degree of economic strain. One pioneer expressed a typical opinion about the second wave residents' inferior financial status:

> I don't think they're as economically stable as we were when we moved in. Because we've heard—and I don't have any research or documentation—some of these houses have been made into Section 8 houses. And I have a problem with that because they're not buying it, so they have no stake in this community like we do. Our stake in the community is that we're buying, and we're not getting any government funding or anybody helping us to take care of our home, where[as] they are.

Though pioneers expressed the sentiment that Parkmont's second wave black residents are *culturally* distinct from them on several dimensions, the main

---

12. See, for example, Osofsky's (1996) history of Harlem.

compositional difference between the two groups seems to be that many new-comers are barely making it in Parkmont. Pioneer Sonya McCall reported that she is concerned that second wave residents have only been able to gain access to Parkmont through low-income rentals and homeownership programs, which she thinks have negatively affected the community. Sonya is now eager to leave Parkmont: "I heard some of them are Section 8. I'm sure there have been a lot of foreclosures. I can't really say how long I'll be here, 'cause I really don't know."

Billy Gordon is a nineteen-year-old second wave resident who lives in a rented row house in Parkmont. His mother, an ex-con and recovering addict, resides in a halfway house, so he stays with his father, stepmother, sister, and his father and stepmother's shared biological child. He told me that as teens he and his sister moved to Parkmont to live with their father, and that in the near future his family plans to purchase the home in which they currently reside. In Billy's view, Parkmont is a very good neighborhood, but it's at risk of decline. Though he is a member of the second wave, Billy thinks the pioneers seem better off financially than the residents in his cohort:

> They were the first blacks, and the whites were probably selling their cribs for a lot of money. If they had enough money to afford it, then they probably did have a couple of dollars. But now that most of the white people left town and other blacks came in? It's probably going down, slowly but surely. This neighborhood compared to other neighbor-hoods, it's pretty good. It's still fixable, and the people who were raised here and were born here care about where they're from and should put forth the effort into getting it fixed. I think it's fixable. I think it's a good neighborhood. It's a beautiful neighborhood.

Mary Smith, a seventy-six-year-old second wave resident, raised her six children in public housing projects as a single mother. She once worked as a tele-phone operator but has been retired for almost ten years. Mary began her tenure in Parkmont as a renter, but her son-in-law recently purchased her home for her. She told me about her dire financial situation when she was younger and how she has continued to struggle with money problems throughout her life. Mary explained how impossible it was for her to locate affordable housing in a safe community and said that this dilemma was the driving force in her move to Parkmont:

> I knew this neighborhood 'cause we used to come out here. There used to be a Jewish bakery up here. It was wonderful. We would come out and get stuff to eat on Sunday. That was a big treat 'cause we were poor. I didn't know anything about it other than that it was predominantly white and Jewish. It didn't bother me. Nobody approached me or acted

> like, "What are you doing up here?" I never had those kind of dealings here....I wanted to relocate, and I wanted to move into an apartment, which I did. I lived there for years. Then the owner sold the place, and they wanted everyone out. I couldn't find an apartment that I could afford. Well, I could afford it, but it was in the bad neighborhoods. All the apartments I really loved, you would be able to pay the rent for a year until they upped the rent. 'Cause that happened to my sister twice. I don't have the kind of income where if it goes up I can pay it. I can't pay it. My kids said, "You gotta buy a house." I said, "I don't want a house." Anyhow, that's how I ended up here. I just started renting. My son-in-law, God bless him, just purchased it....Everybody took care of their property. Now, you find a few houses that don't keep up the property, but must of them do. Most of them do.

Several second wavers told me that they were able to afford a home in Parkmont only because of earlier foreclosures faced by some pioneer families. Lara DiBianco, a second wave resident, is a single woman who had been collecting disability payments, though she was recently employed as a conference organizer for a health insurance company. She purchased her home for only $59,000 from the Federal Housing Authority (FHA). Lara explained that government programs allowed her to purchase a home in Parkmont with almost no money down, but that the responsibilities of home ownership are beyond her financial capabilities:

> I had enough to get the home with a loan and everything, but I didn't have oodles of money. I was FHA. The house has problems, too. I'm in the process of getting an equity loan myself. The garage needs to be redone, and the dishwasher doesn't work, and where the roof leaked, it's gotta be replastered and painted.

Clarice Nellis, a pioneer, complained that second wave residents are unable to afford the expenses associated with homeownership and tend to place a low financial priority on home improvements:

> I think that the people that are moving in now, this is like a stretch for them, so they're barely here. They're working, and the outside of their home is not their focus. They think, "I have to try to pay my mortgage to stay here." I think they're so one-track minded right now that that's their primary focus.

Some second wave residents admitted that they prefer not to spend what little discretionary money they have on home improvements. Mary Smith told me that, many times, her lawn becomes overgrown because she opts not to pay someone to cut it. She explained that her pioneer neighbor often gets fed up with her and intervenes by cutting it when it gets too long for his liking. Mary reported that her home is in need of basic repairs and enhancements, but she cannot afford to make them:

> I had an awning that just went in the trash after this season, so I need a new awning, but they cost a thousand dollars. A thousand dollars is a thousand dollars to me. I'm hoping I can squeeze in the funds to get it replaced, because you have to cook inside without an awning out there in the summertime. Well, that was the beginning of the deteriorating, too.... It's not because you don't want to. That's just the way it is. 'Cause there's a lot of things I want to do here, and they all call for money.

Second wave resident Shonda Suarez is a thirty-two-year-old single mother. Her thirteen-year-old son lives with her mother in the suburbs, but her two other younger children live with her in a rented row house in Parkmont. To help pay bills, her father sometimes lives with her, as well. Shonda's life is very hectic: she works as a department store salesperson and owns and operates a small, fly-by-night daycare center located about fifteen minutes away from Parkmont in a very poor, segregated neighborhood. As an extra source of income, she rents chairs to barbers and hairstylists on the second floor of the daycare center. Shonda moved to Parkmont after getting divorced and hearing from friends that the neighborhood was populated with homeowners and working people. Though she once considered Parkmont to be a higher status black community, she now believes that its level of prestige has declined:

> This is how you can tell if you're in the working class. When you're in the neighborhood, when you wake up in the morning, and every car on your street is gone. Then you know that everybody is getting up and going to work. If you wake up in the morning and everybody cars still parked there on a daily basis, then you know you not in a working-class neighborhood. It's a lot of homeowners here. You can tell people take care of their homes. They're taken care of, as far as the lawn, the outside. That's mostly the homeowners. 'Cause renters, they don't really— not saying all renters—but the majority, they don't really take care of the property. How can I put this? They say Parkmont is more upscale. They say when people move out of Westside to move up, they go to Parkmont. It was considered moving not totally out of the ghetto, but you're moving up to a higher-class neighborhood where the houses are getting more expensive, the income bracket goes up. That was years ago. Now, other areas are considered the nicer ones.

Months ago, Ramell Worthy moved from a nearby low-income black neighborhood to join his fiancée, Aliya Sampson, in Parkmont. They are second wave residents who rely on a combination of disability payments and earned income to get by. Until recently, Ramell was employed as a teacher and social worker, but he is now on disability and is trying to break into the field of real estate. Aliya told me that she purchased their home from a pioneer family, the first black household on her block. Both said that neighborhood racial integration was not a factor in their decision to move to Parkmont since the community had already resegregated by the time of their arrival, but that they wanted to live in a neighborhood like Parkmont because they perceived it to be an improvement in terms of the social class composition of the residents and because they liked the general atmosphere. Ramell explained the unfortunate circumstances that enabled Aliya to afford to buy their home: "Aliya had an opportunity to get this house at a good price, and she jumped on it. It was about to go into foreclosure. It was a black woman here that lived with her mother, and her mother was kind of elderly. They was just trying to really cash out."

Finances were also tight for second wave resident Linda Hopewell. She told me that she grew up just fifteen minutes from Parkmont, in a low-income black neighborhood. Because she was unable to afford a down payment in Parkmont with her savings, and was earning too much money to qualify for many housing programs, Linda cashed in her 401K retirement fund and accepted the associated penalties. She told me the story of her move to Parkmont, beginning with a description of her old neighborhood: "I enjoyed it, but I knew that once I moved out as a single person that I needed to be somewhere that was safe, somewhere that the block was homey, where there were more families and children." I asked if she had felt safe in her former neighborhood, and she said, "Not really. It had gotten to a point where, of course, drugs and gunfire and things like that. I'm not saying that that's not up here either. It is. It's everywhere. But I've never felt unsafe in Parkmont as a single person."

Linda's move to Parkmont did not come at a prosperous time in her life. In a short period, someone had burglarized her former apartment, she had lost her job, and her father had died:

> I was living in an apartment. The apartment had gotten broke into, and I found myself back at my mother's house. Then, a couple months later, I got laid off. My father had just passed, and my mother was there by herself. She was really grieving, so that was really my reason for being there, spiritually.

Though she had not planned it, Linda continued to live with her mother for five more years after her father's death before finally gathering her resources and moving. Linda explained how she had come to own a home in Parkmont at such a hard time in her life:

> I wound up getting a job where I was a temp worker. And then, after like, three or four months, I became full-time. Then, I just stepped out on faith. I didn't have any money saved. At least, I didn't think I had any money saved. I just knew I wanted to move and *he* [Jesus] showed me my 401K, so I wind up taking money out of that and finding money for the house.... It was kind of hard in the beginning because I looked at twenty or thirty houses, and I got so frustrated. My brother lives about four blocks down from here, and I never thought about this part of the area, here. And then, through prayer, I got on the Internet, and the house was right there. I knew when I came here that this was the house, and I've enjoyed it ever since I've been up here. I've never had any problems.

Linda admitted that she was struggling with finances and was not in the ideal position to become a homeowner. However, her recent marriage has relieved some of the burden:

> Once I signed the papers, then I started having doubts. Like, can I really do this? What's gonna happen if I lose my job? You start thinking all these different things, and then you just come back to the reality that you just have to trust Jesus. I have to trust the Lord and knowing that he gave me the opportunity, and that's what I do. And it was hard, but I was able to make it through. I know I was stretching a little bit here within the last two years. But once my husband moved in, we're fine.

Linda's story is emblematic of life as a homeowner for many second wavers. Single, with no cash savings, and only one income, Linda was unable to raise the funds for a down payment to buy a home. When she removed funds from her 401K as part of a "hardship withdrawal" to buy her first home, she had to pay penalties and taxes during the year of the withdrawal, and she also lost the earnings that she would have made from the investment.[13] Like many second wave residents, Linda has continued to struggle with the costs of owning her own home. Yet despite this, she told me that she and her husband consider themselves to be savvy about real estate, and that they aspire to "flip houses," including the one in which they currently reside: "My house has doubled in value, probably more than that. That's one of the reasons why we're trying to renovate the house. We can leave, sell it, and get the money back."

---

13. See Shapiro (2004) for more examples like this.

Many second wave residents explicitly mentioned that financing a first home became far easier in the early part of the 2000s, and they believe that the relative ease of getting a mortgage has contributed to obvious housing turnover in Parkmont. Aliya Sampson, who works as a realtor, echoed the sentiment that Parkmont has become more affordable to blacks as financing options began to open up to families: "I think that a lot of the interest rates now are pretty good for first-time home buyers. If your credit is pretty good, you can get a nice first-time homebuyers program. You can get a good preapproval, which will get you in a better area."

White city-to-suburb migration patterns tend to disturb the fragile compositions of urban neighborhoods, in terms of both social class and family structure.[14] In the aftermath of white flight, Parkmont had far fewer married and two-parent families, more adults working long and irregular hours, and a higher proportion of households with children. With black flight taking hold and relations between pioneers and second wave black residents becoming strained, many pioneers started to scrutinize the comings and goings of people in the homes around them. In addition to noticing economic differences between themselves and the newcomers, pioneers observed that the second wave households often had more varied and unstable family structures.

As a pioneer, Sonya McCall's neighborhood aspirations were not only about racial integration but included the image of stable households and conventional homes where vigilant parents watch over their children. She told me that Parkmont's family structure had changed, and the streets had become overrun with unsupervised children and teens who do as they please during the day. She attributed the deterioration of the neighborhood's social climate to Parkmont's shifting household and family structures:

> It's horrible. I seen it over the years, how the neighborhood has changed. When I moved up here, it was real quiet. You didn't see no boys on the corner. You didn't have all this activity. I think the problem is that when people was moving in, they brought their sons, kids, and a lot of parents. They think, just as long as the kids don't mess up the house, the kids can stay out. They out on the street. I believe it's gonna get worse because the kids are growing up, and they come in, bringing more kids in. They have no control over them. The neighborhood's going to go down.

Like Sonya, many pioneers moved to Parkmont with the expectation that they would live in an environment with a greater representation of nuclear families,

---

14. Frey (1978).

or at least stable households. Their goal was not to achieve a minimal standard of safety from extreme violent crime and brazen disorder; for them, the desire for an improved atmosphere for their families included a neighborhood with a greater representation of conventional families and lifestyles. Pioneer Nina Jones said that she has noticed Parkmont's homes are inhabited by fewer nuclear families and more extended or multigenerational families, which has altered the population composition of both the neighborhood and school:

> I do see a change. I notice a lot of people are living with their parents who brought them up here. Their mom and dad might have bought the house, and maybe they've moved in, or their kids are still in the house. They bought it, because it's like, "Oh I'm trying to move, get a better environment." But now? I just think they are up here to live. Now, you have a situation where a cousin buys a house, and everybody just comes and stays, and then those kids—because they got the address—they go to Lombard.

In the short period of time since she first settled down in Parkmont, the concerns that Nina once had about her former neighborhood have appeared in Parkmont to such a degree that she would hesitate to recommend the community to others. As a teacher at Lombard, Nina believes that she possesses a more complete perspective on the types of families who are moving into the community and the unique sets of problems that they bring with them. Just eight years after arriving, her knowledge about the changes in the profile of residents has led her to decide that she is ready to move. Unfortunately for her, she does not know where to go:

> Right now, we're trying to move. One of my girlfriends wants to move up here, but she's single. I don't recommend it for people who want children or have children. I don't recommend it because you want an area where, number one, the kids can be outside and play. You just never know what's going to jump off here. The neighborhood is failing, and if it's like this now, what's it going to be ten years from now?

Although Nina recognizes that Parkmont is far better than many city neighborhoods, she has become disgusted with the changes in the type and quality of residents. Clearly, for Nina and many other pioneers, the second wave residents are not only different demographically but culturally. Although structural factors have created demographic changes in Parkmont, it is the pioneers' *perceptions* of the *cultural* divide between the groups that are crucial to understanding why so many have chosen to leave.

Cultural Conflict as a Proximate Cause of Black Flight

It is hardly controversial to suggest that in order to get a "feel" for a community and understand its identity, one must gain an understanding of its culture. Tourists flock to urban enclaves to get a taste of the exotic culture of an unfamiliar community, neighbors engage in activism to retain aspects of community culture that they believe are threatened, and longtime residents often teach newcomers about the nuances of a community's culture. Indeed, a neighborhood's cultural dimensions are usually the most riveting parts of community studies. It is no wonder then that many urbanists would argue that culture is central to any holistic understanding of neighborhood change.

In addition to the value of cultural studies for making sense of neighborhood dynamics, investigations into neighborhood culture can provide richer data on ethnic relations within neighborhoods and help counter monolithic misrepresentations of racial and ethnic groups. The groundbreaking, though underappreciated, research of W. E. B. Dubois (1899) demonstrated that the black experience in the United States is diverse, arguing that researchers need to shift the discourse toward cultural understandings of race relations and away from biological ones.[15] Recently, large-scale statistical analyses[16] and in-depth community research have addressed oversimplified depictions of racial and ethnic groups' experiences, with a number of studies breaking new ground by showing the specific ways that modern black communities are socially diverse.[17] For instance, scholars have studied established middle-class black neighborhoods where residents share close bonds and deal with local problems in a cooperative way even though many residents' backgrounds are peppered with criminal histories, addictions, and difficult life events.[18] Additionally, important research on black neighborhoods has provided insights into the challenges and survival strategies of residents in poor, violent, drug-infested communities where "decent" and "street" blacks share residential space.[19] Some have strongly argued that it is imperative for social research to reincorporate the concept of culture or the "sharing of outlooks and modes of behavior" as a causal factor in studies of African Americans, as culture may be the "black box" that is represented by unexplained variance in statistical studies of racial inequality.[20]

---

15. See Anderson (1996) and Bell, Grosholz, and Stewart (1996).
16. Owens and Wright (1998).
17. See Anderson (1999), Lacy (2007), Pattillo (2007), and Pattillo-McCoy (1999).
18. Pattillo-McCoy (1999).
19. Anderson (1999).
20. See Berger (1991), Patterson (2001, 2003), and Wilson (2009).

Culture is, of course, subject to change. The influential sociologist Ernest W. Burgess (1925) argued that urban neighborhoods have a cultural life that is largely shaped by the "sifting and sorting" of families who move into and out of them. Thus, it should not be surprising that the cultural changes that the pioneers have observed in Parkmont have contributed to their rising levels of dissatisfaction and their desire to move. With its densely packed row houses, Parkmont's ecology forces residents to share their living spaces, opening up opportunities to easily observe and judge neighbors' everyday behaviors. As a result, residents' feelings about the cultural aspects of neighborhood change play a large role in perpetuating instability. This sifting and sorting was evident in Parkmont's transition from a white neighborhood to a black neighborhood, and further evidence of cultural change is now apparent as second wave blacks have begun to outnumber pioneers.

Dimensions of Neighborhood Culture and Perceptions of a Divide

The cultural divide between pioneers and second wave residents is inextricably tied to Parkmont's future reputation as a desirable neighborhood. It has been established that perceived differences between groups can translate into neighborhood dissatisfaction and mobility intentions, which are both associated with actual mobility.[21] In his much-acclaimed book, *Disorder and Decline: Crime and the Spiral of Decay in American Neighborhoods*, Wesley G. Skogan (1990) described a process whereby neighborhoods experience physical and social disorder and then face the risk of population change and decline. He argued that when families have problems with neighbors, they often become anxious and dissatisfied. This prompts them to move, if possible, or else to withdraw from the community, isolating themselves from the people whom they find offensive or unsafe.

Culture is an essential part of conflict in Parkmont. Several dimensions of neighborhood culture divide the pioneers and the second wave, reflecting what residents perceive to be radically different worldviews. The cultural messages communicated by residents demonstrate the extent of their personal knowledge about how people should go about living their lives, raising their children, and participating in their community. Since so many pioneers contend with their

---

21. See Woldoff (2002) for an analysis of the effects of social disorder on various forms of neighborhood attachment. See Bach and Smith (1977) and Clark and Ledwith (2006), respectively, for evidence of the links that neighborhood dissatisfaction has with mobility intentions and actual mobility.

own financial challenges, they view cultural differences rather than structural or socioeconomic disparities as the main source of neighborhood conflict. Though willing to acknowledge the structural origins of residents' cultural disagreements, Parkmont's pioneers believe that their new neighbors possess moral shortcomings and lack common sense.

ASSIMILATIONIST ATTITUDES

The word assimilation often brings to mind the process whereby members of an ethnic minority group discard their traditions in favor of those of the dominant group.[22] However, the concept may also be applied to neighborhoods to describe new residents' efforts to conform to the cultural norms of long-time residents. In Parkmont, of course, race complicates this definition. Arguably, the pioneers' decision to move to a white neighborhood reflects a more general desire to assimilate that goes beyond simple respect for the conventions of a new community. Additionally, the ease with which pioneers managed to fit in to Parkmont reflects a shared social understanding (or lack of social distance) between them and the host community of white stayers.

In contrast, second wave residents differ from most pioneers in that they did not move to Parkmont in search of integration. They knew the community was already predominantly black when they arrived, and some even knew that neighborhood was experiencing decline. Additionally, as new residents, the second wave appeared to be neither interested in nor able to merge into the pioneers' cultural milieu, reflecting a more general lack of assimilationist values that goes beyond race. One second wave resident, Rashid Harris, summarized his lack of knowledge about Parkmont and his disinterest in meeting neighbors, saying that he mostly socializes with people from other neighborhoods and prefers to keep to himself: "All I know is since I've been here. I don't really know what was going on beforehand. I never had any trouble. I mean, I know people in the neighborhood, but as far as interacting, I interact with people, but not to get to know anybody."

The topic of assimilation was a major theme in interviews with Parkmont residents when describing their arrival in the neighborhood and efforts to adapt to the new environment. Pioneer Margaret Meadows explained that when she and her husband were first looking to escape the crime and social disorder of their old neighborhood, they were forced to limit their housing search to communities within the city boundaries because of the couple's work-related residency requirements. Though a full-time school nurse, Margaret also holds down two

---

22. See Gordon (1964).

other nursing jobs. What the Meadows family wanted seemed simple, a racially mixed neighborhood with good schools, but the couple soon became dissatisfied with the kinds of people who were moving in and attending Lombard. Like many pioneers, they had begun to contemplate a move to the suburbs. When I asked Margaret what she knew about Parkmont before moving there, she mentioned the racial composition of the neighborhood, its positive reputation, and her family's desire to blend in:

> That not many, or really, no blacks were up here. Italians and people that were Jewish were up here. It was a very good neighborhood. Lombard used to be a good school, but now everybody from all different communities come up here. I don't know what neighborhoods they moved from, but they don't have as much pride in this community as we do. Case in point, there was a house, and we suspected they were selling drugs in that house. I think the drug boys hang out in front. Now, I try not to be out that much.

In drawing cultural distinctions between the pioneers and the second wave residents, pioneer Anne Jackson expressed assimilationist values when she referenced her desire to live in an integrated neighborhood and her attempts to learn about the stayers. She pointed out that when she first moved to Parkmont, many pioneers sensed that the stayers were imposing social pressure about neighborhood norms, but she said the pioneers respected them. Anne emphasized that pioneers were not simply deferring to the neighbors because they were white but were expressing their general respect for the elderly and long-time residents by making an effort to understand them. For pioneers, the transition was not difficult because their values about community life overlapped with those of the stayers. Anne said that the second wave residents seem to be unconcerned about gaining the approval of the pioneers and conforming to the community standards that were already in place when they arrived:

> We came here and wanted to be accepted. It was mostly a white neighborhood. We came in and had no problems. We didn't want to cause any problems. We just wanted to work, take care of the home, fix it up, live, and be happy. The new people that came up here didn't care as much. The first group that came up here, we tried to fit in. We did as everybody else did. We didn't throw stuff around when *we* came in. We would get out and sweep up the front of our house and clean up. To keep it the way it was.

Pioneer Sonya McCall's father, George, lives with her. Recovering from cancer treatments, he spends most days at home, taking care of his granddaughter after school. Like many pioneers, George identifies more strongly with the white stayers than with the second wave residents. He believes that the second wave residents require extra enforcement of social control by pioneers, an indicator of their rejection of community norms. George admitted that he thinks pioneers are less effective at maintaining order than the stayers were and suggested that the loss of long-term elderly whites on his block has caused a breakdown in social control. As an example, he told me about a second wave neighbor of whom he disapproves and how he wishes more stayers were still around to help enforce Parkmont's social norms: "Now, when Joanne [white stayer] and them was over there, we didn't have too much of a problem, 'cause they stayed on top of it. Mr. Henry, he stayed on them. He'd be knocking on the door, 'You get that abandoned car off the block.' He'd call somebody to get it off the street." I suggested to George that some black residents might resent such interventions from white stayers, taking offense at comments that could be perceived as racist, insulting, or judgmental. I said that I thought it might rub black neighbors the wrong way. However, George adamantly rejected this insinuation: "No. They was rubbing us the *right* way. The right way. As soon as they left, you got all this trash back here, and nothing but abandoned cars in the driveway."

African Americans, like all ethnic groups, construct and recognize socioeconomic divisions, often integrating aspects of culture into their constructions.[23] Parkmont's working-class pioneers were often so perplexed, frustrated, and offended by the way second wave residents handled themselves in the neighborhood that they specifically utilized their observations about residents' community values and behaviors to construct universal judgments representing cultural differentiation. In order to assimilate to the Parkmont culture that the stayers and pioneers desire, new residents would have to discontinue their identification with lower-class culture, which includes allegiance to their former neighborhoods, and shift their identities and cultural values to match those of their new neighborhood. However, many pioneers pessimistically expressed the idea that second wave residents seem to have brought "the hood" with them when they relocated to Parkmont and are unable or unwilling to change. Pioneer Sonya McCall put it this way: "I think people just don't care. I don't know where they came from. Some of them may have come from the projects, and they think this is their suburb. See? That's from where they come from. If they came from a rough neighborhood or grew up rough, then that's what they're used to."

Pioneers Lamar and Clarice Nellis are at the end of their rope with their second wave next-door neighbor, whose values and behaviors interfere with their

---

23. See Frazier (1957).

neighborhood quality of life, motivating the Nellis family to contemplate a move. As far as Lamar and Clarice are concerned, the woman who lives next to them represents an increasingly typical profile of Parkmont residents. The couple shared several stories with me about what they consider to be their neighbor's "ghetto" or disrespectful behaviors and attitudes, which they see as major character flaws rooted in lower-class culture and community life rather than minor transgressions. These include defensive and hostile interactions about property maintenance, the failure to share outdoor chores in common areas, a poor sense of priorities, and general ignorance about the basics of how to live on one's own, take care of a home, and be a good neighbor:

> CLARICE: I had a conversation with her about the steps. I said, "We may have to get the steps done because your concrete is cracking, which means eventually, it's going to come over to our side." She said, "No. I'm a single parent trying to do this on my own."
>
> LAMAR: I said, "If you're going to live somewhere, there is ways to do things." Little things. They're not in line with me. I'm not going to fuss and argue over it, but unfortunately we're in row homes. I think it's the baggage they bring from the environment where they come from. Certain things you are taught, you grow up with. It's evident to other people that you choose not to do it, or you haven't been taught the etiquette of homeownership or what to do with the home. For those of us that have lived in homes with our parents, you have to mow the lawn. It's a chore. You have to rake. It's a chore. Your mother or father made you do it, no matter if you wanted to do it or not.

On a winter evening, second wave resident Ramell Worthy pointed to two teenaged boys standing in front of his house, laughing and cursing loudly. Despite the fact that it was dusk, the teens wore sunglasses, and the hoods of their sweatshirts covered their heads. Ramell was mocking and dismissive of them: "Those guys? They're pretending. They're acting like they're selling drugs. They're standing around with their pants hanging down, with their hoods, just hanging." Though he insisted that many teens in Parkmont whom residents find intimidating are just "fronting," Ramell admitted that he is concerned about the future of the neighborhood. He asserted that Parkmont is "not bad yet," but his projection is similar to that of many pioneers: pessimistic. He blamed the decline on the cultural characteristics of new residents and the norms they learned in their old neighborhoods:

> I think it's going to be worse because you're getting a lot of people that are coming in that don't appreciate the property of the neighborhood.

They think they can have the same mentality coming from a worse neighborhood than this. This is a step up, but that doesn't necessarily mean a step up in your personal class, but a step up in a geographical social class. But if it's not a step up in a personal class, it's not going to happen. I can see it by the type of adolescents around, the kids, the teenagers, the young adults. They have this need to look like they're from a worse neighborhood. They have a need to be rougher instead of realizing, "This is an okay neighborhood. We should get clean instead of hanging on the corner." It's their need to identify with this 'hood culture. They don't realize they're in a position to do much better. When their parents get older and when they give their house to them, this is what we'll be left with—those guys that are on the corner. I've seen people selling drugs. I know people selling drugs.

Even though she is a second wave resident who moved from a poor community through the use of a first-time homeowners program, Ramell's fiancée, Aliya, also reported that she has mixed feelings about the cultural impact that second wave residents are having on Parkmont. She blamed the second wave's apparent lack of pride and investment in their homes on the intractable lower-class socialization that is typical of their former communities:

> I think a lot of times people come from a lower-income area, but they may—not to say that people in a lower-income area don't necessarily appreciate their property—but there are some that come from an area where they don't appreciate their property. So then it's the same mind-set. You're moving into a different area, but you still have the same mind-set. I've noticed that here.

When pioneers blame the second wave's lower-class socialization and values for the deterioration of Parkmont, they frequently express disapproval of the way the new residents seem to spend their money. The main complaint is that families should improve the appearance of their homes before buying items or purchasing services that are unnecessary or frivolous. Pioneer Clarice Nellis said:

> My mother always said, "People see the outside of your home first. If you have to choose between straightening up the outside or inside, choose the outside first, and work your way in. *Then* do the inside of your home." She said, "Your home is a reflection of you. Make sure you make your bed, but other things you can let go 'til you can get to it." And their clothes? I see them getting in brand new jeeps, but they don't have a screen door on the front, the blinds raggedy, falling down. I'm looking

at the basics. I don't want to see sheets up in the window. How dare you? When you can go to the value store and buy curtains.

Although she is a second wave resident, Shonda Suarez also attributed the decline in Parkmont's appearance to the way that newer residents with lower-class values prioritize their spending. Confounding class with race and gender, she claimed that single women and blacks are especially less likely than whites and married families to invest adequately in their homes:

> I noticed that at my age—I'm not saying all white people, but a lot of white people—take care of their property more. I think that it has a lot to do with their income bracket. People are out at the mall trying to look good. 'Cause women love to look good, especially African Americans. Our thing is clothes and hair and nails and fashion, jewelry, so the extra money that she [her neighbor with a broken front door] *do* have? Instead of fixing the door, she's out at the mall. I think the values are a lot different between whites and blacks, also. When I first started college, the black guys would walk around with all the name brands, like the Sean John, the Roca Wear, True Religion. Then, you got the white people in college. They're walking around in an old pair of sneakers and jeans they had four years ago. Black people, you would never see them in that. They got to have the latest fashion. They put they money there. That's why they always broke.

Residents' beliefs about the importation of lower- class culture to Parkmont even extended to the quality and appearance of businesses on the strip, with many people pointing out that when neighborhood populations change, the businesses change. Carla Jackson, a social worker and young mother who resides with her parents in Parkmont, is a pioneer. She said that Parkmont's social class decline is especially apparent when walking along the strip, where the newer businesses that have opened largely cater to people without much money to spend. She admitted that some of the service-oriented businesses have responded to common patterns of black consumption preferences. However, she also asserted that "cheap" business owners locate in Parkmont because they perceive that the profile of residents is increasingly lower income and desirous of cheap goods that they would otherwise purchase after traveling to the nearby poor neighborhoods:

> It's not too bad like some of the other neighborhoods, but I think it's gonna get worse because of the things that be going on now. The different stores and the different hangout spots. We have a lot of Chinese stores in here now. We have hair stores. We have stores that have come into the

neighborhood because of the culture that is in the neighborhood. Would you put that hair store in your neighborhood? You wouldn't put it there because there's no need for it. But with the black community, hair is important, nails is important. So they're gonna come, and then the Chinese stores. I think they're accommodating the blacks because the blacks are the ones that spend the money. So why not accommodate them with what they like? But some of the stuff is not positive.

Most second wave residents were not troubled by the appearance of the strip, but Mary Smith, an elderly second wave resident, insisted that the decline in the neighborhood's business climate sends a message to passersby that the residents are mainly low income. Mary disapproves of the stores on the strip that fail to match her memories of the Parkmont that she visited when she was young. In this passage, Mary stopped herself before making a comment about the new "Chinese" stores, a feature of the strip that pioneer residents repeatedly identified to be problem:

> They have businesses up here that are so rinky-dink. I understand if you're in business, and you're trying to make money from the public but.…I don't want to use any racial comments, but they don't keep the glasses in their stores clean. If your business isn't so good that you can't hire anyone, get out there, and do it yourself. And it just could at least look nicer. More cleaner. Where you don't find trash on the ground.…It's a minor thing to get out there and clean the windows for a business when you are trying to entice people to come in. That's about the only thing, but I would say that it doesn't have a nice look.

SENSE OF OWNERSHIP

This dimension of community culture simply distinguishes between residents who seem to care about the community and those who do not. A culture of ownership may be seen as a reflection of the difference between residents with long-term versus short-term orientations toward the community. Residents who intend to live in a neighborhood for years to come are more likely to have a stake in community life and be invested in its future. Pioneers such as Margaret Meadows believe that differences in this cultural dimension represent a major distinction between the two groups of black residents: "It's changing. I still like it for right now because all the people are older people around here, which I consider myself an older person around here. I'm a 'long-term.'"

Unlike the pioneers who moved into a white or integrated community hoping to stay indefinitely, many second wave residents reported that they had never intended to stay for the long term. Second wave residents tended to view Parkmont as a temporary or transitional housing plan, which may explain why building a sense of community has not been a priority for them. For many second wave residents, Parkmont is merely a convenient and safe city neighborhood located close to their extended families—nothing more. Parkmont is enough for them in the present, but many second wave residents expressed aspirations to live in large, detached homes in better communities and saw no need to form social ties or become further involved in the goings-on of the neighborhood.

Second wave resident Rashid Harris exemplifies the short-term orientation to Parkmont that so many pioneers find offensive. He rents a home in Parkmont with his wife, their son, and a child from one of his past relationships. Even though Rashid considers Parkmont to be safer than his old neighborhood, he told me that he had never planned to stay for the long-term: "It's too cramped. If I had my choice, I wouldn't move into the city at all. I don't want to buy a house here. I don't want neighbors. Well, I want neighbors, but I want space in between."

Shonda Suarez also reported that her time in Parkmont is just a temporary living situation. She told me that, unlike the pioneers who moved to the neighborhood with the intention of planting roots, she considers Parkmont to be a stepping-stone until she can buy the house of her dreams. Even though Shonda began renting her home in Parkmont after white flight had largely been completed, she said that she would never be interested in living in the type of community from which so many people have opted to flee. Wanting to follow in the footsteps of the whites and pioneers who have already left Parkmont, her sights are set on a single-family house in the suburbs, but it remains unclear whether her plans are realistic given her limited economic means:

> From what I'm doing, it should put me, in a couple years, to a nicer bracket to where I can afford something nicer to live. I'm looking now, actually. I like Parkmont, but the houses are too small. I have to be where the neighborhood is going up. If I start seeing the neighborhood going down, I'm moving out with the rest of the people that's trying to get out. I'm not going to stay and watch it deteriorate. My grandmother, she been living in her house since 1958. She watched all the white people move out the neighborhood. She watched the neighborhood do a drastic change. If I was her, I might've stayed there, but when the white people left, I'm going. I'm following them. That's the type of person I am. I like to live a certain way. If I feel as though it's going down that much when everybody who was supposed to be in my class range move out, I'm moving too! I wanna go to a more upscale area.

Though Linda Hopewell is a second wave homeowner, she also demonstrated a short-term resident's mind-set when she told me that she maintains a sense

of detachment from Parkmont and "definitely" views her house as an investment "starter" home. In fact, she reported that she did not bother to investigate
the quality of the local schools before moving to Parkmont because she never
planned to stay for long: "I knew that once I would have a child that I would
move to my second house. We do plan to move within a couple years. We're
thinking about starting flipping houses and things like that."

SENSITIVITY TO PHYSICAL AND SOCIAL INCIVILITIES

The idea that persisting problems with neighbors cause residents to consider
moving has been overlooked in discussions of the effects of broken windows
or incivilities. Instead, urban policies have justified the policing of disorder by
focusing on the theorized links between disorder and violent crime. However,
disorder is not simply a factor that may lead to serious crime; it is a cultural symbol representing a shift in the values of newcomers.

To pioneers, disorder is the antithesis of the decency, community citizenship, and aspirations toward upward mobility that Parkmont promised. From
the pioneers' point of view, the implications of disorder are that the neighborhood's quality of life will visibly and morally decline, and, along with the loss,
pioneers' recently achieved residential status and neighborhood identity will
also be threatened. Thus, pioneers are extremely sensitive to social and physical
disorder in the community because of the ways disorder affects their property
values and quality of life, and because it contrasts with the Parkmont they first
knew and desired. Although the pioneers often acknowledged that second wave
residents' behaviors and values result from disadvantaged economic, family, and
neighborhood backgrounds, pioneers were unwilling to excuse the newcomers
or to relax their community standards. In this way, cultural clashes over disorder
have caused black flight to continue because those who are most able to leave
Parkmont often do so. This selective out-migration of residents who are more
stable and community-oriented then causes further neighborhood decline.

Pioneers often stated that their major motivation for moving to the suburbs
is that social disorder and continual problems with second wave neighbors have
started to interfere with their way of life. In contrast, many second wave residents arrived with lower expectations for community conditions, obligations,
and social life. With an absence of memories of Parkmont in better times, second
wave residents often appeared to be more satisfied with the neighborhood than
the pioneers. They seemed to take it for what it is and what they seek from it: a
relatively safe and quiet black urban community.

Pioneers expressed a desire to maintain a relatively pristine community atmosphere, which includes keeping the standards high when it comes to the public
image of the homes and residents, but many second wave residents disagreed

with the pioneers' emphasis on appearance and order and found their criticisms of other residents' lifestyles to be extreme. Pioneer Margaret Meadows described the difference in opinion when it comes to peace and quiet:

> A lot of neighbors share the same values, but the newer people don't. I value my family and my property, even though I don't think that I'm a materialistic person. But those are two things I *do* value. I value the environment of the neighborhood. I love quiet. It's alright for the kids to run around and play, but after a certain time, I'm going to go outside, and if I can hear a pin drop, I like that. I don't like a whole lot of activity. If I want to go to a party, I can *go* to a party.

Inside his home, second wave resident Ramell Worthy considered what might, at first, seem to be an offensive question: whether the second wave blacks are different from the pioneers. But Ramell nodded his head in agreement: "Since I've been here, I've personally put more traffic on this block than anybody else, and I feel bad about that.... I'm not going to say I don't care who I offend, but I'm just saying, until they [the pioneers] understand who I am, then I leave them to judge. Whatever." By "traffic on the block" Ramell meant that he receives many visitors from outside of the neighborhood who come in and out of his home. He told me that the pioneers seem especially overprotective, fearing that the "wrong" people are getting too familiar with the neighborhood, and worrying that outsiders will start "hanging out," or even worse, that such visitors are actually involved in drug deals. Though Ramell identified many differences between pioneer and second wave residents in terms of values (e.g., degree of concern about presentation of self to neighbors) and behaviors (e.g., number of cars on the block, number of visitors), he also perceived the pioneers to be easily offended and said that his infractions are fairly minor and harmless norm violations.

However, Sonya McCall, a pioneer and mother of a young daughter, specifically complained to me about Ramell and Aliya, who are her neighbors. Sonya was angry because the couple owns a van with a broken window that sits in the driveway next to her home. She told me that she had never even seen them drive the vehicle. More important, on several occasions Sonya had seen a group of boys sitting in the van, smoking marijuana. Although she had spoken to Aliya about the situation, the couple had not moved or repaired the van. What bothered Sonya most was that Aliya seemed to think Sonya's complaints were trivial.

This type of neighbor conflict is emblematic of the simmering tension that has emerged between pioneers and second wave residents, each of whom has a very different perspective on what constitutes acceptable behavior in Parkmont and what they are willing to tolerate from neighbors. The pioneers insist that context matters, and when one moves to a row house community with the goal of escaping noise and chaos, the little things matter a lot. Clarice and Lamar Nellis explained how seemingly minor disputes with neighbors can have a cumulative effect:

> CLARICE: Our neighbor only shoveled her half and didn't shovel our steps. It's only a little walkway, and you mean to tell me you only did half? I was hot. It took her longer to do her one little part than it would have to do everything. Now, I'm going to use my deck soon, so I'll have to go over there and tell her nicely she cannot put her trash out there on the deck. She doesn't use trash bags either, just little bags, supermarket bags. We couldn't even use our deck last year.
>
> LAMAR: She has an attitude, too. As nice as you can be, she takes a defensive attitude. She was taking the trash out, and normally we're accustomed to the trash being uniform. She had the trash bags all over the place, and when the wind blows, it blows the trash to the middle of the walkway or driveway. These little bags. So I told her, we use regular trash bags; put your little bags in normal trash bags. She was really annoyed with that.

Second wave resident Rashid Harris summarized what many people believe is typical of the second wave residents' state of mind. When I arrived for our scheduled 10:00 a.m. interview, he asked me to come back later because he had just gotten off his night shift and was drinking beer and "hanging out with his boys." When I returned after his friends left, Rashid reported that his evaluation of Parkmont is that he's "fine with it" and feels safe. He does not perceive decline because he knows that the neighborhood is still far safer than where he used to live. Though Rashid is an adult, he echoed the sentiment of many of Parkmont's children and teens who came from other neighborhoods when he told me that his friends from his old neighborhood think Parkmont is "wack" (i.e., boring, uncool, or lame). Rashid mocked the pioneers' concerns about order, arguing that Parkmont's problems are "just like a molehill" compared to those of his last neighborhood. This kind of trivialization of the pioneers' concerns about social and physical disorder is shared by many second wave residents who patently dismiss the incivilities that the pioneers find so troubling.

In a more unusual case, one second wave resident mentioned that she has become acquainted with several pioneers and has taken the time to understand their strict attitudes about community behaviors. Linda Hopewell shared a story about the pioneers socializing her into neighborhood cultural norms about order that seem counter to those found in many urban neighborhoods. She explained what she has learned about the desirability of block parties from "them":

> We have a block captain who is very good. We don't have any block parties because they don't want a lot of people coming on the block and

messing with our properties. A lot of people think that people will start coming to the neighborhood and start knowing where we are. People from other neighborhoods. Stuff just starts to happen. I mean, when they told me that, I was shocked. When they said, "Well, we don't have block parties." I'm thinking, "Really?" They said, "No. Because people start to come in. They start to mess up your property." And I'm thinking, "I guess they're thinking about the value of the property." They don't want [other] people to come in.

Linda reported that she has come to relate to the pioneers, mainly for financial reasons rather than some larger cultural affinity. Now, out of concern for the value of her home, she has adopted their more stringent attitude toward disorder. Like the pioneers, Linda has already considered moving because she is concerned that forms of physical and social disorder will cause a decline in property values:

> I didn't have a lawn, and I didn't have a garage growing up, so those are things that I do value. The people next door had a dog and three cats, and they let their dog go to the bathroom on my lawn. They owned the house, but they just didn't understand that people like to have a nice lawn. I was told that the people that lived there before them used to get an award for the best lawn within Parkmont. And the people that got it now? You wouldn't think that. [Laughs] But they just didn't understand the concept. Now, next door? I have to get that lawn cut myself. We split it, me and another neighbor. We both don't want to have our lawns looking nice and then the one in the middle look bad. So we just got to the point where last year, every other week or whatever, we just take on the cost of it to keep up the value of the house. People have parties 'til wee hours of the morning. They have music playing. For me, I would just think that a person—once you bought a house—that you would want to keep the value of the house up. That's just me, personally, but everybody's not the same. We were really concerned because of being in the middle of two vacant houses. We really had to think about our property and think about what are we going to do. You know, if we're ready to move. I know we have to do a lot of renovations, but how soon is it gonna be? We've had a lot of people move out within the last couple of years because some people don't keep up their property. That's probably the main thing. We have to think about the value of our property.

Unlike most second wave residents, Linda has come to identify with the pioneers in some ways and is already seeking to move after only a short tenure in Parkmont. Having spent her 401K on this home, she is distressed about its losing its value in the wake of the population change that has already contributed to Parkmont's vacant homes, deteriorating properties, and disrespectful neighbors.

POOR PARENTING AS A FORM OF DISORDER

Though there is a diversity of parenting styles in the United States, when people think about cultural diversity as it relates to parenting, what comes to mind are the unfamiliar value systems and practices of people from different nationalities and religions. Yet, even within ethnically similar groups and communities, parenting values, norms, and practices can diverge and become a source of conflict. Although parenting can be seen as a private matter, it has consequences for communities. In Parkmont, children's public behaviors serve as signifiers of their parents' decency in the home and larger community.

Like many pioneers, Margaret Meadows disapproves of the parenting that she has witnessed among her neighbors. She reported that not only do the second wave residents lack community values and simple respectfulness but their children are out of control and create disorder in Parkmont. Insightfully, she attributed some of the conflict between the pioneers and second wave residents to generational differences in styles of child-rearing. Margaret said that she more closely identifies with the elderly white stayers than younger second wave black residents when it comes to parenting:

> We made sure that our children did the right thing. We watched our children. If it was a neighbor's child, we watched our neighbor's children to see that everything was going okay. But I know people that are moving in now aren't as disciplined. They aren't disciplinarians like we were. The children are doing a lot of things that I wouldn't let my kids do. They out late, walking the dog, and letting them do their business and not cleaning it up, and then somebody step in it. To me, it's a little disrespectful at times. Not all the time. I really don't have that kind of a problem, but I just think, times change and people change. But I think that it's changing for the worse because the kids are a lot different, and they're not as respectful of things as I feel they should be. Another thing, if they're smoking marijuana outside. To me, that's another part of being disrespected.

Pioneer George McCall, Sonya's father, is friendly with many of the white stayers who like to sit outside on their patios, and he often joins them when he goes outside to smoke. George disapproves of the second wave children whom he believes run wild on the streets, creating a disorderly atmosphere. In addition, he is very unsympathetic toward their parents, whom he believes feign innocence: "Our neighbor—that woman—she's got two boys that can't do nothing right. They're in and out. When she goes to work, it's fifteen or twenty of them in the house. When something happens, she goes crying. I told her one day, I said, 'Shut up. You know what's going on in your house.'"

As a teacher, pioneer Nina Jones is especially observant of and sensitive to children's behaviors and especially their respect for adults. She often makes universal judgments about residents' parenting and family lifestyles based on her observations of neighborhood children. Despite the similarities in ethnic background between pioneers and second wavers, Nina believes that even minor indicators of poor parenting indicate that Parkmont's incoming families are beneath her in the social hierarchy:

> The kids walking up and down the street, cursing? I would never, as a child, have cursed in the presence of an adult, but they say "F this" and "F that." Kids sit on your front steps, and you gotta ask them to move just so you can get up your own steps. One day, I had my son outside. I was blowing bubbles, and two girls across the street and some other kids came by. They're teenagers. Then, a whole bunch of little kids came. One had *never* even seen bubbles. So, I'm out there with my bubble machine, and they're busting the bubbles, and they're "F this" and "MF that." I'm like, "All these kids are around. If that's how you talk, and that's how your mom and them talk in your family, you take it there." Oh no, they don't like to see me coming. They do *not* like to see me coming. 'Cause I tell them it's not going to happen here.

To Nina, second wave parents create a negative living environment for Parkmont families, and she finds the parents to be neglectful because their children lack basic manners and have missed out on the most simple and inexpensive childhood enrichment experiences. Like many pioneers, Nina was quite harsh in her assessment of the child-rearing practices exhibited by the second wave residents. As a teacher, Nina understands structural inequality and how it translates into differences in access to athletics, dance classes, and music lessons, but she still viewed the local children's lack of familiarity with bubbles, especially combined with their foul language, as indicative of larger problems in their homes and the general moral failure of their parents.

Leanne Hanson is a second wave resident who lives across the street from Lombard with her mother, husband, and two daughters. On her lawn is a planting of faded silk flowers, and next to the flowers is an oversized white trellis with peeling paint leaning to one side. Leanne has heard pioneers complain about various forms of decline in the neighborhood. She is concerned about the behavior of children in the neighborhood and the school, but overall she is not nearly as troubled as her pioneer neighbors:

> I heard a lot of good things about Parkmont, but I did hear that it wasn't what it used to be. But it was still a good neighborhood. They said that years and years ago, Parkmont was like a melting pot. It was mostly Caucasian. They had Jewish and Korean, and still some mixtures, but it was very peaceful, meaning not a lot of violence, burglary is low, rape is low, not a lot of crime. So I took that as advice, and I wanted to believe that, but you can't believe everything you hear. I did check Lombard, and I heard it was a great school, but it's not how it used to be. That's what I heard, too, but I think it's a good school from what we are deal-ing with now in the city. I think they're one of the good schools left. I think overall it's a good school, but other parents that had children go there and they're grown now will tell me, "Oh, it's good, but it's not like it used to be." I can't say it's not good. I feel it's in a state of decline because I heard so many great things, but I still think the neighborhood is good. I'm not happy with the children in the area from what I have seen. We have neighbors that are graduating from Lombard. They're a little rowdy, and they're getting a little out of hand. Compared to a lot of the areas in the city, I still think it's a great place. I mean, you have to be careful with your children anywhere. I think it's a good place to raise your children.

ATTITUDES ABOUT CRIME, SOCIAL CONTROL, AND COMMUNITY INVOLVEMENT

Pioneers' concerns about the culture of the second wave also extend to the issues of crime, social control, and community involvement. Many believe that crime has been increasing, and they think that the second wave families' tolerance and participation in crime have contributed to the problem. Though Parkmont's crime problems are not as severe as those in many urban neighborhoods, two banks (now converted to a church and a dollar store), several stores, a gas station, and a bar, all located on the strip, have been the sites of armed robberies in recent years. The civic association's minutes have reported that burglaries are a prob-lem, as are nuisance bars. Even at the library, the manager has complained of an "excessive" number of condoms, beer bottles, and drug bags littering the ground. The Laundromat is a site that is especially reviled by pioneers for numerous rea-sons. Pioneers do not want to give the impression to potential home buyers that Parkmont is a poor community, and symbolically, they view the Laundromat as a business that caters to and attracts renters and low-income people who cannot afford their own appliances. Also, based on their experiences in Parkmont as well as in their old neighborhoods, pioneers believe that these kinds of businesses breed disorder because they are poorly maintained, noisy, covered in litter, and they create parking problems. Worst of all, pioneers claim, Laundromats are dangerous, unmonitored places for the loitering of homeless people, teen gangs, drug dealers, and prostitutes, inviting robberies and brawling.

Many businesses have responded to disorder in Parkmont by either withdrawing from the community altogether or increasing security measures in a visible and unfriendly way, including the use of riot gates, surveillance cameras, and discourteous signs about loitering and rules of conduct for students who wish to enter stores. Pioneer Sonya McCall explained how the recent changes in some stores' business hours have affected her:

> The CVS used to be open 24 hours 'cause my daughter used to get sick really bad, and I had to take her to the doctor. I would go there at 3:00 in the morning, get my prescription filled, come home, give her medicine. Now it closes at 10:00, and the pharmacy closes at 9:00 because they been robbed. When they got robbed, that was it. No more. The neighborhood was starting to change then. You can see little things, the merchants closing up, and different things are coming in.

Like many pioneers, Nina Jones thinks Parkmont's young residents now participate in far more dangerous behaviors than she remembers from her youth when she was a student at Lombard. She contrasted three Parkmonts: the old Parkmont of her school days, the one to which she first moved as a pioneer, and the one she lives in now. She made it clear that she does not identify with the second wave residents and seeks to separate herself from the cultural values of newer parents and their children:

> When I was young, it was all about Parkmont. Everything was nice up here. I remember it well. When I moved here in the beginning, it was fine. I would say for the first two to three years I really enjoyed living here. Even up until after I had my son. Then, I was like, "Okay, it's really time to go." I guess my attitude has changed because I have a child. I can't subject him to the things that are going on in this neighborhood. I just, I can't do it. That day with the drug bust when I opened my door, and the people were standing there with guns? I was like, "I can't raise him in this type of environment."

Pioneer Carla Jackson grew up in Parkmont and thinks that, unlike her cohort, the second wave families seem to be desensitized to crime and their own children appear to be involved in it. She reported that she feels intimidated walking along the strip because drug-dealing teens brazenly stand around for hours on end, waiting for customers:

> I go to stores, but I don't *like* to go because the young ones are hanging outside selling drugs. Why would you stand in front? It's not just the way you look, because the white boys look the same. So you can't say that. But why would you stand on that corner for four hours or six hours? Just doin' nothing. Why would you stand there?

Residents who accuse second wave parents of being nonchalant about neighborhood crime may have in mind people like Rashid Harris. Rashid reluctantly moved to Parkmont when his new wife became pregnant because she liked that the neighborhood was safe and near her family's neighborhood. He admitted that his old neighborhood was plagued by disorder and serious crime but said that he had learned to think of that environment as normal:

> I see why some people move, but I feel safe wherever I'm at so it wasn't really about the neighborhood. I was having a son, so I just needed to move from where I was at. I had an apartment by myself. It's a little quieter up here. The life, the style of it, is what my wife considers quieter. She's the boss. Where I lived, it was just noisy, like "people hanging" noise. On my block now, kids go in the house at a certain time. There's some things about my old neighborhood I didn't like, but it wasn't disturbing to *me*. Potheads and gangs and things like that. It was a bad lookin' neighborhood. It's not well mannered like it is here. Where I grew up at, I didn't really think it was a bad neighborhood until I left it. I mean, my friends come here now, so it's cool.

In contrast, pioneer Korrie Dawson remains deeply concerned about a rising tolerance of crime in Parkmont. During my interview with Korrie, we both learned that a man had recently tried to sell a gun to her eighteen-year-old grandson, Brian. Brian shocked Korrie when he interjected with this story about his experiences with crime victimization: "Last week I almost got robbed down the street. Some boy came up to me with a gun. He had a gun in his pocket. He wanted some money. I wasn't having it. So I was talking to him or whatever, but he just walked away after a while and said, 'Gonna get my money.'"

When asked if he felt afraid in Parkmont, Brian just said: "Only at night. People walk around in groups or whatever, like gangs. They're always out here, but people are different at nighttime. Go to any corner store. If they see a weaker person comes up to them, they'll go after them."

Even so, as a newcomer and youth, Brian seemed to share the acceptance of crime that characterizes many second wave residents. He insisted that Parkmont is still a good neighborhood because "there's not too many gunshots." Echoing the comments of many young people who have recently moved from poorer neighborhoods, Brian told me that even though he feels safer in Parkmont, he finds the social scene to be "boring" compared to the high levels of street activity where he used to live. Brian also complained that he feels like an outsider because he has only lived in the neighborhood since his mother left for Iraq. He told me that he misses his old neighborhood friends and does not have friends in Parkmont because he goes to a magnet school located all the way across the city. As a result, Brian spends most of his time with staff members at the JCC, where he works out, and he often visits his girlfriend in his old neighborhood even though he feels afraid when riding public transportation there late at night.

Korrie objected to Brian's blasé attitude about Parkmont's problems, insisting that she knows many pioneer neighbors who are not jaded and who continue to take the incidence of local crimes to heart. To make her point, Korrie told me that her neighbor, an EMT who also sends her children to a magnet school, is so vigilant about the local crime problem that she uses the police radio at work to gather information about violence and shootings that occur in Parkmont. Stressing the importance of the cultural divide between pioneers and stayers, Korrie said that her pioneer neighbors have told her that they want to move out, "so it's not necessarily about color."

Cultural differences in views about crime also extend to attitudes about community involvement and strategies for maintaining social control, such as calling the police. When describing their efforts to deal with emerging problems in Parkmont, pioneers often reported that they try to be active, but many times they are too tired and busy to attend meetings. In contrast, second wave residents reported that the reason they are disengaged is that they view the local problems to be minor and subscribe to a "mind your own business" attitude toward neighborhood issues.[24] This difference in values manifested itself in an interaction I had with pioneer Margaret Meadows:

> MARGARET: Case in point: it was a house that's on that corner. We suspected they were selling drugs in that house, but we've reported it, so.
> R. W.: You called the police?
> MARGARET: That's right. Yeah. We call.
> R. W.: You're not hesitant to call the police?
> MARGARET: No.

---

24. See Woldoff (2006b) for explanations of how fear of crime interferes with informal social control in neighborhoods. See also Woldoff and Weiss (2010), which outlines some of the ways in which black neighborhoods have been negatively affected by anti-snitching cultural norms that discourage reporting crimes to police.

> R. W.: You're not afraid of being a snitch?
>
> MARGARET: Naw. Nope. No. This is where I live, and this is where my kids live, and I want to be protected. So I don't care.

Now consider the case of second wave resident Rashid Harris, who told me that, short of a public rape, he is not inclined to call the police when a crime takes place in Parkmont. His stance on corner drug dealers is in stark opposition to the position that most pioneers take:

> RASHID: Where I grew up, we just grew up minding our business, so I never really pay attention. If it's not bothering me, it's not bothering me.
>
> R. W.: So if you saw something you didn't approve of, would you call the police? If you saw someone selling drugs on the corner, would you call the cops?
>
> RASHID: I don't know about that. Just like I said, it's not my business. Because at the same time that people are selling it, people are buying it, too. So none of this really bothers me. Like I said, it's not my business. It's really not my business. Now, if I saw somebody raped on the corner? Yeah, I'm gonna call the police. That's different because somebody's being violated. That's a big difference. I don't actually think it's the drugs doing something to the neighborhood. It's a petty crime. 'Cause there are drugs in every neighborhood. White, black, whatever neighborhood.
>
> R. W.: At least using drugs. There aren't sales in every neighborhood.
>
> RASHID: Using, yeah. There's not corner sales in every neighborhood. That part of it *is* different. There's drugs everywhere. But like I said, nobody's being violated in that relationship.

Second wave resident Leanne Hanson agreed with Rashid's sentiment that calling the police is only necessary for violent crimes, such as a physical attack or domestic violence. Her elderly mother said that she would not call the authorities even in those violent circumstances: "I would pretend like I don't see it." Leanne confided that she has not called police about incidents such as the teens who smoke marijuana in the car parked in front of her home. She explained how life in her old neighborhood has made her fearful of the repercussions of contacting the police, so she has learned to choose her battles and mind her own business:

> My husband works a lot at night. We're here, just women, by ourselves. Sometimes, when you call the police—and we seen it—the police come knocking, asking if we put in a report. Then people know it was you, and then they're leaving you in the area to deal with these thugs. You never know if they're going to break in or try to hurt you or mess with your

children or mess with your car. So you got to be careful. So I wouldn't say nothin'. As long as they ain't bothering me.

The cynical culture of distrust that residents say has become pervasive in Parkmont seems to have originated from residents' prior experiences with victimization in previous neighborhoods, as in the case of second wave resident Mary Smith, who expressed ambivalence about her safety in Parkmont. Even though Parkmont is not completely removed from violence, Mary considers the community to be an improvement over her last few neighborhoods. However, she has also been traumatized by violent victimization in her past, has few interactions with neighbors, and has personally witnessed signs of violent crime in Parkmont, all of which have tainted her feelings of relative safety. She told me about the crime and disorder in her old neighborhood, which she said are also present in Parkmont:

> Kids, drugs, gunshots. You hear them around here, too. Not often, but you can't escape them really. As far as I'm concerned, it's no matter where you live. People think because they live in lovely neighborhoods, they say they safe. Maybe just a little bit safer. It's everywhere. This is a nice neighborhood. It's a quiet neighborhood, so it's very nice living here. I'm very content here. I think there's been three occasions when I've heard gunshots since I been here, four years. From the sound, one was up that way, one was down that way, and one was down this way. I didn't really expect it, but if you sit down and think about it, guns are everywhere. Everybody is "packing." That's how we live. I mean, even I have a teargas gun.... I don't really know anybody except just the neighbors over here. But one thing, 'cause I'm originally from [another neighborhood], where everybody knew everybody, everybody spoke, and if they didn't, you said "Good morning, good afternoon." I miss that. I've missed that for years ever since I came here.... It's a mixed community with different nationalities. And basically, everybody gets along if you mind your own business.

Like some form of an urban village, black neighborhoods are often depicted in literature, films, and sociological studies as close-knit environments where residents are so close that they socialize, raise each other's children, and even handle crime on their own.[25] In cities with large African American populations, black neighborhoods have historically provided emotional and financial support to residents as they struggled for survival in the face of unemployment, poverty,

---

25. See Naylor (1988), Pattillo-McCoy (1999), Stack (1974), and Trice (1997).

Jim Crow in the South, and segregation and discrimination in the North.[26] Yet this image may also be seen as a sentimentalized oversimplification of black community life[27] since neighbor relationships are often strained by the circumstances that plague many segregated sections of the city, leaving residents divided over the range of problems that disproportionately plague such neighborhoods.[28]

Though Parkmont is now largely a segregated black neighborhood, it stands in contrast to popular depictions of black communities where residents share meaningful and interdependent relationships. Pioneer Anne Jackson explained the social distance that exists among the black residents in Parkmont as compared to her old neighborhood:

> These are my neighbors; they're not my friends. These are just neighbors. That's it. This is altogether a different neighborhood from where I came. These neighbors you speak to, "Hi. How you doing?" But it's not like you go outside and sit on the steps and talk and eat. I was actually more comfortable where I came from. Oh yeah. There was more violence, the guns. There was always something going on. But when something happened, people came to your rescue. We were like a big family. Like this lady up the street here, right up here. One night she had a real bad fire. She lost everything in her house. Everything. We came home, and I said that we need to do something, give something. My husband and I, we gave them some things, and I said, "Just take it." But I don't know them. They don't know me.

Even though crime and disorder were very common in pioneers' and second wave residents' previous communities, there were also far more opportunities to socialize with other residents. Parkmont residents often complained about the lack of organizations and community centers in their new neighborhood. Most reported that even after moving to Parkmont, they continued to attend church in their old neighborhoods. In fact, through all of my fieldwork, I did not meet a single resident who attended a church in Parkmont. In addition, residents' children continued to participate in sports and after-school events at local community centers found in other black neighborhoods within the urban core.

---

26. Cott (2004).

27. Page (1999). Note that such sentimentality may also be, in part, a reaction to the widespread negative imagery of black neighborhoods that has been used to demonize the black family. See Moynihan (1965) for examples.

28. These problems are often seen as constituting a public health problem for blacks. They include but are not limited to the following: lack of quality schools and stable employment; loss of middle class population; exposure to violent crime, drugs, and disorder; and decline of the two-parent family household (Sampson and Wilson 1995; Wilson 1987).

Pioneer Carla Jackson agreed that leaving her old neighborhood meant losing a close-knit community of neighbors. At the time of the move, Carla was already enrolled in a magnet school far from her home, but coming to Parkmont meant that she would transfer to Lombard. Carla described her initial resistance to the move and her eventual acceptance of it: "It was hard for me when I was young, because all my friends and family would round up at the neighborhood, but it was a good move."

Joy Parker, a pioneer, admitted that while she has bonded with some white stayers, she barely knows the black residents and is too busy working to reach out to them. To illustrate the extent to which she feels isolated from her black neighbors, she offered this story about a recent violent crime in Parkmont that had been widely publicized because it involved a politician's son:

> I heard about it at my job. When I am around here, I don't hear nothing. I didn't even get the whole info. I have no clue to be honest because, as I was telling you, I'm always working. I leave for work early in the morning, and I come back late at night, so I don't even know what's going on. You lucky you seen me out here because I don't normally come outside. I never hear nothing 'cause I don't really talk with people around here. There is a lot of wrong things that happen here that I don't hear about 'cause, like I said, I go to work, and I come in. I be so tired. I just wanna go to bed. I'm always working. I work two jobs.

Pioneer Erma Williams, aged sixty-seven, agreed: "I don't know the neighbors very well because I always work, and a lot of them work. So I don't know a lot of the neighbors."

Rhonda Hamilton was one of several pioneers who also admitted that her long work hours interfere with her involvement in the civic association. She complained that the civic association meetings are not what they once were, and only draw between fourteen and twenty people now:

> They have meetings that are scheduled once a month. It should be some more participation than it is. At first, I didn't attend because I would also work at night, but the few times that I've gone, it's just not a lot of participation because people work. They're too tired to come out or they got children or it's homework or something. I've been a couple of times, but it's going to take a lot more.

Pioneers Anne Jackson and her husband attend the civic association meetings, but like other leaders, they are fed up with the lack of participation. Anne acknowledged that residents work long hours, but she also said that the newest residents do not have a sense of alarm about crime because they have been lulled into complacency by the relative safety of Parkmont compared to their former communities. Anne fears their apathy places the civic association at risk:

> I don't think that they have the backing and the support that they should because people don't have time. Most people came from the same neighborhood I came from. So they think, "This is fine to me." It's nice. People keep their little houses up. There's not trash in the street. There's not a whole bunch of gun shootings or people just walking in the street, snatching from you. There's not a lot of that. So they come here. They figure, "It's fine." They just say, "Let me stay in my house and mind my business."

Margaret Meadows, a pioneer, is also pessimistic about Parkmont residents' ability to organize when threats to the community arise. I asked her about the civic association because her husband regularly attends meetings, but she expressed the view that there is not enough participation to sustain the organization:

> It will probably dwindle away. The people that go will still continue to go, and we'll still encourage other people to try to go so it won't just fade away. The only time people really come out is when something's at stake. When there's a crisis, everybody's involved. But other than that, it's just laissez-faire. Whatever. They have less of a stake in the community. Not keeping it up. Not as much pride as we had when we first moved in.

Pioneer Sonya McCall told me that the only Parkmont residents she knows are the elderly whites and the parents of her children's friends. She explained why she is not more involved in the civic association or with neighbors:

> I did go a couple of times to the civic association 'cause they wanted to put a "Stop and Go" in the neighborhood, and I definitely went to that, and I was like, "No." They shot that down. They wanted a twenty-four-hour Laundromat. They shot that down. I was glad for that, and they wanted a check-cashing place up here, and they said "No." I always sign up for my membership. I give them money, but a lot of times I am too tired.... Growing up, for me, everybody knew each other from one end to the other. Here, I just mind my business. I know the parents of the kids my children play with, but if I didn't have kids, I wouldn't know them. I got to know them by being outside. They were watching her when she was little, and they'd come out and talk. But as far as social-izing? No. I don't spend no time with them, I can tell you that. I couldn't tell you half the people on this block. Most of the parents work, but they kids is what's the problem. They know the kid is out doing wrong. They

see them selling drugs and doing everything, and I guess, just as long as the kids bring the money home, it's fine for them.

But even Sonya has given up. Now, when she sees people dealing drugs on her block, she refrains from calling the police because she fears that the dealers will know it was her: "No. I just didn't want to get involved. They start harassing people if you call the police so they would know. They would know. Somehow, they know....I'm hoping I hit the Super Powerball [lottery] so I can get out of here."

In a departure from most pioneers' views, Nina took the fairly extreme position that Parkmont's decline has been so severe that it is now as poor in quality as her previous neighborhood. Nina said that she misses the sense of order that once characterized Parkmont, the loss of which she attributes to white flight, the influx of a younger generation, and an increase in the percentage of renters. She believes that all of these factors have led to a critical mass of new residents with inferior values about family and community:

> Now, to me, the two neighborhoods are both the same. This was an older community, a very quiet, calm community. It was not a lot of kids outside. Not a lot of running around and stuff like that. I saw a six-year-old at that corner store at 8:00 at night, by herself, buying chicken wings. A six-year-old? It's that type of mentality. So they don't care about their kids. They don't care about their property. You never saw trash like it is out here now. Back at home, where my mom lived, it was just starting to kinda go down. You'd see trash, kids outside all the time, a lot of stuff going on, so I was happy to get away from that. Then, it would be funny, 'cause my mom and them would come up here for it to be peaceful. "We're going up to see Nina. It's calm up there." But now it's just the same. Younger people have moved in. It's more blacks up here now. A lot of people rent up here. I didn't even realize it. If only I had! It really changed. You have a lot of Section 8 homes up here now, which there weren't before.

Conclusion

The flight of the pioneers and more recent arrival of their replacements, the second wave, mark a second population shift in Parkmont. This chapter highlights the existence and character of intraracial neighborhood cultural hierarchies, identifies dimensions of neighborhood culture that have the potential to cause cultural clashes, and suggests that there are serious consequences to such conflict. Shared racial identity aside, pioneers and second wave residents diverge in their adherence to codes that form five dimensions of neighborhood culture: (1) assimilationist attitudes; (2) sense of ownership; (3) sensitivity to physical and social incivilities; (4) parenting; and (5) attitudes toward crime, social control, and civic involvement.

In densely packed urban communities such as Parkmont, conflict over these dimensions of neighborhood culture cannot be dismissed as common "border skirmishes." These culture clashes are so all encompassing to residents that the most invested members of the community become dissatisfied and seek to move away. Beyond the study of Parkmont, the dimensions of neighborhood culture uncovered here may be more generally important for understanding other types of changing neighborhoods, including those with high population turnover, populations that are heterogeneous on one or more characteristics, or those experiencing the in-migration of a population that is lower on the social status hierarchy in some way.

There are both similarities and differences between the pioneers who first moved into Parkmont when it was integrating and the second wave of blacks who arrived after it had become predominantly black. Pioneers have more financial and family stability, and their timing of arrival meant that they expected to live in a white or integrated community with a good school. Despite their investment in the community, many pioneers are now interested in moving away, often citing cultural clashes as a main reason for their decreased neighborhood satisfaction. In contrast, the second wave residents feel relatively detached from Parkmont, in terms of both its history and future, and find its problems to be relatively inconsequential. With no memory of another Parkmont, a lack of socialization from long-term elderly white neighbors, and strained relations with pioneers, second wave residents not only tolerate but actually contribute to disorder and crime. With white stayers diminishing in number and pioneers fleeing, Parkmont's future is uncertain.

Outwardly, Parkmont still maintains a pleasant appearance and is relatively peaceful, quiet, and safe. Additionally, in the aftermath of a major U.S. mortgage crisis, homes here cost enough to "price out" many of the city's low-income families. However, pioneers continue to leave in search of greener pastures. Some of the suburbs to which they have moved contain large black populations (some over 70%), but many others are more integrated (10% to 15% black), consistent with the fact that this city's suburbs experienced a significant increase in black population in the 1990s, while retaining high levels of black-white racial separation.

For the foreseeable future, many of Parkmont's pioneers who are municipal workers will continue to search for relatively safe communities within the city's very segregated boundaries, while other pioneers with more freedom to move will continue to search for homes in integrating, affordable suburbs surrounding the city or in nearby states that are within commuting distance to their jobs. Thus, there is cause for hope that Parkmont's social class composition will remain predominantly working class and will never provide a substantial market for serious drug dealing and the violent crime associated with it.

However, as years pass and Parkmont becomes increasingly distanced from its glory days as a desirable "minisuburb," the problems with physical and social disorder and community values may come to matter even more. The cultural divides and lack of involvement that now characterize the community may overpower its ability to stave off undesirable residents, businesses, nuisance properties, and crime. Chapter 7 introduces the narrative of Billy, a young second wave resident whose troubled life epitomizes the social world from which many pioneers believed they were distancing themselves when they moved to Parkmont. Billy explains the difficult journey to Parkmont that many second wave teens have faced, including family crises, neighborhood and school adjustment problems, conflict with peers, involvement in crime, and struggles with letting go of attachments to old neighborhoods and friends. Though on the surface, many second wave families make for unsympathetic figures, Billy's story offers a means to understand them better and sheds light on how and why they are different from the pioneers.

7

BILLY'S NARRATIVE
Clashing in Parkmont

When asked about their old neighborhoods, many of Parkmont's black residents described the things they *didn't* like: "There was a lot of crime and drugs, and I didn't like that." "The schools that were there and different places around the neighborhood." "Two people were killed on my block." "I was mugged over there three times. That's why I carry teargas everywhere I go, and that's why I don't trust anybody." "Down that way? The violence and everything. The drugs, everything that's going on down there, and especially because I have a baby now."

Most black residents moved to Parkmont to live in a place where people were less burdened by segregation, crime, disorder, poor schools, and neighborhood problems. In their view, bad neighborhoods are the common and normal urban residential experience rather than the exception. From this perspective, Parkmont, a recently integrated community with a good reputation, seemed like an oasis that was free from the entrenched problems associated with city life. With its semisuburban feel, affordable homes, neat lawns, and highly regarded school, incoming black residents viewed the neighborhood as a retreat from their own residential histories in the inner city. However, Billy Gordon, a nineteen-year-old who moved to Parkmont as part of the second wave, schooled me on the realities of life in the neighborhood and why his experiences and those of many second wave residents differ from those of the pioneers.

My day with Billy started out at his father's modest barbershop, a black-owned business on the strip, and a place where casual conversations revealed a great deal about the lives of younger residents. On a hot July afternoon, I sat waiting for Billy in the shop. His father, Ray, is a forty-year-old U.S. Army veteran and second wave resident. Ray wore a neat haircut, a crisply new and stylish athletic jersey, and extra long denim shorts. As he cut a man's hair with an electric razor, we were joined by several customers who seemed impatient to have their turns.

In the background a soccer match was on television, though Ray had muted the volume and the sounds of a popular hip-hop song filled the small room. The shop was stocked with artifacts of Afrocentric symbolism and black pride. Several framed posters hung on the walls to remind customers of the African origins of humankind, including depictions of human migration patterns across the globe and a timeline of black religious history. A stereo with a pile of rap and R&B CDs, posters displaying black men's hair styles and one offering special prices for senior citizen cuts on Wednesdays, and a large poster advertising "Urban Talent Showcase: Street Mafia" all gave the space a cluttered feel. Leaning against one of the walls was a telling symbol of community life in Parkmont: a door with a steel security gate waiting to be installed.

One man, tired of the delay, asked about making an appointment. Ray let him know that he does not get enough business to take appointments: "I ain't that big. I'm a little dude." Ray is a proud entrepreneur, but he seemed to be struggling to make ends meet. A few days earlier, he had aggressively tried to sell a baseball hat to me. Athletic gear is apparently a side business for him. He and his wife, Neala, had just opened a women's beauty salon next door where I had my hair done once, but it would go out of business after less than a year.

As customers talked, I heard about the troubles in the lives of Parkmont's newest black families—school problems, criminal involvement, family breakups, and the need for money to pay bills and debts. At one point, a teenager named "Beats" entered. Below his long, baggy shorts, he wore an electronic ankle bracelet used to track criminal offenders after their release. Everyone in the shop greeted Beats and some men commented on his long absence from the neighborhood. "I heard that you was giving away lyrics now," said Ray, commenting on Beats's reputation as a rapper. Beats downplayed the quality of the recording of his music that had been circulating around the neighborhood, but Ray and others in the shop objected to his modesty and urged him to be more consumer-oriented and in the capitalist spirit: "It don't matter if *you* like it, as long as people buying it." After the entrepreneurial pep talk, Ray lowered his voice and said, "Beats, you stay focused, and don't get into no more trouble. You be in the [recording] booth and school as much as possible."

A few minutes later, a young teen ran into the shop and loudly asked everyone, "Who got shot last night?" According to the television news and gossip around Parkmont, a gunman fatally shot a pizza deliveryman just a few blocks from the shop; many young people who hang out on the strip had been talking about it. With no sign of shock about the shooting, the customers exchanged stories about what they had already heard about it. A few moments later, Billy entered and greeted everyone. Then, we left the shop and walked to the patio of the nearby public library to talk in a more private place.

Billy, along with his father, stepmother, and siblings, lives in a rented home in Parkmont. Like many second wave children in Parkmont, he has siblings from his mother and father's relationship as well as from their relationships with other people. Though on the surface his appears to be a stable, nuclear family—with Billy in college, living in a married, two-parent household, and having a father who owns his own business—this family has dealt with considerable volatility and hardship. It does not take long to recognize that they, like many second wave residents in Parkmont, are struggling. Parkmont's streets are far better than other parts of the city, but this façade masks the troubles of a community where new residents are having difficulty staying afloat, and most are fairly alienated from community life and their neighbors.

This life history chapter moves us from Billy's original neighborhood to Parkmont, the site of his troubled teen years, and then to his current life as a cautious college student who lives four hours away and only returns to Parkmont during breaks. Because of his young age, recent graduation from Lombard, and the abundant time he has spent hanging out at his father's shop, Billy considers himself quite knowledgeable about Parkmont, and especially about the experiences of neighborhood youths. This chapter considers the similarities and differences between pioneer and second wave families, with special attention to stated differences in cultural values and consequential behaviors.

Escaping "Typical" Ghetto Life

A key goal shared by most of Parkmont's black residents, pioneers and second wave residents alike, was to escape the serious crime and poorly performing schools that were ubiquitous in their old neighborhoods. This desire to flee reflects the fact that the city's many black communities tend to be deeply troubled by poverty, crime, and unemployment. Such neighborhood-level problems are caused, in part, by city-level problems with segregation, suburbanization of jobs, gains in immigrant Asian, Latino, and black populations, and selective population decentralization, all of which have resulted in the loss of middle-class and white residents.

Parkmont's second wave residents seemed especially aware of these problems because they were the ones who had most recently left neighborhoods where blight and danger were the norm. Billy explained the sad state of his old neighborhood: "It just was bad. Still is. Typical stuff—drug selling, shootings.

I know I would've been involved in all that stuff if I had stayed down there." While Billy conveyed a negative evaluation of his old neighborhood, he was simultaneously nonchalant about the tragedy of his experiences there. Having lived in a segregated, poor, and crime-ridden community for so long and so recently, Billy has developed a more general sense of normalcy about the existence of violence and crime in urban neighborhoods. His use of the word "typical" demonstrates that he, like many second wave residents, found it unremarkable that his former neighborhood was riddled with so many serious problems.

This is not to say that Billy approved of the state of affairs before; nor did he live fearlessly in his day-to-day life in his old neighborhood. In fact, part of the reason that Billy seemed both disapproving of and desensitized to the harsh realities of his old neighborhood was that the problems there closely mirrored those of his own family: "I was used to the shootings, but I didn't like that stuff. I didn't like to see the drug addicts walking around. I knew my mom was one." Unlike the typical pioneer in Parkmont, Billy viewed members of his own family as epitomizing the set of problems that plague so many urban neighborhoods.

Parents "Doing Their Own Thing"

Everything changed when Billy moved to Parkmont. The drive-by shootings, the constant threat of being robbed, and the daily sidewalk traffic of crack addicts that characterized his old block were no more. But these were not the only changes; the circumstances of his move were such that he also had to contend with the personal trials of establishing a life with a whole new family.

Billy's mother is addicted to drugs and has been largely absent from his life. His father only became involved in his upbringing after the death of Billy's grandmother, who served as his legal guardian. His grandparents raised him in their home, located in Westside, a very poor black neighborhood: "I didn't live with my parents. I lived with my grandparents at the time, and they felt comfortable there because they lived there for a while. So they weren't gonna go nowhere." When I asked about his parents, Billy described his strained relationship with each of them:

> They wasn't doin' all right when I was down there. My mom, in and out of jail. My dad, he was just doin' his own thing, but he came through. My dad, he did more than my mom. He came through around birthdays, maybe Christmas or stuff like that. My mom, she came through once in a blue. I'm in touch with her. I just seen her when my sister graduated from high school the other day. She comes during stuff like that, and

I still talk to her and stuff. I lived with my grandmother 'til I was like twelve, and then she passed. My grandfather passed when I was in fifth grade, so we really didn't have nowhere to go because my parents, they were doing their own thing. So my dad—I'm not saying he *had*—but he kind of *had* to step up to the plate. That's the way I look at it. Unless we were just going to be in foster care or something like that. So I feel like he *had* to step up to the plate.

I surmised that Billy felt like his father was forced to take him in. Billy said, "I don't know what would have happened. I think about that a lot. See, I don't really know. I'll never know because it's already happened now. We here."

Married family households are relatively uncommon among Parkmont's second wave families. Instead, the newest Parkmont residents have more varied arrangements that are either intended to help pay bills on time and provide childcare or else are the unfortunate result of life events that have split families apart: single women living with young nieces and grandchildren, sometimes along with their own children; divorced or never married single mothers living with their own children but also renting out a room to a sibling or even a parent; single women, both young and middle aged, cohabiting with and caring for aging parents; single women of various ages living alone; and unmarried couples living with shared children as well as children from past relationships.

Unmet Expectations and a Segregated School

Like many successful inner-city black students, Billy did not attend his old neighborhood's poorly rated school. Both of the schools located in his old neighborhood are counted among the most persistently dangerous ones statewide. Billy's grandparents were outraged by the conditions there, so they sent him to an integrated school located about an hour away by public transportation. Billy explained: "I went to school at Northside. I used to take the bus because of the neighborhood. Well, the school, and then, the neighborhood. Period."

Though Billy loved his school and did not want to transfer to Lombard, his father promised that moving to Parkmont would offer an even better life than he had with his grandmother because he would have access to both a safe neighborhood and a reputable school. However, the reality was far different. Both Lombard and its surrounding neighborhood had resegregated by the time of Billy's arrival. In addition, Lombard was failing academically and residents said that it was notorious for frequent disciplinary problems, which occurred not only among students but also between students and teachers. Billy complained of overcrowding at Lombard. Because it was originally built as an elementary school and later expanded to include children from kindergarten and up, Lombard's high school students are confined to one floor, while the rest of the school building is for children in lower grades.

I asked Billy whether he had heard of Parkmont before he moved here: "Yeah, but only from what I was hearing about Lombard." The only time Billy had even heard about Parkmont was in reference to its school, which people said had a good reputation. I asked Billy to talk about some of his expectations about Parkmont and how they matched up to reality: "Didn't nothin' really match. Not really. Because there was a lot of black people here when I came here, and the school wasn't really good. I didn't look at the teachers and all that stuff as being really good. It was better when I was at my other school, so I was like, 'What the heck did I really change for?'"

Billy told me about how different his former school on the Northside was from Lombard: "My friends were there. That was a good school. It was bigger, had better opportunity. They have more sports: football, basketball, others I can't even name. More activities, more people." I asked if his friends at Northside had lived around that neighborhood, and he said, "A lot of them did. A few of them didn't. They were like me, kinda like commuting." Billy said that he did not realize that leaving the ghetto for Parkmont would mean trading an integrated school experience for a segregated one and missed the diversity of his friends at his old school: "White, black, Puerto Rican, Chinese. There was like a mix. That's what I'm used to."

High expectations for Lombard and Parkmont were aspects of Billy's case that contradicted my interviews with many second wave residents. As with many pioneers, his views were based on information from older blacks he knew who were bused into the neighborhood years ago. In the following excerpt, Billy described his image of what going to school in Parkmont was going to be like:

> It ain't how they said it was going to be. Down my old way, I knew a girl that went to Lombard, and she was saying that it's a good school. I can only remember one white person in every class that I probably had. It was probably the same way for my sister [laughs]. At the time, I thought it was more because I kept hearing that it was a good school. I thought it was more white people. Then my cousin graduated from there in '94 or '91 or something like that, a while back, and she was telling me when she was there, it was like a ton of white people.

Thus, Billy once lived in a neighborhood far more dangerous and disorderly than Parkmont, but his grandparents made a special effort to send him to more reputable and integrated school way across town. His father insisted that he switch

schools to attend Lombard, and Billy, like many Parkmont youth, was saddened
to leave his old school and friends. However, he was also excited, having heard
about Lombard's well-regarded reputation from family, friends, and neighbors.
He assumed that like his other school, Lombard's student body would have a sizable population of white students. This anticipation of a racially mixed school
was integrally tied to his perception that the school would be of high quality, but
in a strange turn of events it was not until he moved to Parkmont that he began
to attend a segregated, black school.

Billy's expressions of disappointment with both Parkmont and Lombard
sounded similar to complaints made by pioneers. Although pioneers had already
figured out that Lombard is no place to send their children to school, the second
wave parents and children were just beginning to learn this. Billy's tendency to
link racial integration to his anticipation of school and neighborhood quality
was also characteristic of residents who were relying on older information about
Parkmont from the generation of blacks who were bused in. Residents who
learned about Parkmont from the "bused generation" often conveyed the feeling that they had been duped—victims of a residential "bait and switch" caused
by white flight. The local school, Lombard, was often the strongest source of
disappointment to parents, children, and teens. Like so many black residents in
Parkmont, Billy was fully aware of the neighborhood's recent white flight, and
race was a topic that he did not want to skirt.

Neighborhood Identity and Clashing Youth

Parkmont residents who are in the know think that too many of Lombard's students commute in from outside neighborhoods. The younger people who attend
Lombard were better able than their parents to provide details about how this affects students. The account below represents Billy's view of the composition of the
student body at Lombard and how it has created a special set of problems there:

> It's weird because everybody in Lombard is not really from this neigh-
> borhood. Everybody comes from so many different neighborhoods. It
> kinda clashes. It's starting to clash now. People gotta prove points. Stuff
> here, stuff there. Even if they live in the neighborhood, they not usually
> originally *from* this neighborhood. Like, even me. It's just getting like
> that now. Clashing and people wanting to prove themselves—that they
> can do this or where they're from is like this. If they all came from one
> place, it would be a lot more peace. Especially, being moved here. Like,
> if me and you both moved from Northside, just because we both moved

out of Northside together, I could probably talk to you. I'm from Northside and you from Northside, and we would probably become friends or something like that.

Billy's discussion of his experiences at Lombard returned to the topic of race. He insisted that once Lombard resegregated, students from other neighborhoods began to flow in, even though Lombard no longer needed integration busing. Billy suggested that even after the school became completely black, many students continued to commute from other neighborhoods, which led to violence when students from different communities conflicted with one another. I asked Billy how many students come from other neighborhoods, and in his answer he said that the intraracial conflict at Lombard consisted of fights between bused in students and second wave students, neither of whom wanted to be associated with Parkmont's reputation as a "soft" neighborhood:

> BILLY: I'd say more than half were from other places. Even if some people are in this neighborhood now. It's recent. Real recent.
>
> R. W.: So, they're still attached to their old neighborhood?
>
> BILLY: Yeah, I would say that.
>
> R. W.: And they want to show that they are not from this neighborhood?
>
> BILLY: Basically. Exactly.
>
> R. W.: Because this neighborhood isn't really tough or....
>
> BILLY: Not at all. *I'm* not saying that, but that's the way *they* look at it.
>
> R. W.: Is that what you mean when you say they are trying to prove that they are not from here?
>
> BILLY: Definitely. They're not from Parkmont, even though they live here now.
>
> R. W.: And so why are other kids coming to Lombard? Why don't they go to a school near them?
>
> BILLY: Because they're moving here. Like me, they could be living in their neighborhood, and maybe they thought that Lombard was this good school or something. They might think that they're getting into a good school like I did, but it was getting crazy kinda. Is this like snitching or something if I give you details? There were like, riots in that joint. There were fights every day, and then it was crazy because it was so many young people, like ninth graders and stuff, trying to fight everybody. The hallways are so tight because they put lockers in there. It was really tight and a lot of bumping going on. A lot of beef got said, and a lot of fights broke out just in the hallway. Big riots, people getting trampled over, people who ain't even in it getting hit. It got crazy after a while.

Many of Lombard's second wave students resemble their parents in that they feel conflicted about their neighborhood identity and allegiances. On one hand, they know that Parkmont is safer, more attractive, and more economically stable than many black city neighborhoods. However, on the other hand, the community leaves much to be desired, and to many young people, it is nothing special or worth fighting for. Like many of Parkmont's second wave youths, Billy remains attached to his old neighborhood. As new residents attending a school with so many children from other neighborhoods, second wave young people are reluctant to show weakness. Being from Parkmont, a neighborhood that lacks notoriety on the street, has made teens quick to demonstrate their affiliations with the lower-income, tougher neighborhoods where they once lived and with which they still identify.

Billy elaborated further on the ways in which the racial homogeneity in Parkmont is misleading for those trying to understand the culture of the community. He explained that the diversity of neighborhood loyalties and peer conflicts are not just found at school but can also be observed on the streets of Parkmont:

> People might just look at the color, like it's just the black people moving in. But it's people coming in from so many different places and so many different ways of living and so many different mind-sets of how they go about things. It's from where they are *actually* from. It's just clashing and colliding. It's just crazy. People, when they move here, want to come up and think it's really *sweet* and just take over or something like that. Like, "I'm in charge up here" or "I'm the toughest guy up here." It is safe. It's definitely safer than other neighborhoods. I can tell you that. Stuff you hear about other neighborhoods don't really happen here, but I'll tell you that there's a lot of people up here now that just not from the neighborhood. It's like they're bringing their own 'hood and what they know here. It's so difficult when you come into contact with somebody, and you never know what they might do. I keep myself small. I know almost everybody up here, but it's the difference between knowing them and being able to speak to them and *really* being cool with somebody. I'm cool with only, like, four people.

In Billy's view, Parkmont is a "sweet" place to live to outsiders because it is uncharted territory. Anyone can move to the community and have a chance to be the "top dog." As he sees it, Parkmont's dubious status as a new and "soft" black neighborhood has resulted in conflicts over respect and territory. The neighborhood problems cannot be simply categorized or traced solely to racial change, drugs, or gangs. And even though Parkmont is relatively safe, Billy believes that residents can only successfully navigate the culture clashes by becoming guarded in public places.

The conflicts over culture and identity have divided Parkmont's black population. Because many second wave parents have not embraced the preexisting cultural codes in their new neighborhood, second wave children have also struggled to shift their cultural orientations, friendships, and loyalties. The second wave children are far more likely to attend Lombard than the pioneers' children, who attend Catholic schools, private schools, charter schools, or magnet schools. Thus, the newest Parkmont children are far more enmeshed in the social life of the neighborhood than their pioneer counterparts. According to Billy, Parkmont feels unsafe because it is filled with unfamiliar people who are originally from outside neighborhoods. Whether it is an authentic way of life or just posturing, second wave teens are perceived to be living according to a more threatening set of codes, similar to those that were the norm in their former neighborhoods. Youth feel pressured to adhere to the cultural codes from their old neighborhoods, which in part, persist in Parkmont because of the steady influx of new residents from similarly poor, high-crime areas. Second wave children often try to prove themselves in an effort to "represent" their street credibility and identification with their previous neighborhoods. As Billy explained, Parkmont's intraracial cultural clashes are magnified for youth, making for a volatile community atmosphere.

Drugs

Having come from worse communities, many of Parkmont's adults, teens, and children have had direct experience with dealing drugs or have had close friends and family involved in dealing drugs. I learned about Billy's time selling drugs when he told me why his grades in high school were not as good as they could have been: "I had a job for most of high school and other stuff. I was workin', playing ball. Girls were in there, too. A little bit of drugs; not major, just marijuana. I don't use. I'm talkin' 'bout sell-wise." When I asked what he bought with the drug money, Billy told me, "Oh, gear! [Clothing]. I ain't into that stuff no more, though. I stopped. I just looked at it as, like, extra. It was so easy to do. I just looked at it like extra cheese or extra money." As might be expected in a community mostly populated by working people with stable jobs, Billy did not sell drugs out of economic need. In fact, he worked as a security guard in an upscale mall located downtown. Like many neighborhood youths, the opportunities and desire to deal drugs were closely tied to Billy's family problems and his move to Parkmont.

Billy emphasized that selling drugs was not the center of his life, saying that he also attended school, played on the basketball team, had a job, and was very interested in girls. However, he also reported how important it was at Lombard to conform to the materialism that characterizes popular teen culture. The money from his job and family was not enough to keep up with his peers, so he said that he had to resort to drug dealing to buy the extra clothing and items required for his friends to consider him "in style." Initially, Billy felt unconcerned about the consequences of drug dealing and dismissed the crime as an obvious, easy way to obtain money. He told me that, at that time, he was focused on the lucrative nature of drug dealing and not the possibility of getting caught at a young age and entering the criminal justice system.

The absence of Billy's father and his father's practice of routinely taking back the material things that he once provided as a punishment for Billy's bad behavior further fueled his receptiveness toward drug dealing. It was obvious that Billy holds a deep resentment toward his father and is guarded around him. Billy told me that he prefers to be independent, which in high school meant buying sneakers and clothing with his own money from work and drug dealing, although he admitted that Ray would buy him something if he asked:

> My dad would say, "Yeah." But I'm the type that never really asks for stuff. I get that stuff on my own. I wouldn't take the money, even though it's my pop. I don't like making people feel like I owe them anything. I didn't live with him. Stuff just went down. Like, if I was to do bad or something, he'll take stuff back from me. That was just when I was younger, like if my grandma would say I was acting up or whatever. He wouldn't step in. He'd be like, "Give me the clothes. Give me the stuff I bought you back." I'd be mad, because how can you buy somebody somethin' and then take it back?

Like Billy, many second wave residents revealed that the damaging personal struggles from their old neighborhoods followed them to Parkmont. Billy moved to Parkmont because his grandmother died, his mother was in and out of jail and drug rehabilitation centers, and his father felt obligated to take him. His interview shows that the material demands of teen popularity, his negative experiences with his father's parenting, and Parkmont's opportunities for teens to deal drugs all combined to lead him down a risky path.

The fact that moving to Parkmont did not insulate Billy from the opportunity to sell drugs and that he engaged in risky behavior does not mean that Parkmont has not been an improvement over his old neighborhood. Despite the general recognition that the neighborhood is not what many residents had hoped for, many children and teens there seemed to believe that they were part of a special group who had escaped far more dangerous places. Most young people I met aspired to success by following predictable pathways, since being conventionally successful and out of the drug world are shared values among most Parkmont residents. Yet it is no wonder that Billy became involved with drug dealing, given his assertion that the drug trade has become so prevalent in his community:

> I was probably fifteen the first time [I sold drugs]. When I came across the opportunity to get something bigger [amount of marijuana] in twelfth grade, I did that. And then I stopped. *Everybody* is going to know someone who's selling drugs. Just being *here,* like fifty to one hundred people sell. I wasn't selling for nobody. You can just find who's carrying what, and you buy. I would just buy the stuff for myself, and get all the work myself. I bought what I wanted and sold it. But I was just tired of it, because I'm not trying to go to jail and all that crazy crap. I wasn't afraid. I think a lot, so I'm not trying to be in jail and all that. That's not the path that I'm trying to go.

Closely aligned with Billy's insistence that he was not a big-time dealer was his assertion that he never found drug dealing to be fulfilling as a life pursuit. However, the main reason that Billy seemed willing to discuss the drug-dealing life that he left behind was that he did not believe that it was grossly immoral or troubling. As he saw it, he only sold marijuana, and he bought the drugs and sold them himself, rather than being part of a crew or gang. In a worse neighborhood where people might have known that Billy was selling on his own and making good money doing it, he might have become a target for muggers or more established drug dealers. The relatively safe nature of Parkmont, instead of protecting Billy, actually eased him into the drug trade by allowing him to feel comfortable selling alone.

Since Ray runs a barbershop located only a block from the school, I wondered if he knew about Billy's drug dealing. Billy said he was able to conceal his behavior from his street-smart father, partially by having a regular job on the side. However, Billy alluded to the fact that his father had once been involved in drug dealing, and he said that Ray has a suspicious nature, so he seemed to know what was going on:

> My dad will confront me about something even if he got the slightest idea about anything. When you're a barber, you know a lot of people involved in many different things. Friends that do that, friends that do this, friends that *sell* that. One of his friends that I've been around since we moved here, he's into a little of this and that. I was just talking to him one day. I've known him for like six years now, so we just walked out the side of the barbershop together, and that's it. This is when I was in college, too. And my dad thinks that I'm doing something. Like,

I'm selling drugs up at college or somethin' like that. And he asked my cousin, "What's up with Billy? What's up with him and Mark walking out the barbershop?" Like, dang, man. "You can't say somethin' to me or ask me?" He didn't even ask me. He just asked my cousin, "What's up? Is he selling drugs?" He'll say anything if he thinks it at all. Now, I'm older. I'm in college now, and I've got too many other plans.

Though many second wave families consider their values to be superior to the people from their old neighborhoods, they are aware that Parkmont's pioneers have even more middle-class or conventional cultural ideals. Billy's downplaying of his involvement in the drug-dealing subculture reveals the way that the second wave Parkmont youths use different levels and distinctions of drug dealing to demonstrate their more respectable cultural orientations. For instance, having a crew seemed more deviant to Billy than dealing drugs alone. Additionally, he seemed proud that that he had quit selling at age eighteen and has since embraced his new social status as a college student.

Ties to the Old 'Hood and Getting Involved in the New One

Billy had very few positive things to say about his old neighborhood, and the few pleasant memories that he did share were brief. His last neighborhood was a dangerous place populated with drug addicts. It was a community where teens— even those with street savvy—lived every day with the fear that there was a possibility of getting shot. So, what aspects of life there *does* Billy miss? The people. The intimate ties with the good people he knew are all that he really misses. He said that he knew everyone in his old community and had close, trusting bonds with many neighbors on his block. Like so many second wave residents, Billy seemed unable to let go of the community of which he was once a part.

Billy explained that the people from his old neighborhood were much closer than the neighbors in Parkmont. Before moving, he and his grandparents had strong ties to neighbors, but this type of neighborly closeness was not present in Parkmont at the time that Billy arrived. In rapidly changing neighborhoods like Parkmont, where Billy lived out his teen years, close neighbor relationships can be difficult to nurture. In more established and stable black neighborhoods and in communities where fewer people work the long hours that people in Parkmont do, neighbor relationships are easier to find and are often more intimate.

Thus, even after six years away from his old neighborhood (a lifetime for a teen), Billy has continued to keep in touch with his friends from the old neighborhood: "I got a couple of friends down there that were really like my brother's friends. They were three years older than me, but I'm still cool with them. Two went to college and everything, one of them just graduated from college, and I still keep in touch with them." And Billy is not alone. Many second wave residents reported that they often go back to their old neighborhoods to visit with former neighbors, family, and friends; sometimes, their friends even make the journey to Parkmont. Like most second wave residents, Billy realizes his old neighborhood was a far from ideal living situation, but he still feels attached to it. He insisted that the people he stays in touch with are the good ones—those who have succeeded through conventional means. Unlike others who visit their old neighborhoods for excitement or "to mix it up," Billy goes to see his friends who, like him, are college students. As he said, "I'm not trying to hang with old buddies who're getting into trouble."

Yet Billy explained that he and his family are like most second wave residents, uninvolved in community life and rather isolated. He said that second wave residents have a set of norms and values that run counter to pioneers' ideals of participation and involvement in community affairs. As an example, Billy elaborated on his own father's unwillingness to attend neighborhood civic association meetings despite the fact such meetings could be beneficial to the future of his home, family, and business. According to Billy, Ray's customer base includes many people involved in crime, and he enjoys being in the middle of the action and "in the know." Billy thinks that his father attaches more importance to maintaining these customers' business than to improving Parkmont's quality of life:

> We ain't used to no meetings and stuff like that. We probably not paying attention to it. We probably just doing what we got to do for *our* life, going to work or whatever we're doing, and going to sleep. Before, people here were probably really into where they live at and their neighborhood and stuff like that. Now, it's probably a lot of "this is where I live" type people. The only difficult part for my dad—I don't know how to put it—is we got so much clientele that's into stuff [crime]. Most of our clientele are working people, but then we got a lot of clientele that is into stuff like that. It's hard, especially for a barbershop. It's hard for businesses like that. You got so many different types of people, you just got to stay humble, man. You won't believe what people talk about. My dad likes to know what's going on.

At times, Billy seemed pessimistic about Parkmont's future, and like many residents he stated that the neighborhood is getting worse. When he specifically mentioned emerging problems with violent crime, I asked what incidents made him think that serious crime was becoming an issue, and he said, "How about last night somebody got shot?" Repeating the news that the men in the barber-shop had gossiped about before Billy's arrival there, Billy explained that someone in Parkmont had just been murdered, providing very clear evidence that deadly violence *has* reached this relatively sheltered community.

Although Parkmont is safer than residents' old neighborhoods, it shows signs of decline. Some of the problem is compositional; Parkmont needs residents who have economic and family stability. However, in terms of culture, residents must identify with Parkmont, have a shared value system, and stay involved in neighborhood and school life. Many disadvantages, complicated family problems, and unexpected school and community conflicts have set the stage for unfortunate residential experiences and teen outcomes in Parkmont.

Despite having better odds at success than many urban youths, Billy came to Parkmont during a decade that saw the loss of throngs of white residents and black pioneers, as well as a collapse in the real estate market. It is still too early in the history of this newly black neighborhood to say how far or fast the school and neighborhood will deteriorate. The pioneers struggled at first with the rapid loss of the white population, but were determined to do their part to maintain a clean, safe community. However, the small coalition of active neighbors is only loosely organized, and many remaining pioneers plan to leave the neighborhood in the coming years. With fewer and fewer pioneers remaining to take the lead in community efforts to deal with disorder, crime, and school problems, the fate of Parkmont lies with the second wave.

Unfortunately, the second wave's economic and family instability, timing of arrival, and cultural value systems and identities work to further inhibit the growth of networks and investments in Parkmont. With the presence of school children from all over the city, and with the most stable residents and their children absent from the neighborhood all day, second wave residents struggle. Like Billy, many lack a sense of their place in the social order of Parkmont because the community is characterized by population change and intraracial cultural conflict. Whatever the similarities between the pioneers and the second wave, the differences are real.

Parkmont's newest parents and children are not making the needed social investments in Parkmont, and, for youth in particular, neighborhood attachment is undermined by situations at school and on the street where they often feel the need to publicly demonstrate that they do not identify with the neighborhood. The problematic presence of outsiders at Lombard has been exacerbated by white flight and the pioneers' decisions to send their children elsewhere for school. Unaware of other options and less capable of negotiating the bureaucracy of the city's school system, well-intended second wave parents send their children to Lombard and hope for the best.

The question of good schools is essential to any study of residential mobility and neighborhood change, and this case is no different. Chapter 8 takes a closer look at Lombard, once "the gem" of the neighborhood, highlighting its crucial role in white flight and black flight from Parkmont. It suggests that, just as it always has, Lombard will continue to play a pivotal role in Parkmont's demographic changes for years to come.

8

SKIPPING SCHOOL

The Negative Effects of a
Neighborhood Institution

> You know what? Lombard, back in the day, when I was in school, it
> was the school to go to. That was one of the premier high schools.
> You could look at [the black students at Lombard], and you could
> tell that they came from a different environment. Lombard was *the*
> school. In our minds, we were like, "Wow. Lombard. That must be
> the thing."
>
> —Ramell Worthy, second wave, aged thirty-eight

> Lombard used to be the fourth or fifth best school in the city, but
> now it's horrible. The education is lousy. Everything's just horrible
> over there. Like, they don't care anymore. Well, the neighborhood
> changed, so all the stuff that it *did* have and offered to them then?
> When people migrated out of here, the education migrated, too. How
> can you go from being one of the best schools in the city to where
> the people in Parkmont don't even want to send their children there?
>
> —Anne Jackson, pioneer, aged fifty-five

Families often decide to move when there is a mismatch between their real living
situation and the neighborhood and housing scenario that they desire.[1] Age, family structure, housing space, and budget all factor into residents' views of their
residential status as they plan to move. However, another important factor that
drives families' mobility choices is their perceptions of the local schools. Such
heavy attention to neighborhood school quality is merited since public schools
are a key way in which neighborhoods indirectly affect children.[2]

The role of schools in blacks' residential satisfaction and mobility decisions is understudied. Much of the research on black mobility patterns emphasizes economic constraints and the limits of economic models for explaining
black mobility in the face of housing discrimination.[3] In Parkmont, parents'

---

1. See Brummell (1979), Hanushek and Quigley (1978), and Speare (1974).
2. See Ennett et al. (1997) and Teitler and Weiss (1996).
3. South and Deane (1993).

perceptions of Lombard played a major part in their decisions to move to the neighborhood, and their observations of the school continue to influence migration patterns.

This chapter examines change in Parkmont through the lens of Lombard, its local school. I begin with pioneer families, many of whom continue to live in Parkmont, but send their children to schools in other parts of the city to avoid the shortcomings in educational and behavioral control at Lombard. I then turn to the second wave residents and their children. Because pioneer children have effectively migrated out of Parkmont for schooling, the second wave children who largely attend Lombard fail to benefit from the presence of pioneer children in the classroom. Aggravating this problem, many parents who reside in the city's worst neighborhoods still believe that Lombard is a relatively good school and often make special efforts to send their children there, either through legitimate transfer programs or by providing school administrators with fake Parkmont addresses. As a result, Parkmont's second wave children miss out on the positive cultural influences of the neighboring pioneer children while continuing to have most of their peer contact with children further down the cultural and economic hierarchies—children who may, in many cases, be from the very neighborhoods that Parkmont's black residents sought to escape when they moved here.

Going On Reputation: Choosing Parkmont for Its School

On the last day of school before the summer of 2006, Lombard experienced an incident that, to many Parkmont pioneers, epitomizes the problems with the local school. As luck would have it, I happened to visit the school on this day. In the hallway were the metal detectors that are required at all city schools because of the district's numerous incidents of gun violence against principals, teachers, and students. Next to the detectors, just outside of Lombard's auditorium, were large, beautiful statues depicting children playing and reading. I had seen and admired these statues many times, but on this day they were splattered with red and blue paint. And in case there was any hope that the vandalism was just a harmless prank, smashed and broken pieces of plastic and hardware were scattered on the hallway floor in a trail leading to the computer lab. I later learned that, just days before, teachers had unpacked brand-new Mac computers, and on that day, they had all been destroyed beyond repair.

Even in the midst of this drama, the school year was coming to a close, and much work remained to be done. I watched Lombard's teachers clean their classrooms and conduct inventories of school supplies. Students wandered in and out of the front office, and I listened to their anxious conversations as they talked about what had happened to their school. In the front office, Dana Steinberg, an administrator, handled numerous interruptions from phone calls, PA announcements, staff, and students while she explained the vandalism incident to me:

> We believe it was some students. We have an after-school program that uses our facilities, but is not really a part of Lombard. It's a federally funded after-school program called "Lighthouse." We're assuming it was some kids who came through the door that they use, which is at the side of the lunchroom. There *is* a guard there, but only until 6:00, and the program runs 'til 8:00. I definitely think they were students—middle school, anywhere from sixth or seventh grade. And they took paint from Lighthouse, and they threw it all over figures that we had here of students, all over the walls and the floors, the auditorium. They went down into the lunchroom area, and they busted the refrigerator. We have an idea who did it from the kids. Kids talk about stuff like that. I'm not surprised because the student that would have initiated it is a pretty angry individual. We have a lot of those students here.

According to the National Center for Educational Statistics data for 2008–09, Lombard, Parkmont's only school, has once again become segregated (94% of the students are black in elementary grades and 97% are for the high school grades), and it is now largely low-income (with more than 66% of elementary school students eligible for the city's free lunch program). Lombard, a nonmagnet public school, may also be labeled an academic failure. In the 2009 school year, 49 percent of third graders scored "proficient" on state standardized tests for reading (57% for math). By high school, the situation becomes far worse. For eleventh graders, 21 percent were proficient in reading (7% for math).

As Dana Steinberg mentioned above, conduct problems are also prevalent at Lombard. Even with an all-day police presence of three officers as well as metal detectors at the school entrance, student misbehavior incidents are frequent. Lombard's environment is also less than ideal because students spend their days in chaotic and crowded classrooms, hallways, and schoolyards. Since Lombard serves students from kindergarten through twelfth grade, it offers very few extracurricular and recreational activities, especially for its high school students. Additionally, many of Lombard's students come from outside neighborhoods all over the city, as evidenced by the noisy clusters of students who wait for city buses to depart from Parkmont after the last bells ring for the day.

Like whites, African Americans move both because of "push" factors that drive them away from their current residences and "pull" factors that draw them into certain communities. Though whites in large metropolitan areas tend to live in suburban neighborhoods,[4] which often have satisfactory schools, the situation is quite different for African Americans who reside in metropolitan areas. They are about twice as likely as whites to live in the central city,[5] and they often reside in segregated black neighborhoods[6] where their local schools are at risk.[7] Such neighborhood disparities are especially severe in Northeastern cities like the one in which Parkmont is located, which has a large black population and a high degree of black-white segregation.[8] Given that school characteristics are especially important to parents of school-aged children,[9] it makes sense that many of Parkmont's pioneers give great weight to this aspect of the neighborhood environment and self-selected into a community with a school that they deemed worthy of their children.

In general, pioneers selected Parkmont under the impression that they were buying in to a neighborhood with a highly reputable public school, but most have since concluded that Lombard's students and staff are suffering difficulties. Making matters worse, in August of 2008 Lombard changed principals for the third time in a decade. The problems at Lombard are especially alarming since it was considered one of the best public schools in the city from the 1970s on through the early 1990s. Its students often went on to college, and its faculty positions were highly coveted among city teachers who were looking for a safe environment with motivated, prepared students and involved parents. Back when it was first built, Lombard parents especially appreciated that their children attended a true neighborhood school.

Many pioneers told me that they specifically moved to Parkmont for its school and that the importance of education in their choice of community was second only to their insistence on a neighborhood that was safe from violence and drugs. Despite trying their best to find a safe neighborhood *with* a good school, many pioneers admitted that they possessed incorrect information or relied upon faulty assumptions in conducting their search. When I asked what gave them the impression that Lombard was a desirable school for their children, there were three common answers: (1) they took it for granted that a school in a recently white neighborhood would be of high quality; (2) they accepted as valid the outdated reports about Lombard's reputation, often based on their own memories or the advice and distant childhood experiences of friends, family, and acquaintances; or (3) they followed recommendations from realtors and school district officials who told them that Lombard was relatively good for a city school.

---

4. Lamb (2005).
5. McKinnon (2003).
6. Logan (2002).
7. Card and Rothstein (2006).
8. Logan (2002).
9. Downs (1981).

Sam Wilson, Parkmont's civic association president, places an extremely high value on education and said that he chose the neighborhood with that in mind, under the impression that Lombard was a high quality school. Sam told me that, unlike many pioneers, he had been personally familiar with Parkmont from his teenage years working as a pizza deliveryman. He had largely assumed that the school had maintained its good reputation. Still, he asked around, even seeking the advice of the principal of his alma mater, a magnet high school:

> The principal thought that Lombard was still a great elementary school, and when I got here it was. My oldest daughter really liked her second-grade teacher, and it was a good school, a very good program. And the same with her third-grade teacher. She loved her third-grade teacher. And fourth grade.

Like Sam, Sonya McCall, a pioneer and single mother, relied on word of mouth and was impressed by Parkmont's reputation, but she has since changed her mind. She explained that her initial opinion of Lombard was based on stories from her adult friends who were bused in years ago:

> Quite a few of the people I work with, co-workers at the post office, they told me they went to Lombard. I was shocked. That was back when there wasn't that many blacks that was there. One of them said her mom fought to get her in there, so that's how she went. So I was like, "Oh, okay." But, no more. I don't think nobody really wants their child to go to Lombard. Maybe *someone* do, but *I* don't. When I first went to Lombard to register, there was somebody that told me, "Don't put her in that school." And then I called the school district, and they was telling me, "Do you know how many parents would want their child to go to Lombard? 'Cause they had just built the addition—the schoolhouse. So I went and checked it out, and I liked the part that was the schoolhouse. It was separated, but as soon as she got out of third grade, they told me she was going to the big building, and I didn't want that.

A few pioneer parents reported that they went forward with the move to Parkmont even though they had already become aware that Lombard's respectable reputation was fading. However, pioneer Nina Jones justified her decision by saying that, at the time, she was a single woman with no children, so she was not as concerned about the school. Even so, Nina remembered that when she purchased her home, the couple selling the house to her warned Nina about the school:

> The people here before us had a daughter and didn't want her to go to Lombard High School, so they moved out 'cause the school started to

change. The school definitely started changing by then. Everything. The demographics of it has changed. The city school system just wasn't what they wanted. They weren't going to offer her daughter all the things they wanted her to have, so that's why they moved.

Pioneers Clarice and Lamar Nellis moved to Parkmont because family members recommended Lombard to them, but now they send their young son to an elementary magnet school, and they intend to send him outside of the neighborhood when he is old enough to attend middle school: "Our parents told us that Lombard was good. We knew Lombard was a pretty good school, but Clarice's concern was that it might go down over time. Just now, Clarice was telling me about their test scores. She was saying that they are really bad."

Negative Evaluations of Lombard: Blaming White Flight

From the perspective of someone standing outside of the main building, Lombard appears to be a good school. Aside from the remains of some empty bags of potato chips and a few crushed soda cans on the front lawn, the property is free of the typical signs of urban decay. Instead of the graffiti that is seen on the outside walls of many city schools, Lombard's main building features a very moving and colorful mural depicting African American students studying. Lombard has one of the largest school sites in the city, with the main building (grades four through twelve), the adjacent "schoolhouse" for younger children (kindergarten through third grade), and a spacious recess yard all taking up an entire block.

Janice O'Neill, a pioneer, explained that Lombard "was part of the reason why I moved here," but told me that she has removed both of her children from Lombard. She said that the profile of students and families has changed and has hindered teaching effectiveness:

> Lombard's horrible. Lombard *was* an excellent school, 'cause I believe they built it specifically for Parkmont. And it was K to 12, and there's only maybe one other one in the whole city. I don't know if it was a combination of such a vast amount of people moving and the exodus of people that moved up into this area *with* children, but the school is really not able to accommodate them. And unfortunately, for some reason, black parents tend not to participate as much. I don't know if it's because we got to work more or whatever to make the same salary as, perhaps, someone else, for various reasons. So there was less participation, and it also seems like the quality of the children is deteriorating.

Not to blow my own horn, but I have raised good kids, not like these bad kids that want to cuss you and act inappropriate towards teachers in class and not have respect for others and all that. There's a lot of that up there. If you have to work in that environment, over time you don't teach as effectively. People getting stressed. Anybody working in a stressful environment, their work is going to deteriorate.

Janice, who is a nurse, explained that she is required to live in the city because she is an emergency worker. In fact, she moved to Parkmont as a part of her hospital's housing incentive program, which geographically expanded in the 1990s to include Parkmont. However, other pioneers, such as Margaret Meadows, who is a school nurse, recently have been released from residency requirements and now want to move away from Parkmont to provide better schooling for their children. Unfortunately, Margaret's husband's EMT job still restricts their housing search to the first-ring suburbs where homes tend to be too expensive for them, but she still aspires to find a community with a better school than Lombard:

Now, I want to live somewhere close, but that borders the city. The school district dropped their residency requirement about seven or eight years ago. In the suburbs, the school districts are better, and that's what I want for my kids. My two youngest children are eleven and nine, and I don't like the city school district and the education that they're receiving.

For the majority of pioneer parents who cannot afford private schools, Lombard is often the main factor that provokes black flight.

Another recurring theme reported by pioneers was that racial segregation is to blame for Parkmont's school problems. Pioneers reported that they did not notice Lombard's decline until after white flight was complete and black flight had already begun. For instance, pioneer Margaret Meadows argued that Lombard is no longer well funded, and she attributes the disinvestment in the school to white out-migration and the associated loss of white students:

I believe my son's school [outside of Parkmont] is a little bit better because he's in a smaller school, and he gets mentally gifted services, so he gets a little bit extra. My daughter goes to Lombard. The school's changed. That school had more resources when the neighborhood was white than it does now because the school has gone downhill. As a matter of fact, my husband and I are looking to take my daughter out. If I could leave in the next three to five years, I would leave, because of the school district. That is the main thing for me, especially with my kids, because I would love it if I could afford to send both of them to private school. If I could send the both of them there, I would feel a lot better.

Another pioneer, Kenny Washington, a mechanic, lives on one of the blocks facing Lombard. He too, blames white flight for the change in the character of the student body, but his main complaint is that the loss of white residents has interfered with accountability and social control at the school. He said that crowds of students routinely hang around Parkmont for hours after classes end, acting "very rowdy." According to Kenny, back when Parkmont was racially integrated, police officers would come to the schoolyard at the close of the day to usher the students, many of whom lived in other neighborhoods at that time, to the bus stop. However, with Parkmont now dominated by working black families, few residents remain at home during the day to call the police. Kenny said that even when black residents are around to call, police are unable to distinguish between the students who live in Parkmont and those who are bused in because the whole neighborhood population is now black.

Student Body Composition: Black Flight in the School

When speculating about the causes of Lombard's downfall, the pioneers were just as likely to blame the second wave blacks as they were to blame white flight. After all, white flight had come and gone, and the pioneers' most proximate and daily concerns have been with the people now living next to them. The pioneers reported that Lombard's students are of low quality in terms of behavior, attitude, and preparation, reflecting the black-flight pattern in Parkmont as a whole. Lack of parental involvement, poor behavioral control, and problems with classroom management were most frequently cited as evidence that Parkmont's second wave families produce poor students and undesirable peers. Nina Jones, a pioneer parent who is also a teacher at Lombard, believes that she has an especially credible perspective on the children who now form the core of Lombard's student body:

> They're not taught to value education. They're not taught to respect their teachers. If you don't have classroom management, you can't teach anything. This is even at kindergarten. This is how they come into school. You have kids who you'll call the parent and say, "They didn't do their homework," and "I need you to come up for a meeting." Or we have something where when children are really failing or having difficulties, and you write them up and put them in this special program. And you have these meetings where the parents come in. It's like a team, you know? You all sit down and talk. But parents will not come. I could

scream. I have a little girl in my class. She's seven. She sat in second grade for half the year, and then the mother realized she shouldn't have been in second grade. She should have been in first grade. What's up with that? And the mother did not come for the meeting. I could've strangled her because of all the help that we could've set up for her. If we don't have the parental consent, we can't do anything. These are the people that live up here. You see their attitude?

Pioneer Janice O'Neill expressed similar concerns about the ways in which the cultural values of second wave parents and children affect the school environment at Lombard. Like many pioneers, Janice has tried to keep her children away from Lombard students. She suggested that the affordability of Parkmont has attracted a different class of residents whose children largely contribute to problems at Lombard:

> I think it's because people that are moving in are worse. Now, *everybody* just movin' in. This neighborhood is cheap compared to a lot of places. The children, they just not good kids, and that's what happened up at Lombard. Just out of control. That's why my son had to get out of there. The kids were evil. They were really giving him a hard time. Find another victim. I had to get him out of there.

In response to my questions about the "bad kids" of second wave parents, one school official provided a unique perspective and told me about recent violent incidents involving Lombard's students and their families. James Herman, a forty-nine-year-old Lombard police officer, gave me a tour of the school grounds, and then we talked in front of the metal detector area where he signs in the many late-arriving students. I was interested to learn that Officer Herman actually graduated from Lombard and participated in the city's busing program. After marrying at age nineteen, he served in the U.S. Air Force and now works as a police officer as well as a marriage counselor, a Baptist minister, and a deacon.

Officer Herman informed me of a recent news story about Lombard students who were arrested for robbing several pizza deliverymen and for robbing college students who were attempting to withdraw money from ATMs. We also discussed a 2005 incident in which a Lombard student's mother and older brother violently attacked the principal. In addition, I asked Officer Herman about a story that Amber Miller, a nineteen-year-old graduate of Lombard, told me. I met Amber at the Parkmont hair salon owned by Billy Gordon's stepmother. Amber had already moved away from Parkmont as part of the wave of black flight, but she said that she was afraid of groups of young men who loiter in front of the bus stop and the "gangs" of girls who would harass her in the bathroom at Lombard. Officer Herman grumbled about exaggerated rumors and assured me that Lombard is relatively safe. He reminded me that the youngest children are safely isolated from the teenagers in the "schoolhouse" building, which does not even have metal detectors. He also expressed optimism about the fact that he "mostly finds knives and maybe a few guns" via the metal detector at the main school.

However, the problems that parents complain of at Lombard can even be found at Parkmont's nearby preschool, which none of my informants' children have attended, despite its convenient location a half block away from Lombard. In the mid-1990s, when younger whites still lived in Parkmont and the preschool had a different owner, neighborhood children filled every available vacancy. I talked to preschool staff members about the types of children who are now enrolled there. Katie Kress, the head teacher, said that none of the children are white and all receive low-income subsidies. She described the challenges of teaching the kinds of children who attend Parkmont's preschool:

> They just seem to have a hard edge to them, even the really small ones. It's like they've already lived a life before. They're two and three years old, and the things they described that they've seen and they've heard! A lot of them come from single mom families, so they'll come in, and they'll tell us about mom's boyfriends or say, "We stayed at grandmother's house because Mom went out." I'm thinking these are three and four-year-olds. They shouldn't be exposed to this. A few of them have come in and said "My dad's in jail." I'm like, "Okay." I just leave it. I don't ask why. I just let it go. And the mother will come in when they fill out our paperwork, and I'll say something about the father. And they'll be like, "He's incarcerated." I'm like, "Okay, that's fine, okay."

Although some residents in Parkmont are concerned about the practice of busing in students from other neighborhoods, most pioneers seem to think that the "problem students" at Lombard are not the outsiders, but the children of second wave parents. As a teacher, pioneer Nina Jones knows the students and where they live, and as a resident she has observed that the problems that are usually found in other parts of the city have recently crept into Parkmont. She described the time she witnessed police conducting a street-level drug sweep to take dealers off of a corner on the strip:

> I think it's [serious crime] here. Even though there a few that kinda come up from other neighborhoods, still most of them are from up here. On the strip one day, there were kids up there, and [the police] blocked off all of the strip. And when I finally got around, and maneuvered my way up, I saw it was boys who went to Lombard. They were laying on the floor, like

laying on the ground, handcuffed and everything. I was like, "Those are the kids that I knew from Lombard." They were like ninth, tenth grade.

Lamar and Clarice Nellis explained that they, like many pioneers, want their preschool-aged son to attend a racially integrated school, but they also emphasized that behavioral standards are especially important to them. They have been searching for a school with a safe environment that promotes learning, as well as one that advances assimilationist cultural values. Although the family is not Catholic, the couple has been sending their son to a Catholic preschool, and they reported that they are reluctant to allow him to play with Parkmont children. Lamar explained the way his views about second wave residents have influenced his decisions about their son's education and contact with peers:

> What I see is there's no ownership, and when there's no ownership, there's no real values. Where's the values? My son has one friend that he plays with here, but a lot of his friends are from outside of the neighborhood because of his school. He didn't go to the daycare here, whatever that place is. Clarice was in the educational field. There were certain things we require. Early foundation is very key to us. The way the children are, the way the teacher speaks, the way the individuals go about certain things were very important to us because that's what the child mimics. The school that he goes to currently has maybe 5 percent blacks. It's a predominantly white school and Asian. He feels comfortable. I want him to feel comfortable, but yet he can fit in well going to his cousin's house and playing on their block, you follow me? Now, we're at the point that he's six, and so his vocabulary is very important to us, the way he speaks. He has a lazy tongue [a speech impediment], so we're working with him on certain things, but they tease him in certain environments, you know? We tell him, "You live in America. Standard English is what you are supposed to speak." Because in a different environment, they may speak broken English.

Though Lombard's flaws are many, the pioneer parents seemed most concerned about behavioral problems, or as one parent said, "The tone. When we go up there, there's kids running around, all outta control. And just, it's not in order." I was able to witness the classroom environment firsthand when Lombard administrators allowed me to observe a seventh-grade math class one day. I was surprised to see most of the children repeatedly leaving their seats and walking around the classroom without permission, playing games with calculators, and sleeping with their heads on their desks, as the teacher yelled at the students, and wrote the worst offenders' names on the board as part of a list of students to be punished. However, what really shocked me was the fight that broke out between two boys, with one threatening to dislocate the jaw of the other as he loudly called him a "motherfucker." Many of the students looked at me with embarrassment, but the teacher seemed unfazed by the outburst and by the end of class had written down the names of six children whose parents she planned to call because of disciplinary problems. When I told Nina Jones, the pioneer and teacher at Lombard, she said, "Oh, I'm used to that, and I teach first grade. That happens. It even happens in kindergarten." Later, after the classroom confrontation, I began to feel more optimistic about Parkmont's learning environment because the heavyset boy sitting next to me in class kept raising his hand and providing the correct answers to math problems, but then he told me: "I was left back from last year. I already did this all before."

Pioneer Sam Wilson said that Lombard is not well-equipped for educating children, but he maintained that behavior problems were the key factor that led him to remove his daughters from Lombard:

> It started to go downhill. My father would come back and report to me what he witnessed in the school, but I thought he was just overreacting. Then, my wife would do the same, talking about the behavior in the schoolyard, the behavior in the classrooms. Yeah, and for a while they didn't have the appropriate textbooks. They didn't have enough supplies in the school. So then I went there one day, and we quickly decided that we would send them to Catholic school for the next academic year. And since we're Catholic, it was fine for us to do that.

Pioneers take great pains to improve the educational lot of their children. Their stories show the specific motivations and strategies of the most informed, involved, organized, and able segment of Parkmont's parents. Many have placed their children in a wide range of schools in the city and suburbs, such as charter schools, elite private schools, Catholic schools, and magnet schools. Although originally the convenience of a good neighborhood school was central to their decision to move to Parkmont, the pioneers' children now travel across the city on buses and trains to attend higher quality schools, sometimes in more dangerous, high-poverty neighborhoods. Pioneer Sonya McCall explained her daughter's time at Lombard and the decision to remove her:

> She went there until the third grade, but I snatched her out of there! That school was horrible! Kids fightin', beatin' up the teachers, and I was talking to my next-door neighbor, and she was like, "Try a magnet school." Okay, so I said that I'm going to try to get her in there, and they accepted her. So she goes there now. She's went there since fourth grade.

Sonya seemed unsure about where her daughter would eventually attend high school. It was especially sad to listen to her young daughter confide that she often worries about where she will attend school. She struggles with math and fears that the city's magnet high schools will be too selective for her to gain admittance.

Janice O'Neill was among the many pioneer parents who also removed their children from Lombard after her high hopes for the school were shattered:

> I think when we first came up here it was nice, but then there was like a rapid deterioration. 'Cause I was like, "Oh, the school's good. I'll move here." I knew, given my income, what I could afford as far as not paying for a private school. So I said, "Okay. If I'm going to send my child to a public school, let me send them to the best one available to them." And that's what I thought I was doing, but it turned out it wasn't that way. My daughter, she did go there 'til the eighth grade, but I immediately got her out, and my son is being home-schooled now because he's special ed.

Michelle Mitchell, a pioneer and single mother of two, explained that her daughter is now enrolled at a charter school after a brief time at Lombard. Less than a year after I interviewed her, I learned that Michelle had moved away from Parkmont. Before the move, she described the complicated and stressful arrangements involved in transporting her daughter from Parkmont to the charter school, which was located across the city:

> Did my daughter tell you she takes the bus? She takes the bus in the afternoon because there's a forty-five-minute difference from the time she gets out of school until the time I get off work. So now she has a cell phone, and it's just for emergencies, and when she's on the bus she turns it on. I take a bus to work. But yeah, she takes the bus, which runs to my sister's house, and I've established a relationship with the bus driver. She knows where to sit and everything. I mean, at first I was a nervous wreck, but it's okay now.

For many residents, the only alternative for a high-quality residential neighborhood with a good school is to move to the suburbs, but this option is usually out of reach. Pioneers Lamar and Clarice Nellis want more for themselves and their son and now plan to move, though Lamar still feels conflicted about the suburbs:

> I have mixed feelings. If I was married with no children, I would want to live in the city, because you're able to get to everything. I like the diversity. I like different types of people. I like to entertain. I like to socialize. I like good people, and I don't want to drive everywhere I go.

But I have a son, and the school is important, and the social life for him is important. He needs a different mind-set. I'd prefer suburban life, but the economy sorta gets to me, because you gotta drive everywhere now, and that's gas and things of that nature. Clarice wants to move up. I think she wants to start teaching college. She wants to get into that, so she has goals for herself, and I really feel it makes sense for us to say good-bye to Parkmont.

Outsiders: Busing and Fake Addresses

Busing is a common complaint among Parkmont residents. In the late 1970s, the city adopted a school desegregation policy that honored parents' requests to transfer their children to schools that are located outside of their home neighborhood. This policy was similar to those in many cities with court rulings that forced integration by busing black children into white neighborhoods to attend schools that had lower percentages of blacks. Often, the receiving schools' student bodies were completely white, as was the case with Lombard.

The city has three main types of high schools: special admission (e.g., magnet schools), citywide admission (e.g., students from other neighborhoods may attend), and neighborhood high schools. Most of the city's schools have a "feeder area" or neighborhood boundary for students who are below the high school grades, although it is possible for younger students to request a transfer. In eighth grade, all students fill out high school application forms to apply to a maximum of five schools in any combination. On these forms, students must inform the district if they plan to attend their neighborhood or "feeder" school, or they must rank their school preference list. These requests for transfer out of the feeder school are ordered according to school space and a lottery system. Students who are not accepted to their preferred schools are eligible to attend their local feeder school. Once in high school, students seeking a transfer may select up to five schools, but no single school is guaranteed.

The city policy is that only local children may attend Lombard unless they officially apply for a transfer and are accepted. Thus, parents in nearby neighborhoods sometimes use fake addresses to ensure that their children are in safe schools, usually conveniently located near their homes. Parkmont residents have long been concerned about the outside students who commute to Lombard, whether they attend legitimately or not. I asked Dana Steinberg, the Lombard official, about this, and she told me that Lombard's principal is aware of residents' concerns about outside students coming in, overcrowding the school, and hanging around the neighborhood. Dana said that the principal has cracked down on the use of fake addresses, but she told me that the fraudulent use of addresses at Lombard is not a new phenomenon. Even when Lombard was a predominantly white school, white students from nearby integrating neighborhoods would use fake addresses to attend Lombard. She elaborated the pioneers' concerns about Lombard and the long history of "outsiders" at the school:

> Parents were upset that they came to this neighborhood for a better school and hopefully, a better education, and what happened was kids were using relatives' addresses—grandparents, aunts that live in the neighborhood. They were coming in with fake IDs, fake address information, and the classrooms were overcrowded. We've always had this situation. We've always had the problem because what happened was white kids that lived down the hill should have gone to their neighborhood school, but it was kind of changing, so they wanted their kids up here. They would come here, and how they would come here is they would use somebody's address. This was not an African American thing. This was done before. And the principal—maybe I shouldn't say this, but I believe that the principal at the time did it to keep this neighborhood white and to keep the school white by having more whites come here. Back then, you couldn't just go to other schools. There had to be space. And so, there was never space because we were full with other white kids.

Thus, the interplay between school and neighborhood predates the integration of Parkmont, as does the intraracial conflict. When Parkmont was a Jewish community with a smattering of Italian and Irish families, whites from other neighborhoods used fake addresses to attend Lombard and were a source of tension. Soon, non-Jewish white ethnics moved into the community en masse. When blacks began attending Lombard, white families removed their children from the school and moved away, and soon black students dominated the school and black families began to integrate Parkmont. Today, Parkmont is a black neighborhood, and its parents are concerned about children from other communities attending Lombard, spending time in the neighborhood, and possibly moving in. However, like the whites before them who worried about "outsider" whites invading their local school, Parkmont's black parents are worried about outsider students who are also black.

"I wish the school was better," Carla Jackson, a twenty-four-year-old pioneer, said to me. On a wall in her living room was her framed college degree. Carla's son's education, meanwhile, remains uncertain. Like many pioneers, Carla thinks the busing is a major cause of Lombard's problems:

> Parkmont is real small. I think it's only about four blocks long either way. It's not big. If you stand in the middle of Parkmont, you might have

four blocks to the north, four blocks to the south. Two blocks east and west. So it's not that big. You have the school right in the center. Like I said, Lombard was excellent, but you know, the problem with Lombard is very easy to solve. If you're not from this neighborhood, you can't go to this school. If you would stand where the bus stops, every child that gets off this bus to go to Lombard is not from the neighborhood.

Many residents described the use of fake addresses by "outsiders" at Lombard. However, I noticed that outsider students often had some kind of connection to a Parkmont family. For instance, on several occasions second wave residents told me that the children who I would often see in their homes did not live there. These children were family members who attended Lombard by using the addresses of their aunts, cousins, and grandmothers.

Some residents blame the outsider students for the neighborhood problems that spill over from the school. Stayer Sadie Underwood was pessimistic about the futures of Parkmont and Lombard. She provided her view of the causes of the decline:

> It's going downhill, definitely. When I walk on the strip I see the difference. The strip is filthy because the kids, they buy the drinks, bottles, cups, and paper goods. Oh, it's dirty. It's absolutely filthy. And there's a lot of kids who are bused in to Lombard, and they're the ones who leave the mess.

Again, the topic of the school is one on which pioneers and stayers often agree. Pioneer Margaret Meadows echoed Sadie's sentiment that students from outside neighborhoods have ruined Lombard and tend to disrespect Parkmont and its residents:

> The school tries to tell us that they're trying to get everybody [non-Parkmont children] out of Lombard, but it's not true. I stand there and watch the kids get off the bus. Sometimes, they get off the bus, and they throw things down. I ask them to pick it up. And then, they might cuss me out. But I told them, "Look, the trash can is right here. Why do you get off the bus and throw things down?"

Pioneer Michelle Mitchell said that the parents she knows are fed up with the school system, and they view Lombard as representative of the failure of city schools. She believes that one can tell that Lombard's students are out of control from the way they dress and carry themselves:

> People are sick of public schools, whether it's Lombard or another school. They're just sick of public schools. You know who sends their kids here? A lot of people that don't live in Parkmont, and they think

Lombard is better than other public schools. They really do, and it surprises me. I just feel that you're missing out when you're not exposed
to other people and other things. Oh my god! That school's changed a
lot. I see the kids that go there. I look at the way they dress when they
go to school. It's like, "Don't you guys have a dress code when you go to
school? Is there somebody checkin' you before you come in?" Like sayin',
"Girl, that skirt is a little too short."

As she told this story, I remembered that Lombard students are required to
wear a "uniform" consisting of a white polo shirt and khaki bottoms, but very
few students adhere to the dress code and many even wear clothing that offends
teachers. For instance, one day while I was waiting for an interviewee, two tenth-
grade boys talked to me about Lombard, but neither was wearing his uniform
despite the fact that school had just let out. One boy was an honor roll student
who politely asked me for advice about financial aid for college; he was clearly
worried about his mother's ability to afford his education. The other boy, his
classmate, wore a necklace with a pendant depicting a marijuana leaf. He was not
trying to be rude, but as we talked he did not make eye contact and he habitually
spat on the ground.

Officer Herman believes that outside students and Parkmont families are
both to blame for the behavior problems at Lombard. He verified for me what
many Parkmont residents suspect, which is that many Lombard students are
from other communities, and their parents commit address fraud to gain admittance. At the same time, like most people I interviewed, Officer Herman said that
Parkmont's own parents share some of the blame for students' conduct problems. Although he empathizes with Parkmont's working-class parents who have
long hours and cannot supervise their children at home, this did not change his
assessment that neighborhood parents are a large part of the problem in the
school and community:

Many parents work two jobs and overtime to make ends meet. They
can't always keep up homes and watch kids. A lot of kids are latchkey.
Lots of kids use fake addresses to be here or they live with aunts and
grandmothers. Also, a lot of kids are relocated [for their own safety]
to Lombard because they were witnesses in [criminal] cases involving
peers at a local school. Kids from other areas are not supposed to be at
Lombard, but when a problem occurs, we often find out that the kid's
info doesn't match up, and he's from another area.

Pioneer Sam Wilson took an even stronger stance than Officer Herman on the
local nature of the problems at Lombard. He said that most Lombard students

are from the neighborhood and cited a recent Parkmont baby boom as a cause of school struggles:

> There's overcrowding. That's a major part of it. There's just too many students there, and they're primarily from here. There's just been a population boom here. The people who have moved in have a lot of families with small children, so it's just a lot of kids here, and everybody's in that one building. That, coupled with a lack of resources. It's just not an optimum situation for anybody. That's part of it. It just devolved. Everybody isn't as able as we are to send our kids to private school.

Many Parkmont parents are incredulous that parents from other neighborhoods would want to send their children to Lombard. As pioneer Nina Jones said, "A lot of kids come from where I used to live and farther down. I don't know what the parents see is so great about Lombard, because I wouldn't send my dog there." Even though Nina teaches at Lombard, she thinks that the "decent" parents send their children elsewhere, and she plans to do whatever it takes to do the same:

> Especially the parents that have it together. They're on the ball. My son's not going to Lombard. If we're still living here, which I hope that we're not, but if we're still living here, he won't go there. We wouldn't send him there. He would go somewhere in the suburbs. I would figure out a way. I have people. I know people over there. I have a lot of friends from college, and I made a lot of friends over on the suburbs side.

To many whites, when a neighborhood shifts from white to black, it symbolizes inevitable decline. However, this is not always the case for the pioneers, who consider themselves to be successful, hard-working, and responsible parents who are proud of being African American. Many pioneers in Parkmont, whether by choice or because of the limitations placed on their residential mobility options, have taken a more nuanced "wait and see" attitude about neighborhood racial change than the whites before them. Unfortunately, now that some time has passed, many do not like what they are seeing. The intragroup dynamics at Lombard reflect the ways in which Parkmont has changed and provide a glimpse into how it may look in the future.

When Intraracial Means Invisible: Shifts within Black Communities

Busing introduced racial change at Lombard in the 1970s and was intended to create a more diverse school environment and provide greater educational equality. In 1985, Lombard was formally praised for its integration policy when it was presented with a letter that remains prominently displayed in a trophy case in front of the auditorium, right across from the main office. The letter offers Lombard "commendation for being one of 71 desegregated public schools" and for providing an "integrated learning experience" and a "desegregated environment" for learning. It closes by saying that the "lives of these students will forever be enhanced … by the racial, ethnic, and religious harmony" experienced at Lombard. When I was reading it, I could not help but notice that oddly juxtaposed next to the letter in the trophy case was a framed photo of Lombard's most recent class of high school graduates. Every student in the photo was African American. This change from white to integrated to black is obvious because of the visibility of the students' skin color. Less visible, but still important, are the shifting dynamics *within* black communities that continue to affect the composition of Lombard's study body, and ultimately, Parkmont as a whole.

Within Parkmont are two subgroups of blacks, each of whom has had to adapt to the reality of urban schools. The pioneers have made do by working multiple jobs and long shifts to send their children to expensive schools, homeschool their children, place them in magnet schools, or use fake addresses in suburban areas so their children may attend the public schools in the wealthy first-ring suburbs. Their children travel long distances, leaving early in the morning and returning home just as it gets dark outside. Parents must constantly arrange networks of friends, family, and after-school programs to help with transportation and caregiving. Second wave families often opt for Lombard, at least in part because their children are younger and because these families are less knowledgeable or engaged in their children's education. Many black residents eventually decide to leave Parkmont altogether, only to once again search for a better place for their families to meet some basic needs: safety, effective education, and positive social influences.

Further complicating matters is the introduction of a third group who is engaged in educational pursuits in Parkmont: the children who are bused in to Lombard but who still live in the ghetto. Well-intentioned parents across the city, rightly or wrongly, believe that Parkmont has more to offer their children than their own communities do, and they go to extreme lengths to improve their lot. These families rarely have the means to provide their children with a home in a community as safe as Parkmont, so sending them to the school there is the next best thing.

Lombard is increasingly composed of second wave students and outsider students from low-income communities. As far as the pioneers are concerned, these two groups share more in common than do the pioneers and the second wave, so pioneer parents have withdrawn their children from the school. Although seemingly a benign development at first glance, the withdrawal of pioneer children from Lombard has, in fact, altered the pattern of neighborhood cultural influences on second wave children. Specifically, second wave children are deprived of the positive influences of the pioneer children who do not attend Lombard and are away from the neighborhood much of the time. At the same time, second wave children remain exposed to the cultural influences of outsider students from disadvantaged neighborhoods. Thus, simply residing in Parkmont fails to pull the second wave toward the culture of the pioneers, as expected. Instead, second wave children are guided toward the values and behaviors of children who live in far worse communities and often come from more disadvantaged family circumstances. In fact, some behavior problems exhibited by second wave children may not be blamed solely on their parents, as the pioneers claim, but may be attributable to the hidden influence of their social networks at school.

Thus, pioneer and second wave adults' conflicts over cultural scripts are exacerbated by what goes on with Parkmont children who attend school at Lombard. The second wave students at Lombard contend with peer socialization that discourages them from identifying with Parkmont and from adopting more assimilationist and prosocial community attitudes, norms, and behaviors. All of this affects the Parkmont environment by further igniting pioneers' grievances against their neighbors, discord that does not bode well for the future of the community in terms of the metrics that originally made the neighborhood attractive to pioneers. For pioneers and second wave residents alike, the story of Lombard furthers our understanding of the difficulty of escaping high-poverty communities and the far-reaching effects of schools on neighborhood life.

School migration patterns have affected Parkmont throughout its history. The problems that recently have emerged at Lombard overlap with the timing of the neighborhood's massive population change, but they also serve as a leading indicator of future changes in Parkmont's composition. The main reason that Parkmont residents first lobbied to build a local school was so that parents could avoid sending their children to an integrating school that was located nearby. When Parkmont was still a Jewish neighborhood, residents became concerned about the Italians "from down the hill" sneaking into the school by using fraudulent addresses. Shortly after their children began attending Lombard, Italian families began to buy homes in Parkmont. Simultaneously, busing for integration was implemented, so white parents' concerns about Lombard were then diverted to the black children who were coming into Parkmont for a better education. After Lombard integrated, it began to resegregate and become predominantly black, triggering white flight. The final chapter in this story is that of black flight as pioneers prefer that their daughters and sons attend schools outside of their own community and away from the influence of the children of second wave residents. At the same time, children from worse neighborhoods across the city now compete to gain entry to Lombard, creating an unexpected and unwanted community presence.

It is striking that so many pioneers entered Parkmont with misleading impressions of Lombard, heavily relying on reputation and advice from others. They have had to lower their expectations and rethink their plans, but they retain their high aspirations. Though Parkmont's black families are diverse, all embarked on their moves with a shared hope that their children would live and learn in a safe, enriching environment. Like immigrants in search of a better life in a new country, these parents used the best of their knowledge and abilities when they selected Parkmont as their destination. Packing up their lives and leaving familiar places was difficult, both financially and socially, but many arrived with a sense of enthusiasm and possibility that was shattered when they confronted the reality of the school that awaited their children.

Contrary to popular images of parents of urban students as passive or uninvolved, many of Parkmont's parents can be seen as innovators. Unlike many upwardly mobile whites who simply relocate to suburban communities with more desirable school districts, black urban residents must contend with rigid constraints on their residential choices. Few can move to the neighborhoods that contain the schools they seek, either because of finances, city job requirements and incentives, or family obligations. Thus, the parents who are most committed to their children's education are constantly engaged in a quest to find an appropriate school. There is no question that families' efforts to gain access to schools outside of Parkmont demonstrate a high level of awareness about Lombard and a commitment to education. What their neighborhood cannot provide, they will.

9

CONCLUSIONS
Understanding the Cultural Dynamics of Neighborhood Change

Many anecdotal stories of white flight conclude when whites make their mass exodus from a neighborhood. There is no need to follow up because it is assumed that what will transpire is known: the inevitable, clear-cut, neighborhood racial change "death spiral." Many anticipate this sense of doom well in advance, which is why school and neighborhood racial integration so often lead to the community phenomenon that is labeled "white flight."[1] Whereas white flight marks the end of an era for those who leave, it is just the beginning for the newcomers and old-timers who choose to remain.

My study of Parkmont begins where the literature on white flight ends. In this book, I have described the structural and cultural dynamics that occur in the aftermath of racial integration. The story of Parkmont makes it clear that race remains an important category of analysis in community research, but it also illustrates the complexities of race effects as neighborhoods continue to change. Interracial cooperation and increased agency for both the pioneers and stayers represent clear, positive outcomes of the changing racial composition of Parkmont, but there are also stressors that trigger further change in the form of black flight. Even though in retrospect it may seem obvious that rapid white flight often creates conditions that lead to a later phase of black flight, this consequence often goes unnoticed.[2] Following the neighborhood of Parkmont through two distinct phases of change forces us to reconsider absolutist assumptions about

---

1. See Armor (1978), Cummings (1998), Ginsburg (1975), and Rieder (1985).
2. Krase (1982).

the aftermath of white flight, such as rapid ghettoization, interracial tensions, and intraracial unity.

I began my study of Parkmont with a focus on black-white neighbor relations and the observation that not all of the whites who stayed were simply "left behind" as victims of economic circumstance. Instead, I learned that stayers decided to remain in their longtime community for a variety of reasons, many of which had nothing to do with a financial inability to move. Though I did not initially expect to study intraracial tensions, along the way I found that differences among black residents were also present in Parkmont and that researching this aspect of social relations added much to understanding the phenomenon of neighborhood change. Ultimately, Parkmont's story is about a neighborhood's multiple stages of change over time.

In Parkmont, I found an opportunity to study the negotiation of race, class, age, neighborhood longevity, and power after white flight. Differences in demographics and culture were sometimes complex when they seemed simple and sometimes simple when they seemed complex. The individuals in this study did not passively accept the imposed categories of race and age and the assumed associations with social class in predictable and deterministic ways. In many cases, stayers transcended dichotomous ways of thinking and adjusted their views of the new residents, reclassifying pioneers based on their newly formed personal relationships and the newcomers' abilities and efforts to share Parkmont's identity as an orderly neighborhood with a sense of ownership over the future. However, the second stage of neighborhood change brought forth conflict that resulted in destabilization as the pioneers and second wave residents could not reach a compromise about the high-stakes issue of neighborhood quality of life.

Pioneers' very strong views about second wave residents' behaviors and values should not be dismissed as minor or petty disagreements over lifestyle or habits. Pioneers made universal judgments about the changing cultural milieu of the neighborhood, and second wave residents represented an affront to pioneers' very identities. As pioneers saw it, the newest residents would never think of Parkmont as anything more than a disposable community. Thus, with a sense of hopelessness about the possibility for successful interventions to deal with intraracial conflict, the pioneers' dissatisfaction and fears about the future festered and resulted in black flight.

The case of Parkmont provides evidence that white flight, often seen as a topic from the past, is still relevant. Yet by studying the aftermath of white flight in the modern era, new questions are raised about the causes and consequences of white and black flight, the social meanings of integration, and the ways in which neighborhood values and behaviors can be either a unifying or dividing force. By following through after the dust of white flight has settled, the cultural milieu of neighborhood change becomes illuminated, making it clear that places like Parkmont are sites of hope in some ways, but remain vulnerable to more subtle transitions that cannot be detected by simply perusing census statistics on racial composition and ethnic change.

Lessons about Stayers, Pioneers, and Cross-Racial Neighboring

Parkmont's story changes and complicates the way that we think about race, white flight, and black neighborhoods and invites readers to consider the aftereffects of racial change. This book tells a neighborhood story, while also providing an intimate portrait of elderly whites who age in place and offering insight into what it is really like for black working-class families in the city as they balance family life, work, and school with their search for a suitable place to live and educate their children. Below, I summarize the ways in which the study of Parkmont contributes to understanding the dynamics and culture of neighborhood change in urban environments.

Stayers' Agency: Aging in Place and Interacting with Pioneers

The existing literature on elderly white stayers focuses on earlier eras and generally fails to value residents' decision making. Parkmont provided an unusual opportunity to study stayers, in part because of the time-sensitive nature of the fieldwork. During the data collection, many of the oldest people were moving to assisted living facilities, and some had died. Their stories, explanations, and lived experiences have shed much light on this poorly understood group. The evidence from this study points to the lesson that whites who stay in their communities after white flight deserve a careful analytical treatment, one that investigates their motives and extends to their relationships with new black neighbors. In the twenty-first century, white stayers are not the scared, hateful xenophobes historically depicted in the media and in some case studies.

Many people are puzzled and chagrined by white elderly residents who decide to stay in their neighborhoods after white flight. This confusion and frustration is especially noticeable among the younger family members of such stayers. My study of Parkmont shows that, on the whole, once blacks move in, white stayers experience a great deal of pressure to move away from their long-time homes. Despite what many believe, most of them actually *can* afford to do so. Choosing to leave would certainly go far in quieting the concerns of their families and friends. This is what makes the stayers' decisions to stay seem so surprising and irrational to outsiders, as well as to the people closest to them.

There is a Yiddish expression that summarizes stayers' attitude about aging in place: Abi gezunt! (As long as you're healthy!) Stayers clearly represent a certain type of person. They are involved, aware, and active participants in most aspects of their lives, including their mobility decisions. Rather than passively reacting to change and simply following the crowds who flee in fear, they attempt to maintain a sense of normalcy as they age. Stayers' decisions to remain in Parkmont, even as others question their lucidity and openly pass judgment on the loss of status to their beloved community, might be seen as the ultimate expression of agency.

Blacks Help Stayers to Age in Place

Like everyone, stayers make their housing decisions within a context of constraints. Elderly people vary in terms of their economic limitations, access to assistance from family, levels of independence, health, physical abilities, and availability of other housing opportunities that match their preferences. However, a select group chooses to stay. It is true that members of this group feel especially attached to their homes and neighborhoods. But just as important is the fact that black residents simply do not scare stayers enough to inspire them to drop their lives and move. Even before white flight, stayers had relatively low levels of prejudice toward blacks, and since white flight took hold of Parkmont, this racial tolerance bloomed into a sense of openness. As stayers continued to age in place next to black families, opportunities for contact with black neighbors emerged, and the possibility of meaningful cross-racial neighbor relationships materialized.

Without the pioneers, many stayers would not have been able to remain in their preferred residential situation as long as they did. By providing routine help with daily chores and housework, pioneers took some of the burden off of the aging stayers who increasingly struggled to complete even minor tasks. In so doing, pioneers also are likely to have prevented injuries and, in some cases, criminal victimization of these elderly residents.

However, for the many stayers who have lost a spouse and receive few visitors, pioneers provided more intense forms of help that go beyond the instrumental favors often expected of neighbors. Whether pioneers are keeping company with the stayers, taking their emergency calls in the middle of the night, driving them to the hospital, caring for them as they recover from an illness or injury, checking up on them to make sure that all is well when things seem to return to normal, or making sure that their homes are safe and secure, pioneers function as an essential part of stayers' lives and contribute greatly to their overall well-being.

The days when the black pioneers first arrived in a white neighborhood are long gone, but the effects of this period of integration remain obvious in Parkmont. Further, it is clear that stayers' initial efforts to show a welcoming attitude toward pioneers were not unreciprocated. After all, the pioneers had some idea of what they were getting into when they specifically selected a predominantly white neighborhood, and in turn many of them made special gestures to reach out to the aging stayers living next to them. A failure to acknowledge this reality of white-flight contexts would prevent an understanding of the significance of the black residents for stayers' everyday lives as they age in place. Stayers rely on pioneers for companionship, a shared sense of neighborhood identity, and most important for the help that allows them to remain in their homes into the later stages of old age.

Black Residents Receive Benefits from Stayers

Pioneers also benefit from being with long-time residents who share similar values. For instance, pioneers sprinkled their neighborhood stories with details gleaned from the stayers whom they know. This transmission of neighborhood culture helps pioneers to gain a sense of neighborhood history and continuity. In a sense, these pioneers are "social preservationists" who view the stayers as crucial in the safeguarding of a community that has an authentic, cohesive, and orderly feel.[3] This explains some of the pioneers' efforts to prolong their elderly neighbors' tenure in Parkmont.

When the pioneers first arrived, the white stayers were hyperaware of the black newcomers, and with little else to do during the day, many reached out to welcome them. However, pioneers reported that they, too, benefited from stayers' efforts to reach out and socialize them into neighborhood norms. Even though the pioneers were looking forward to life in an orderly, low-crime neighborhood, they appreciated the pleasant change of having so many elderly "watchers" who were invested in Parkmont and who took the time to educate them about community norms, including neighborhood upkeep, local services, and how to handle problems that might arise.

Finally, many pioneers reported that they enjoyed the emotional and social rewards from neighboring with older people, whose values they shared and respected. Through daily conversations, birthday parties, or when involved in the occasional care of children, stayers and pioneers learned about each other's culture, shared in family celebrations, and provided emotional support during hard times. In some cases, even after pioneers moved on and stayers went into

---

3. Brown-Saracino (2004).

retirement homes, the relationships established in Parkmont continued in the form of phone calls, visits, cards, and gifts.

In summary, this study of Parkmont shows us that researching racially changing communities is much more than just a way to learn about population shifts in cities. Neighborhood change can, at least temporarily, open opportunities for friendship that cross the lines of race, age, and ethnicity, contributing to a stronger community. White stayers in Parkmont are not categorically racist, xenophobic, fearful senior citizens who feel trapped by circumstance. Black pioneers do not resent the white stayers or long for the social comfort of neighborhood racial homogeneity, and they do not bring crime, disorder, and anti-community subcultures with them to Parkmont. The deep cultural description and analysis of Parkmont's white flight illuminates the potential for mutually beneficial neighbor relations between dissimilar groups who are often perceived as unfortunate presences to be tolerated rather than as assets for people in search of lives that are fulfilling on both personal and community levels.

The Destabilizing Force of Rapid Change

Although Parkmont has provided positive experiences and opportunities for residents, the rapid pace of population change has also damaged the neighborhood in many respects. Whereas some literature on race and community depicts close-knit urban black neighborhoods as places where everyone "keeps up on" each other, other research shows a more complex picture. For instance, African Americans tend to prefer mixed neighborhoods, and most would be happy to enter a white community, as long as it contains some black residents,[4] though the degree of blacks' preferences for integration varies across cities[5] and states.[6] However, the white-flight phenomenon makes it clear that whites' preferences are not compatible with those of blacks in the long run. As a result, integration is often a transitional phase in U.S. neighborhoods that brings forth further shifts in community life.

Racial Change: Stayers to Pioneers

The pioneers' decisions to enter a predominantly white neighborhood are central to the story of Parkmont. Pioneers are distinct from the second wave because

---

4. Krysan and Farley (2002).
5. Farley, Fielding, and Krysan (1997).
6. Johnson and Brunn (1980).

of two factors: population selection processes and timing. Regarding the first concept, it is well known that differential interneighborhood migration patterns exist across groups and that certain populations "self-select" into particular kinds of neighborhoods.[7] In Parkmont, the pioneers were the people with knowledge of the community, financial means, and quasi-assimilationist values that are associated with the willingness or desire to move into a white neighborhood. Pioneers chose to move into a white community; this choice required both familial and economic resources and a particular set of attitudes.

Although Parkmont's white leavers obviously did not recognize this, the pioneers contradict the popular image that equates neighborhood racial integration with decline. The whites who fled Parkmont can be seen as similar to those described in a study that asked white survey respondents why they would flee an integrated neighborhood.[8] Many of those whites, instead of reporting racist attitudes toward all blacks as a group, focused on the negative features that they associated with racially mixed communities. Yet in the case of Parkmont, the amenities that whites most feared losing were often nearly identical to those that the pioneers were seeking.

Although large numbers of lower income residents can create conditions that lead to neighborhood decline, Parkmont's incoming pioneers were not poor. They purchased their homes, often at relatively high prices, and had stable incomes and steady working-class jobs. This basic similarity in socioeconomic status and desired amenities between Parkmont's whites and the black pioneers shows that racial change need not be equated with social distance or a lack of shared understanding between groups.[9] This community represents a case where the incoming blacks in the 1990s were economically comparable to white residents, presenting no threat to future property values. In fact, many white stayers, judging the pioneers by their cars, jobs, and home improvement efforts, reported that they perceived them to have a better socioeconomic status than the white residents who had left.[10]

The timing of arrival also had a major impact on the ways in which pioneers were socialized into neighborhood life and on their sense of community history. Because they arrived in Parkmont when it still had a large presence of whites who were long-term residents, pioneers benefited from arriving in a place where residents were highly invested in the neighborhood. Elderly stayers, risking accusations of paternalism, socialized new residents into the role of a Parkmont

---

7. Crowder, South, and Chavez (2006).
8. Krysan (2002).
9. See Cover (1995) and Park (1924).
10. See Northwood and Barth (1965) for other instances of this pattern.

homeowner. Because of their resources, values, and desire to live in Parkmont, the pioneers fit in well from the start. However, by their own admission, they were unfamiliar with neighborhoods that were low in crime, clean, quiet, and well maintained. Rather than feeling offended by nosy stayers, pioneers felt relieved to be in a place where they were welcomed and where people seemed invested in the future. This is what they had hoped for, and they internalized the values and behaviors that matched their own and seemed to predominate in Parkmont.

Parkmont's transitions highlight a lesson about the cultural conflicts associated with "tipping points" of population change. Malcolm Gladwell (2000) popularized the idea of tipping points associated with rapid change, but tipping points (also known as threshold effects, contagion theories, and critical mass models) have long fascinated demographers who study segregation.[11] In Parkmont, critical masses of whites rapidly fled, creating an ecological milieu of instability that triggered further change. These structural factors have limited pioneers' abilities to realize their preferences.[12] Although fair housing laws have attempted to eradicate discrimination and eliminate many of the forces that have historically contributed to segregation, many other factors remain in place such that racial integration and community stability frequently remain distant dreams for African Americans.

Population change in Parkmont was extremely rapid, as indicated by the census data presented in table 1 (see the appendix). This is important because rapid neighborhood change has long been viewed as a disorganizing force in communities.[13] When populations turn over quickly, communities fail to socially integrate, and the process of learning and teaching neighborhood social codes is degraded.[14] Like all new residents, pioneers struggled to establish themselves and gain a new sense of place identity. Why did they struggle? One reason may be that pioneers, though similar to their white predecessors in terms of income and education, were far less diverse than the original white population, which included residents with a range of ages and family structures. Pioneer households were mostly families with multiple children and adults who worked long hours. These new families had little of the leisure time and presence that is needed to foster neighborhood guardianship. Thus, as blacks replaced whites, Parkmont's new population profile contained more working families, more children, and more single parent households, changes that left the community vulnerable.

---

11. Classic examples of research on the nonlinear aspects of racial residential segregation include Granovetter (1978), Quercia and Galster (2000), Schelling (1971), and Schwab and Marsh (1980).

12. See Adelman (2005) for quantitative evidence about the mismatch between blacks' preferences for integration and their ability to realize those preferences.

13. Shaw and McKay (1942).

14. See Freeman (2006) and Thomas and Znaniecki (1995).

Cultural Change: Pioneers to Second Wave

No sooner had the pioneers begun to gain a sense of neighborhood pride, identity, and social integration than the second wave arrived on their heels. This new group filled the large number of vacant homes left by older whites and pioneers fleeing Parkmont because of poor schools, the loss of racial integration, and various threats to neighborhood quality of life. In order for pioneers to be role models, the second wave of newcomers would have had to think of pioneers as respected leaders who were there to help others become a meaningful part of a stable, functioning community. Parkmont seemed so promising to the many pioneers who looked forward to becoming the heirs to a beloved and respectable neighborhood, but for too many of them, the instability resulting from white and black flight created inhospitable conditions for maintaining the desired quality of life.

Elderly whites in Parkmont were passing on the baton of community organization to a population of young, busy pioneer families with only a short history in the neighborhood. With younger whites fleeing and the stayers aging, Parkmont needed families and residents who could serve as authorities on neighborhood social norms. New residents need time to gain authority, knowledge, and networks, but the short period of time between the entry of the pioneers and the influx of the second wave blacks thwarted the ability of pioneers to become custodians of a unified community culture. Consider the difference between an elderly stayer who has been in the neighborhood for forty years communicating neighborhood norms to a pioneer and a pioneer who has been in the neighborhood for only a few years attempting to do the same thing to a second wave resident of approximately the same age.

These problems were further exacerbated by perceived differences in values and behaviors between pioneers and the second wave. Cultural values clearly emerged as an important source of division between Parkmont's two groups of black residents. With such large numbers and with little meaningful or positive contact with stayers and pioneers, the second wave residents seemed to have their own subculture that did not conform to Parkmont's community norms and more assimilationist values.[15]

It is true that the problems in Parkmont are far less serious than those in many urban black neighborhoods. Additionally, it might be expected that pioneers would have welcomed the chance to have neighbors who were racially, and presumably culturally, more similar to them, relative to whites. However, the input from pioneers in this study reveals that simply being black does not immunize residents from concerns about the disorderly behaviors of their neighbors.

---

15. Fischer (1975).

The second wave's norms, values, and codes of behavior proved difficult for the pioneers to counter or overcome.

Making matters worse, when pioneers disapprove of second wave residents' behaviors, they tend to make more holistic judgments about their values. Elijah Anderson (1999) described "decent and street" families and their standards of life in poor, high-crime areas. He showed the troublesome encounters that occur in communities where families have similar racial backgrounds but very different cultural orientations and public behaviors. I found evidence that a similar dynamic occurs in less marginal areas. In Parkmont, the second wave residents are looked down upon because of the ways in which they parent, neglect their homes, fail to participate in neighborhood life, and carry themselves in the public spaces within the community.

Unlike Anderson's work, which suggests that residents share the same values but have developed different codes of behavior to survive the difficulties of the urban economy, Parkmont residents view behaviors as an extension of values. Parkmont is not just any neighborhood to the pioneers; it is the first place they have lived that feels like they have "made it," and they are unwilling to let it slip away. They have invested a great deal of economic capital and energy in their dream of a peaceful community. To pioneers, the second wave residents who violate the codes of behavior have fundamentally different values. When second wave residents play loud music, litter, and let their children run the streets, they may not realize it but they are separating themselves from the pioneers. Unable to change the values of their newest neighbors, pioneers opt to pack up their belongings and flee. Thus, culturally diverse neighborhoods are not sustainable when the nature of the diversity is focused on differences in opinions about what a neighborhood is for.

Pioneers and stayers share a vision of community that goes beyond second wave residents' individualistic, dwelling-centered orientations. Major cultural differences among groups about the core values of neighboring and citizenship are difficult to overcome. Incremental change, had it occurred, might have cushioned the impact of the second wave residents, allowing Parkmont to become established as a black community with a strong sense of identity, an active organization, and a longer history of social networks.

Social Disorder Affects Mobility Decisions

Neighborhood stability promotes collective efficacy, a shared sense of values, trust, and a willingness to intervene, which together deter serious crime.[16] The

---

16. Sampson, Raudenbush, and Earls (1997).

case study of Parkmont suggests that similar mechanisms explain the influence of social disorder on neighborhood migration patterns. In Parkmont, lack of stability has interfered with the community's ability to realize shared values and goals. Today, pioneers and second wave residents do not get along, and they believe that they each hold different values about appropriate community behaviors, participation in community problem solving, and what constitutes a serious local problem requiring intervention.[17] Without solidarity toward shared goals in Parkmont, selective out-migration and decline have flourished.

As the neighborhood resegregated, Parkmont's black residents began to move. Pioneers knew that whites would not replace black leavers, but hoped that the second wave residents would have stable incomes and similar values.[18] It might have been expected that pioneers would just learn to live with what they perceived to be a decline in the quality of life in Parkmont. After all, the police and the general public tend to accept social and physical disorder as part of their image of what goes on in black neighborhoods,[19] and they may see disorder as a minor problem for a black neighborhood. Quality of life issues in neighborhoods are often dismissed or viewed as a low priority in cities, and some researchers are skeptical about the role of social and physical disorder in neighborhood decline. Even when problems with incivilities are addressed, efforts to deal with these problems are often mocked. For example, police departments in many cities have been criticized for enacting quality of life policing. Detractors think "broken windows" policing is based on a set of classist assumptions and values, and they dismiss it as a mere fad that places undue emphasis on incivilities.[20] However, quality of life was a key factor in pioneers' original decisions to move to Parkmont, which is why it is so hard for them to change their expectations.

Practically speaking, many pioneers have been reluctant to leave Parkmont because they find it to be a convenient and affordable community. When pioneers explained their rationales for moving away from Parkmont, they repeatedly emphasized that newer residents' values, behaviors, and intraracial hostilities about neighborhood life were the driving "push factors." Although pioneers were willing to tolerate white flight, and almost all had figured out ways around the poorly performing neighborhood school, they drew the line when it came to infringements on basic quality of residential life. These conditions have been a disappointment to many pioneers who once viewed their move to Parkmont as a major life milestone. The incivilities that have accompanied the second wave residents' in-migration are an affront to the life that the pioneers sought out and

---

17. Taylor (2001).
18. Blackwell (1975).
19. Meares and Kahan (1998).
20. Bursik and Grasmick (1993).

to which they have become accustomed, one that they characterized as a quiet, safe, clean, well maintained, pleasant environment with stable property values.

The pioneers who want to move on are simply unwilling to wait for the further decline that they once witnessed in their previous neighborhoods—extreme violence and declining property values—to take control of the their living situation. Thus, although black residents in other parts of the city might perceive the changes in Parkmont as trivial, pioneers perceive a fundamental and inescapable social distance from second wave blacks, and they view the increased social and physical disorder as a serious threat. With a rising sense of residential dissatisfaction and an increasing feeling of estrangement from neighbors, pioneers watch their peers pack their moving trucks, and they make plans to do the same.

Policy Implications of Continuous Neighborhood Change

To the extent that metropolitan areas continue to change, the neighborhoods within them also will transform. Assuming that a substantial degree of stability is positive and necessary for communities to thrive, how can neighborhoods maintain stability? What happens when new arrivals do not appear to share the same values as those who settled at an earlier time? How can groups be persuaded to stay when they feel threatened by newcomers? The people of Parkmont have created a life for themselves in a community that was recently abandoned by whites. The racial change was not merely cosmetic but was accompanied by changes in neighborhood family structure, social networks, and values. I conclude by considering the policy implications that arise from my in-depth interviews in Parkmont.

In general, researchers who are interested in community stability often focus on extremely distressed neighborhoods,[21] but stability is important for all neighborhoods, and it is a key factor in nurturing a sense of community identity.[22] Community identity promotes involvement and personal investment, but when the residents of a neighborhood are constantly changing, their community identities also continue to shift.[23] In general, Parkmont has a high rate of home ownership, which has been shown to promote longer lengths of residence and better property maintenance.[24] However, pioneers' preferences about neighborhood

21. Zielenbach (2000).
22. Hummon (1990).
23. Downs (1981).
24. Rohe and Stewart (1996).

quality, combined with the fragility of black home ownership, which often necessitates two incomes, a stable high-paying job, and highly competitive mortgage packages, created conditions in which housing turnover occurred more frequently than expected. Thus, given the strong role that home ownership plays in civic engagement, careful policy efforts to prevent foreclosure are important. In light of the foreclosure crisis that first became widely apparent in 2007 and that has disproportionately affected black communities in the United States, policies that assist borrowers at the earliest signs of trouble could benefit entire neighborhoods and could prevent the neighborhood distress caused by widespread foreclosure for years to come.

At the same time, noneconomic factors are also a neglected, but important, part of instability in places like Parkmont. Many pioneers cited the lack of institutions that cater to the needs of working black families as a problem for retaining and attracting quality residents, and research on other communities supports this claim.[25] The synagogue and Jewish Community Center are key institutions for those Parkmont residents who are members, but they are no longer adequate or ideal. Parkmont's black families need their own churches, youth recreation centers, and activities to feel at home.[26]

Arguably, the most broken institution in Parkmont is the school, which most residents find to be a disgrace. There are many benefits of attending a neighborhood school, but across the city neighborhood schools are rarely seen as the best option for students. Despite the pioneers' hope, Parkmont proved to be no different in this regard. Though it is not poor and remains relatively safe from the very worst crime that occurs on a daily basis in many black neighborhoods in the city, Parkmont has not been the panacea for black families fleeing urban problems, and many families cited the school as a major source of their dissatisfaction with the neighborhood. As the demographic composition of the school changed, the more academically successful students selected out of Lombard and into college-preparatory magnet schools. Today, the kinds of parents who are concerned and informed about local educational opportunities are unlikely to locate to Parkmont if they are aware of the quality of its neighborhood school.

A stable business district would also do much to encourage a sense of place for residents. Parkmont's "strip" is a block in search of an identity. After catering to Jews and Italians, then facing abandonment and disinvestment, it is in need of a diverse set of restaurants, stores, and services that cater to black families as well as nearby whites, but that are not perceived as downscale or "ghetto." Almost all residents who arrive in Parkmont like the idea of being able to walk anywhere to

---

25. Wilson (1987).
26. Kinney and Winter (2006).

get the things they need, but they want more of a choice than Popeye's, Chinese take-out, and hair-braiding salons. They want a streetscape that looks attractive and reasonably upscale, feels safe, and attracts a mix of people.

One way to reverse the pattern of selective out-migration of businesses and residents might be for neighborhood town watches to improve their organization, focus on a range of issues, and become inclusive of all blocks. Remaining pioneers are concerned about declining property values and addressing these concerns could prevent their departure from Parkmont. Neighborhood organizations could also focus on incivilities and properties that residents consider to be public nuisances. Homes in need of repair, renovation, and cleanup often have a detrimental effect on the morale of residents and threaten the health and viability of the entire neighborhood. Neighborhoods that fail to visibly demonstrate a sense of pride are likely to have difficulty retaining and attracting high-quality residents.

Pioneers explained that they are especially concerned about social disorder, a problem that goes beyond worries about property values to encompass concerns about whether Parkmont provides a positive socialization experience for their children. Research suggests that pioneers' concerns are legitimate. Disorder is linked to fear of crime and withdrawal from the community.[27] It also has far-reaching negative effects on many dimensions of residents' attachment to their neighborhoods, such as sentiments or feelings about the community, evaluations of its quality, residents' neighboring behaviors, and their efforts to solve problems.[28] Thus, preventing disorder is a major priority for neighborhoods undergoing rapid change. To assuage residents' fears and build the solidarity that is needed to maintain organization, disorder and incivilities must be taken seriously by community members, police, and the research community. Even though Parkmont's cultural divides are partially manifestations of structural issues, the causes of the behaviors matter very little to pioneers, and they have a low tolerance for excuses. What matters to them is changing the behaviors that interfere with their peace.

How can differences be managed? In addition to attracting newcomers who already share pioneers' values, pioneers must step up and reach out to educate incoming residents about commitment to citizenship in Parkmont, including social norms, rules, and policies, and involvement in schools and neighborhood organizations. All of this teaching and organizing require a great deal of effort from pioneers, many of whom work long hours and have many obligations outside of their community. Neighborhood organizations and block captains can

---

27. Skogan (1990).
28. Woldoff (2002).

play a key role in socializing and mentoring new residents without appearing to be oppressive bullies. For instance, as is common in condominiums and developments with homeowner associations, city neighborhoods like Parkmont can maintain a handbook of community rules, residents can encourage one another to get involved in the process of developing these local rules, and block captains can help residents resolve problems through mediation.

The Future

When I was growing up, starting in fifth grade I would take public transportation deeper into the city to attend a magnet school, and while riding the buses and trains I would watch people get on and off at the "black stops" and the "white stops." In this way, I received an early education about the fact of black-white neighborhood racial segregation; it was a daily part of my early experience of city life. When I would ask adults why blacks lived in separate neighborhoods from whites, the answer was always the same: people like to live with their own groups—it's just more comfortable. Sometimes, the "clannishness" explanation would also include a mention of the fact that blacks live where they can afford to live—the black areas. Even today, when I discuss my research with strangers, acquaintances, family, friends, students, and colleagues from other fields, the assumption is that blacks live in urban segregated black neighborhoods because they prefer it or else they simply cannot afford integrated communities. However, the story of Parkmont is a much more complicated narrative of what people want out of their communities and what it is like when their neighborhoods change around them.

Ideally, neighborhood change occurs slowly with a core group of respected residents and organizations that manage residents' concerns and deal with any problems that arise. However, as long as whites equate racial change with decline, and as long as housing markets are flooded with vacancies that invite residents with different codes of community life, rapid changes will continue to destabilize communities and that ideal will remain unrealized. After lifetimes of struggle for equal access to housing and neighborhoods, housing laws have eradicated legal forms of discrimination. Still, the long-anticipated access to neighborhoods where blacks and whites coexist, attend school together, and work together to maintain a shared community vision usually has proved elusive.

Ultimately, integrated, stable communities with a high quality of life can exist only when long-time residents stay and newcomers with similar values enter. How that can be achieved in a society that views racial change as a threat to safety and property and in cities with selective out-migration of whites and

middle-class blacks, poor schools, and declining tax bases remains almost as unclear as it was when white flight took hold in cities during the 1950s.

For many decades, Parkmont represented a close-knit, white, working-class
urban community. Today, it represents a relatively good black urban community. In
the 1990s, pioneers arrived in a white but integrating neighborhood with dreams
of a peaceful residential life where the streets were safe and quiet, neighbors shared
values about home ownership, family, and community norms, and properties retained their value. Though pioneers were surprised by how quickly most of their
white neighbors fled, they thought that population stability would set in and a
sort of equilibrium would take place. After all, the pioneers had bonded with the
older white stayers and had no reason to think that the second wave of incoming
blacks would not share their goals and conform to the environment that awaited
them.

Instead, the flood of housing sales in Parkmont and the low cost of mortgages
in the 1990s and early 2000s allowed a wider range of people to come into the
area. Unfortunately, the shortcomings of the new residents were felt most sharply
by the black pioneer families, so it is not surprising that many remember the
period of integration as a high point and view the second wave with disdain. In
general, the second wave did not come searching for integration and had little
contact with white old-timers. With black pioneers so busy with work and family, second wavers also failed to benefit from meaningful contact with the black
residents. Simultaneously, institutions such as the school, library, synagogue,
businesses, the civic association, and local newspaper became destabilized. Instead of equilibrium and unity in this newly black neighborhood, black flight
erupted. Dissatisfied pioneers began to leave Parkmont in search of the amenities they wanted when they first arrived: integration, better schools, and neighbors who share their values. Today, the housing market has slowed, yet the black
population in Parkmont has continued to churn. The cultural divide between
the remaining pioneers and second wave residents has become more obvious
and tense.

These findings represent a continuation of an important tradition of research
on neighborhood racial transitions. Sociologists have long been interested in the
causes of neighborhood racial and ethnic change, and the major findings from
the classic invasion-succession, filtering, and life cycle models of neighborhood
transition have provided great strides in accumulating knowledge about the
causes of neighborhood population turnover.[29] At the same time, few studies have
illuminated the longer-term, dynamic cultural environments of neighborhoods

---

29. See Lee, Spain, and Umberson (1985) and Schwirian (1983).

in the aftermath of white flight. This study adds to the traditional white-flight research by offering data about what happens to people who stay behind, how they make residential decisions, the ways they interact with newcomers, and the culture of such communities as they continue to change. To the extent that neighborhoods where elderly white stayers and black working-class pioneers co-exist are commonplace in many cities, understanding them as cultural sites is important for shedding light on the social experience of white flight for the groups left to coexist and for understanding the subtle ways that such areas continue to change.

Neighborhood change can take many forms. The typical model of white-flight communities where angry stayers are pitifully left behind is an outdated generalization that attempts to dismiss and oversimplify the complicated nature of race relations in the wake of white flight. Similarly inaccurate is the assumption that white neighborhoods that become black will be characterized by a transcendent racial unity that negates important differences among blacks in terms of family structure and class composition, timing of arrival, residential preferences, parenting styles, and attitudes about the responsibilities, values, and behaviors that constitute a decent and peaceful community setting. As I have shown throughout the book, being white in a changing neighborhood does not mean having no choice and living in fear. Similarly, being black in a black-flight neighborhood does not translate into passive acceptance of change in the name of racial solidarity or leveled standards for community life. Just like other Americans, whites and blacks are diverse in terms of their values, behaviors, tolerance, life experiences, and aspirations.

Appendix

Table 1. Parkmont population and housing characteristics (1970–2000)

	1970	1980	1990	2000
Percentage white	99.6	98.5	92.2	33.2
Percentage black	0	0.2	2.2	58.8
Percentage black homes owner-occupied	0	100.0	13.3	73.7
Homeownership rate	78.8	79.1	73.4	73.6
Total population	9,313	7,677	7,271	7,768

Source: U.S. Census Bureau SF1.

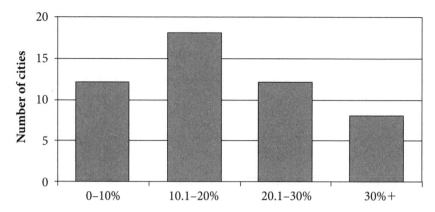

Percentage of neighborhoods experiencing white flight

FIGURE 1.   Frequency of white flight in the fifty largest U.S. cities, 1990–2000. *Source:* Geolytics Neighborhood Change Database (NCDB). See notes in chapter 1 for the definition of white flight and the criteria for neighborhood inclusion in data set.

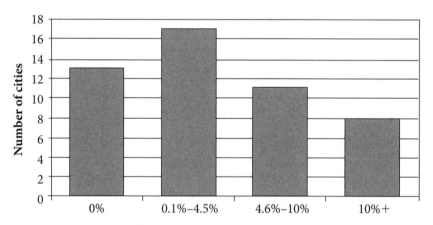

Percentage of neighborhoods experiencing white in-migration

FIGURE 2.   Frequency of white in-migration in the fifty largest U.S. cities, 1990–2000. *Source:* Geolytics Neighborhood Change Database (NCDB). See notes in chapter 1 for the definition of white in-migration and the criteria for neighborhood inclusion in data set.

References

Adelman, Robert M. 2005. "The Roles of Race, Class, and Residential Preferences in the Neighborhood Racial Composition of Middle-Class Blacks and Whites." *Social Science Quarterly* 86(1): 209–28.

Akers, Ronald L., Anthony J. La Greca, Christine Sellers, and John Cochran. 1997. "Fear of Crime and Victimization among the Elderly in Different Types of Communities." *Criminology* 25(3): 487–506.

Aldrich, Howard E. 1975. "Ecological Succession and Racially Changing Neighborhoods: A Review of the Literature." *Urban Affairs Quarterly* 10: 327–48.

American Association of Retired Persons (AARP). 1996. "Understanding Senior Housing into the Next Century: Survey of Consumer Preferences, Concerns, and Needs." Washington, D.C.: AARP.

Anderson, Elijah. 1978. *A Place on the Corner.* Chicago: University of Chicago Press.

——. 1990. *Streetwise: Race, Class, and Change in an Urban Community.* Chicago: University of Chicago Press.

——. 1996. "Introduction to the 1996 edition of *The Philadelphia Negro,*" in *The Philadelphia Negro: A Social Study,* by W. E. B. Dubois, ix–xxxvi. Philadelphia: University of Pennsylvania Press.

——. 1999. *Code of the Street: Decency, Violence, and the Moral Life of the Inner City.* New York: W. W. Norton.

Armor, David. 1978. "White Flight, Demographic Transition, and the Future of School Desegregation." *Rand Paper Series.* Santa Monica: Rand Corporation.

Bach, Robert L., and Joel Smith. 1977. "Community Satisfaction, Expectations of Moving, and Migration." *Demography* 14: 147–67.

Bay, Mia. 1998. "The World Was Thinking Wrong about Race: The Philadelphia Negro and Nineteenth-Century Science." In *W. E. B. DuBois, Race, and the City: "The Philadelphia Negro" and Its Legacy,* edited by M. B. Katz and T. J. Sugrue, 41–59. Philadelphia: University of Pennsylvania Press.

Bell, Bernard W., Emily R. Grosholz, and James B. Stewart. 1996. *W. E. B. DuBois on Race and Culture: Philosophy, Politics and Poetics.* London: Routledge.

Berger, Bennett M. 1991. "Structure and Choice in the Sociology of Culture." *Theory and Society* 20(1): 1–19.

Berube, Alan. 2001. "Racial Change in the Nation's Largest Cities: Evidence from the 2000 Census." Brookings Institution Center on Urban and Metropolitan Policy. Census Series, April. Washington, D.C.: Brookings Institution.

Bickford, Eric. 1997. "White Flight: The Effect of Minority Presence on Post–World War II Suburbanization." University of California, Berkeley. http://eh.net/Clio/Publications/flight.shtml.

Billig, Miriam. 2004. "Supportive Communities, an Optimum Arrangement for the Older Population?" *Journal of Sociology and Social Welfare* 31(3): 131–51.

Blackwell, James E. 1975. *The Black Community: Diversity and Unity.* New York: Harper and Row.

Blakeslee, Jan. 1978. "White Flight to the Suburbs: A Demographic Approach." *Focus: Institute for Research on Poverty Newsletter* 3(2):1–4.

Boaz, Franz. 1894. "Human Faculty as Determined by Race." *Proceedings of the American Association for the Advancement of Science* 43:31.

Bobo, Lawrence, and Camille L. Zubrinsky. 1996. "Attitudes on Racial Integration: Perceived Status Differences, Mere In-Group Preferences, or Racial Prejudice?" *Social Forces* 74: 883–909.

Brown-Saracino, Japonica. 2004. "Social Preservationists and the Quest for Authentic Community." *City and Community* 3(2): 135–56.

Brummell, Arden C. 1979. "A Model of Intra-Urban Mobility." *Economic Geography* 55(4): 338–52.

Bryan, Thomas M., and Peter A. Morrison. 2004. "New Approaches to Spotting Enclaves of the Elderly Who Have Aged in Place." Paper presented at the annual meeting of the Population Association of America, April 1–3, Boston, Massachusetts. Bures, Regina M. 2009. "Moving the Nest." *Journal of Family Issues* 30(6): 837–51.

Burgess, Ernest W. 1925. "The Growth of the City: An Introduction to a Research Project." In *The City,* edited by R. E. Park, E. W. Burgess, and R. D. McKenzie, 42–62. Chicago: University of Chicago Press.

Bursik, Robert J., Jr., and Harold G. Grasmick. 1993. *Neighborhoods and Crime.* New York: Lexington.

Butler, Edgar W., Ronald J. McAllister, and Edward J. Kaiser. 1973. "The Effects of Voluntary and Involuntary Residential Mobility on Females and Males." *Journal of Marriage and the Family* 35(2): 219–27.

Card, David, and Jesse Rothstein. 2006. "Racial Segregation and the Black-White Test Score Gap." *Journal of Public Economics* 9 (11–12): 2158–84.

Carp, F. M. 1976. "Housing and Living Environments of Older People." In *Handbook of Aging and Social Sciences,* edited by R. H. Binstock and E. Shanas, 244–71. New York: Van Nostrand Reinhold.

Carr, Leslie G., and Donald J. Zeigler. 1990. "White Flight and White Return in Norfolk." *Sociology of Education* 63(4): 272–82.

Charles, Camille Zubrinsky. 2000. "Neighborhood Racial-Composition Preferences: Evidence from a Multiethnic Metropolis." *Social Problems* 47(3): 379–407.

——. 2003. "The Dynamics of Racial Residential Segregation." *Annual Review of Sociology* 29(1): 167–207.

——. 2006. *Won't You Be My Neighbor? Race, Class, and Residence in Los Angeles.* New York: Russell Sage.

Chevan, Albert. 1982. "Age, Housing Choice, and Neighborhood Age Structure." *American Journal of Sociology* 87(5): 1133–49.

Clark, William A. V. 1987. "School Desegregation and White Flight: A Reexamination and Case Study." *Social Science Research* 16(3): 211–28.

Clark, William A. V., and Valerie Ledwith. 2006. "Mobility, Housing Stress, and Neighborhood Contexts: Evidence from Los Angeles." *Environment and Planning* A 38: 1077–93.

Clotfelter, Charles T. 1976. "School Desegregation, 'Tipping,' and Private School Enrollment." *Journal of Human Resources* 1(1): 28–49.

Cott, Nancy F. 2004. *No Small Courage: A History of Women in the United States.* New York: Oxford University Press.

Cover, Daniel J. 1995. "The Effects of Social Contact on Prejudice." *Journal of Social Psychology* 135: 403–5.

Crowder, Kyle. 2000a. "The Racial Context of White Mobility: An Individual-Level Test of the White Flight Hypothesis." *Social Science Research* 29: 223–57.

——. 2000b. "Racial Stratification in the Actuation of Mobility Expectations: Microlevel Impacts of Racially Restrictive Housing Markets." *Social Forces* 79: 1377–96.

Crowder, Kyle, and Scott J. South. 2008. "Spatial Dynamics of White Flight: The Effects of Local and Extralocal Racial Conditions on Neighborhood Out-Migration." *American Sociological Review* 73(5): 792–812.

Crowder, Kyle, Scott J. South, and Erick Chavez. 2006. "Wealth, Race, and Inter-Neighborhood Migration." *American Sociological Review* 71(1): 72–94.

Cuddy, Amy J. C., and Susan T. Fiske. 2002. "Doddering but Dear: Process, Content, and Function in Stereotyping of Older Persons." In *Ageism: Stereotyping and Prejudice against Older Persons,* edited by T. D. Nelson, 3–26. Cambridge: MIT Press.

Cuddy, Amy J. C., Michael I. Norton, and Susan T. Fiske. 2005. "This Old Stereotype: The Stubbornness and Pervasiveness of the Elderly Stereotype." *Journal of Social Issues* 61: 265–83.

Cummings, Scott. 1998. *Left Behind in Rosedale: Race Relations and the Collapse of Community Institutions.* Boulder, Colo.: Westview Press.

DeJong, Gordon F., and Robert W. Gardner, eds. 1981. *Migration Decision Making: Multidisciplinary Approaches to Microlevel Studies in Developed and Developing Countries.* New York: Pergamon Press.

DiMaggio, Paul. 1997. "Culture and Cognition." *Annual Review of Sociology* 23: 263–87.

Dougherty, Conor. 2008. "The End of White Flight." *Wall Street Journal,* July 19, A1.

Downs, Anthony. 1981. *Neighborhoods and Urban Development.* Washington, D.C.: Brookings Institution.

Drake, St. Clair, and Horace Cayton. 1945. *Black Metropolis.* New York: Harcourt, Brace.

DuBois, W. E. B. 1899. *The Philadelphia Negro: A Social Study.* New York: Lippincott.

——. 1903. *The Souls of Black Folk.* Chicago: A. C. McClurg and Co.

Duneier, Mitchell. 1992. *Slim's Table: Race, Respectability, and Masculinity.* Chicago: University of Chicago Press.

——. 1999. *Sidewalk.* New York: Farrar, Straus, and Giroux.

Durodoye, Beth A., and Angela D. Coker. 2007. "Crossing Cultures in Marriage: Implications for Counseling African American/African Couples." *International Journal for the Advancement of Counseling* 30(1): 25–37.

Early, Gerald Lyn. 2003. *This Is Where I Came In: Black America in the 1960s.* Lincoln: University of Nebraska Press.

Ellen, Ingrid Gould. 2000. *Sharing America's Neighborhoods: The Prospects for Stable Racial Integration.* Cambridge: Harvard University Press.

——. 2008. "Continuing Isolation: Segregation in America Today." In *Segregation: The Rising Costs for America,* edited by J. Carr and N. Kutty, 261–78. New York: Routledge.

Ennett, Susan T., Robert L. Flewelling, Richard C. Lindroth, and Edward C. Norton. 1997. "School and Neighborhood Characteristics Associated with School Rates of Alcohol, Cigarette, and Marijuana Use." *Journal of Health and Social Behavior* 38(1): 55–71.

Faircloth, Christopher A. 2002. "The Troubles with 'Celebrity': Community Formation in Senior Public Housing." *Ageing & Society* 22(5): 563–622.

Fanon, Franz. 1967. *Black Skin, White Masks.* New York: Grove Press.

Farley, Reynolds. 1996. "Racial Differences in the Search for Housing: Do Whites and Blacks Use the Same Techniques to Find Housing?" *Housing Policy Debate* 7(2): 367–85.

Farley, Reynolds, Elaine Fielding, and Maria Krysan. 1997. "The Residential Preferences of Blacks and Whites: A Four-Metropolis Analysis." *Housing Policy Debate* 8: 763–800.

Fasenfest, David, Jason Booza, and Kurt Metzger. 2004. "Living Together: A New Look at Racial and Ethnic Integration in Metropolitan Neighborhoods, 1990–2000." Washington, D.C.: Brookings Institution.

Feagin, Joe R. 1991. "The Continuing Significance of Race: Antiblack Discrimination in Public Places." *American Sociological Review* 56: 101–16.

Fischer, Claude S. 1975. "Toward a Subcultural Theory of Urbanism." *American Journal of Sociology* 80(6): 1319–41.

Fitzpatrick, Kevin, and John R. Logan. 1985. "The Aging of the Suburbs: 1960–1980." *American Sociological Review* 50(February): 106–17.

Frazier, E. Franklin. 1957. *Black Bourgeoisie*. New York: Collier Macmillan.

Freeman, Lance. 2006. *There Goes the 'Hood: Views of Gentrification from the Ground Up*. Philadelphia: Temple University Press.

Frey, William H. 1978. "Population Movement and City-Suburb Redistribution: An Analytic Framework." *Demography* 15(4): 571–88.

——. 1979. "Central City White Flight: Racial and Nonracial Causes." *American Sociological Review* 44(3): 425–48.

——. 1994a. "Minority Suburbanization and Continued 'White Flight' in U.S. Metropolitan Areas: Assessing Findings from the 1990 Census." *Research in Community Sociology* 4: 15–42.

——. 1994b. "The New White Flight." *American Demographics* 16: 40–48.

——. 2002. "Escaping the City and the Suburbs." *American Demographics* 24: 6.

——. 2003. *Boomers and Seniors in the Suburbs: Aging Patterns in Census 2000. The Living Cities Census Series*. New York: Brookings Institution.

Frey, William H., and Reynolds Farley. 1996. "Latino, Asian, and Black Segregation in U.S. Metropolitan Areas: Are Multiethnic Metros Different?" *Demography* 33: 35–50.

Galster, George C. 1990. "White Flight from Racially Integrated Neighborhoods in the 1970s: The Cleveland Experience." *Urban Studies* 27(3): 385–99.

Galster, George C., and Heather Keeney. 1993. "Subsidized Housing and Racial Change in Yonkers, New York." *Journal of the American Planning Association* 59: 172–81.

Gamm, Gerald H. 2001. *Urban Exodus: Why the Jews Left Boston and the Catholics Stayed*. Cambridge: Harvard University Press.

Gans, Herbert. 1962. "Urbanism and Suburbanism as Ways of Life: A Reevaluation of Definitions." In *Human Behavior and Social Processes,* edited by A. Rose, 625–48. Boston: Houghton-Mifflin.

Geertz, Clifford. 1973. *The Interpretation of Cultures*. New York: Basic Books.

Giddens, Anthony. 1984. *The Constitution of Society: Outline of the Theory of Structuration*. Cambridge: Polity.

Giles, Howard, and Scott A. Reid. 2005. "Ageism across the Lifespan: Towards a Self-Categorization Model of Ageing." *Journal of Social Issues* 61: 389–404.

Ginsberg, Yona. 1975. *Jews in a Changing Neighborhood: The Study of Mattapan*. New York: Free Press.

Gladwell, Malcolm. 2000. *The Tipping Point: How Little Things Can Make a Big Difference*. Boston: Little, Brown.

Goffman, Erving. 1963. *Stigma: Notes on the Management of Spoiled Identity*. Englewood Cliffs, N.J.: Prentice-Hall.

——. 1971. *Relations in Public: Microstudies of the Public Order*. New York: Basic Books.

Goodwin, Carol. 1979. *The Oak Park Strategy*. Chicago: University of Chicago.

Gordon, Albert Isaac. 1959. *Jews in Suburbia*. Boston: Beacon Press.

Gordon, Milton M. 1964. *Assimilation in American Life: The Role of Race, Religion, and National Origins*. New York: Oxford University Press.

Granovetter, Mark. 1978. "Threshold Models of Collective Behavior." *American Journal of Sociology* 83(6): 1420–43.

Greenbaum, Robert, and George Tita. 2004. "The Impact of Violence Surges on Neighborhood Business Activity." *Urban Studies* 41(13): 2495–2514.

Griswold, Wendy. 2005. "The Sociology of Culture." In *The Sage Handbook of Sociology*, edited by C. Calhoun, C. Rojek, and B. Turner, 254–66. Thousand Oaks, Calif.: Sage.

Hagestad, Gunhild O., and Peter Uhlenberg. 2005. "The Social Separation of Old and Young: A Root of Ageism." *Journal of Social Issues* 61(2): 343–60.

Hanushek, Eric A., and John M. Quigley. 1978. "An Explicit Model of Intra-Metropolitan Mobility." *Land Economics* 54(4): 411–29.

Harris, David R. 1999. "'Property Values Drop When Blacks Move In, Because....': Racial and Socioeconomic Determinants of Neighborhood Desirability." *American Sociological Review* 64: 461–79.

Harrison, Roderick J. 2002. "Moving Out When Minorities Move In (Analysis of the 'White Flight' Phenomenon)." *American Demographics*, June 1.

Hartigan, John, Jr. 1999. *Racial Situations: Class Predicaments of Whiteness in Detroit*. Princeton: Princeton University Press.

He, Wan, Manisha Sengupta, Victoria A. Velkoff, and Kimberly A. DeBarros. 2005. "65+ in the United States: 2005." *U.S. Department of Census Current Population Reports*. Washington, D.C.: U.S. Government Printing Office.

Heflin, Colleen M., and Mary Pattillo. 2006. "Poverty in the Family: Race, Siblings, and Socioeconomic Heterogeneity." *Social Science Research* 35: 804–22.

Herbert, Christopher E., and Eric S. Belsky. 2008. "The Homeownership Experience of Low-Income and Minority Households: A Review and Synthesis of the Literature." *Cityscape* 10(2): 5–60.

Herbert, Christopher E., Donald R. Haurin, Stuart S. Rosenthal, and Mark Duda. 2005. "Homeownership Gaps among Low-Income and Minority Households." Washington, D.C.: U.S. Department of Housing and Urban Development, Office of Policy Development and Research.

Hill, Shirley A. 1997. "Ethnicity and the Ethic of Caring in African American Families." *Journal of Personal and Interpersonal Loss* 2: 109–28.

——. 2001. "Class, Race, and Gender Dimensions of Child Rearing in African American Families." *Journal of Black Studies* 31(4): 494–508.

Hirsch, Arnold, R. 1983. *Making the Second Ghetto*. Chicago: University of Chicago Press.

Hochschild, Arlie Russell. 1973. *The Unexpected Community*. New York: Prentice-Hall.

Horton, Derrick, Beverlyn Lundy Allen, Cedric Herring, and Melvin E. Thomas. 2000. "Lost in the Storm: The Sociology of the Black Working Class, 1850 to 1990." *American Sociological Review* 65(1): 128–37.

Hummon, David Mark. 1990. *Commonplaces: Community Ideology and Identity in American Culture*. Albany: State University of New York Press.

Immergluck, Dan. 1999. "Cities and Finance Jobs: The Effect of Financial Services Restructuring on the Location of Employment." A discussion paper prepared for the Brookings Institution Center on Urban and Metropolitan Policy, November.

Jacobs, Jane. 1961. *The Death and Life of Great American Cities*. New York: Random House.

Johnson, James H., and Stanley D. Brunn. 1980. "Residential Preference Patterns of Afro-American College Students in Three Different States." *Professional Geographer* 32: 37–42.

Jonas, Andrew E. G. 1998. "Busing, 'White Flight,' and the Role of Developers in the Continuous Suburbanization of Franklin County, Ohio." *Urban Affairs Review* 34(2): 340–58.

Kasinitz, Phillip. 1992. "Bringing the Neighborhood Back In: The New Neighborhood Ethnography." *Sociological Forum* 7(2): 355–63.

Katz, Michael B., Mark J. Stern, and Jamie J. Fader. 2005. "The New African American Inequality." *Journal of American History* 92: 1.

Katz, Peter. 1994. *The New Urbanism.* New York: McGraw-Hill.

Keith, Pat M. 1977. "Perceptions of Needs of the Aged by Ministers and the Elderly." *Religious Research* 18(3): 278–82.

Kennedy, Maureen, and Paul Leonard. 2001. *Dealing with Neighborhood Change: A Primer on Gentrification and Policy Changes.* Washington, D.C.: Brookings Institution.

Kinney, Nancy T., and William E. Winter. 2006. "Places of Worship and Neighborhood Stability." *Journal of Urban Affairs* 28(4): 335–52.

Koebel, C. Theodore. 2002. "Analyzing Neighborhood Retail and Service Change in Six Cities." Blacksburg, Va.: Virginia Center for Housing Research.

Krase, Jerome. 1982. *Self and Community in the City.* Washington, D.C.: University Press of America.

Kraus, Neil. 2000. *Race, Neighborhoods, and Community Power: Buffalo Politics, 1934–1997.* Albany: State University of New York Press.

Kruse, Kevin M. 2005. *White Flight: Atlanta and the Making of Modern Conservatism.* Princeton: Princeton University Press.

Krysan, Maria. 2002. "Whites Who Say They'd Flee: Who Are They, and Why Would They Leave?" *Demography* 39(4): 675–96.

Krysan, Maria, and Reynolds Farley. 2002. "The Residential Preferences of Blacks: Do They Explain Persistent Segregation?" *Social Forces* 80: 937–80.

Lacy, Karyn R. 2007. *Blue-Chip Black: Race, Class, and Status in the New Black Middle Class.* Berkeley: University of California Press.

LaGory, Mark, Susan R. Sherman, and Russell A. Ward. 1988. *The Environment for Aging: Interpersonal, Social, and Spatial Contexts.* Tuscaloosa: University of Alabama.

Lamb, Charles M. 2005. *Housing Segregation in Suburban America since 1960.* Cambridge: Cambridge University Press.

Lamont, Michèle, and Mario L. Small. 2008. "How Culture Matters: Enriching Our Understanding of Poverty." In *The Colors of Poverty: Why Racial and Ethnic Disparities Persist,* edited by D. Harris and A. Lin, 76–102. New York: Russell Sage Foundation.

Lassiter, Matthew D. 2007. *The Silent Majority: Suburban Politics in the Sunbelt South; Politics and Society in Twentieth Century America.* Princeton: Princeton University Press.

Lauria, Mickey. 1998. "A New Model of Neighborhood Change: Reconsidering the Role of White Flight." *Housing Policy Debate* 9(2): 395–424.

Lee, Barrett A., Karen E. Campbell, and Oscar Miller. 1991. "Racial Differences in Urban Neighboring." *Sociological Forum* 6(3): 525–50.

Lee, Barrett A., Daphne Spain, and Debra Umberson. 1985. "Neighborhood Revitalization and Racial Change: The Case of Washington, D.C." *Demography* 22(4): 581–602.

Lee, Barrett A., and Peter B. Wood. 1991. "Is Neighborhood Racial Succession Place-Specific?" *Demography* 28(1): 21–40.

Lee, Judith A. B. 2001. *The Empowerment Approach to Social Work Practice.* New York: Columbia University Press.

Lee, Ronald, and John Haaga. 2002. "Government Spending in an Older America." Washington, D.C.: Population Reference Bureau.

Levine, Hillel, and Lawrence Harmon. 1992. *The Death of an American Jewish Community: A Tragedy of Good Intentions.* New York: Free Press.

Lewis, Oscar. 1959. *Five Families: Mexican Case Studies in the Culture of Poverty.* New York: Basic Books.

———. 1966. *La Vida: A Puerto Rican Family in the Culture of Poverty, San Juan and New York.* New York: Random House.

Lieberson, Stanley. 1981. *A Piece of the Pie: Blacks and White Immigrants since 1880.* Berkeley: University of California Press.

Lincoln, Yvonna S., and Egon G. Guba. 1985. *Naturalistic Inquiry.* Newbury, Calif.: Sage Publications.

Linde, Charlotte. 2009. *Working the Past: Narrative and Institutional Memory.* New York: Oxford University Press.

Lofland, John. 1972. "Analytic Ethnography." *Journal of Contemporary Ethnography* 24(1): 30–67.

Lofland, Lyn H. 1973. *A World of Strangers: Order and Action in Urban Public Space.* New York: Basic Books.

Logan, John R. 2002. "Separate and Unequal: The Neighborhood Gap for Blacks and Hispanics in Metropolitan America." Albany, N.Y.: Lewis Mumford Center for Comparative Urban and Regional Research.

Maly, Michael T. 2005. *Beyond Segregation: Multiracial and Multiethnic Neighborhoods in the United States.* Philadelphia: Temple University Press.

Massey, Douglas S., and Nancy A. Denton. 1993. *American Apartheid: Segregation and the Making of the Underclass.* Cambridge: Harvard University Press.

Maurrasse, David J. 2006. *Listening to Harlem: Gentrification, Community, and Business.* New York: Routledge.

McKinnon, Jesse. 2003. *The Black Population in the United States: March 2002.* Current Population Reports, Series P20–541. Washington, D.C.: U.S. Census Bureau.

McPherson, Miller, Lynn Smith-Lovin, and James M. Cook. 2001. "Birds of a Feather: Homophily in Social Networks." *Annual Review of Sociology* 27: 415–44.

McRoberts, Omar. 2003. *Streets of Glory: Church and Community in a Black Urban Neighborhood.* Chicago: University of Chicago Press.

Meares, Tracey L., and Dan M. Kahan. 1998. "Law and (Norms of) Order in the Inner City." *Law and Society Review* 32(4): 805–38.

Meyer, Stephen Grant. 2001. *As Long as They Don't Move Next Door: Segregation and Racial Conflict in American Neighborhoods.* New York: Rowman and Littlefield.

Molinsky, Andrew. 2007. "Cross-Cultural Code Switching: The Psychological Challenge of Adapting Behavior in Foreign Cultural Interactions." *Academy of Management Review* 32(2): 622–40.

Molotch, Harvey. 1972. *Managed Integration: Dilemmas of Doing Good in the City.* Berkeley: University of California Press.

Moynihan, Daniel Patrick. 1965. *The Negro Family: The Case for National Action.* Washington, D.C.: U.S. Department of Labor, Office of Policy Planning and Research.

Myrdal, Gunnar. 1944. *An American Dilemma: The Negro Problem and Modern Democracy.* New York: Harper and Brothers.

Naylor, Gloria. 1988. *The Women of Brewster Place: A Novel in Seven Stories.* New York: Penguin Books.

Newport, Frank. 2007. "Black or African American?" *Gallup Public Opinion Poll.* Princeton: The Gallup Organization.

Nobles, Wade. 1985. *Africanity and the Black Family: The Development of a Theoretical Model.* San Francisco: Black Family Institute Publishers.

Northwood, Lawrence K., and Ernest A. T. Barth. 1965. *Urban Desegregation: Negro Pioneers and Their White Neighbors.* Seattle: University of Washington Press.

Nyden, Philip, John L. Lukehart, Michael T. Maly, and William Peterman. 1998. "Chapter 13: Conclusion." *Cityscape: A Journal of Policy and Research* 4(2): 261–69.

Osofsky, Gilbert. 1996. *Harlem: The Making of a Ghetto, Negro New York, 1890–1930.* New York: Harper and Row.

Ottensmann, John R. 1995. "Requiem for the Tipping Point Hypothesis." *Journal of Planning Literature* 10(2): 131–41.

Ottensmann, John R., and Michael Gleason. 1992. "The Movement of Whites and Blacks into Racially Mixed Neighborhoods: Chicago, 1960–1980." *Social Science Quarterly* 73(3): 645–62.

Ovadia, Seth, and Rachael A. Woldoff. 2008. "White Flight, White Inmigration, and Stable Diversity: Race in America's Urban Neighborhoods, 1990 to 2000." Paper presented at the Annual Meeting of the American Sociological Association, Boston, August 1–4.

Owens, Michael Leo, and David J. Wright. 1998. "The Diversity of Majority-Black Neighborhoods." *Rockefeller Institute Bulletin* 8: 1–20.

Page, Phillip. 1999. *Reclaiming Community in Contemporary African-American Fiction.* Jackson: University Press of Mississippi.

Park, Robert E. 1924. "The Concept of Social Distance as Applied to the Study of Racial Attitudes and Racial Relations." *Journal of Applied Sociology* 8(6): 339–44.

Patterson, Orlando. 2001. "Taking Culture Seriously: A Framework and an Afro-American Illustration." In *Culture Matters: How Values Shape Human Progress,* edited by L. E. Harrison and S. P. Huntington, 202–18. New York: Basic Books.

——. 2003. "Culture of Poverty, Poverty of Culture." presentation at the Annual Meeting of the American Sociological Association, Atlanta, August 16–19.

Pattillo, Mary. 2007. *Black on the Block: The Politics of Race and Class in the City.* Chicago: University of Chicago Press.

Pattillo-McCoy, Mary. 1999. *Black Picket Fences: Privilege and Peril among the Black Middle Class.* Chicago: University of Chicago Press.

Pritchett, Wendell. 2002. *Brownsville, Brooklyn: Blacks, Jews, and the Changing Face of the Ghetto.* Chicago: University of Chicago Press.

Putnam, Robert D. 1995. "Turning In, Turning Out: The Strange Disappearance of Social Capital in America." *Political Science & Politics* 28(4): 664–83.

——. 2000. *Bowling Alone: The Collapse and Revival of American Community.* New York: Simon and Schuster.

Quercia, Roberto, and George Galster. 2000. "Threshold Effects and Neighborhood Change." *Journal of Planning, Education, and Research* 20: 146–62.

Rawlings, Lynette A., Laura E. Harris, and Margery Austin Turner. 2004. "Race and Residence: Prospects for Stable Neighborhood Integration." *Neighborhood Change in Urban America* Series (3): 1–9. Washington, D.C.: Urban Institute.

Renzulli, Linda A., and Lorraine Evans. 2005. "School Choice, Charter Schools, and White Flight." *Social Problems* 52(3): 398–418.

Rieder, Jonathan. 1985. *Canarsie: The Jews and Italians of Brooklyn against Liberalism.* Cambridge: Harvard University Press.

Rohe, William, and Leslie Stewart. 1996. "Homeownership and Neighborhood Stability." *Housing Policy Debate* 7(1): 37–82.

Rossi, Peter H. 1955. *Why Families Move.* New York: Free Press.

Saltman, Juliet. 1990. *A Fragile Movement: The Struggle for Neighborhood Stabilization.* Santa Barbara, Calif.: Greenwood Press.

Sampson, Robert J., Stephen Raudenbush, and Felton Earls. 1997. "Neighborhoods and Violent Crime: A Multilevel Study of Collective Efficacy." *Science* 277: 918–24.

Sampson, Robert J., and William Julius Wilson. 1995. "Toward a Theory of Race, Crime, and Urban Inequality." In *Crime and Inequality,* edited by J. Hagan and R. D. Peterson, 37–56. Stanford: Stanford University Press.

Schafer, Robert. 1999. "Determinants of the Living Arrangements of the Elderly." Working Paper No. W99–6. Joint Center for Housing Studies. Boston: Harvard University.

Schelling, Thomas C. 1971. "Dynamic Models of Segregation." *Journal of Mathematical Sociology* 1: 143–86.

Schneider, Benjamin. 1987. "The People Make the Place." *Personnel Psychology* 40(3): 437–53.

Schwab, W. A., and E. Marsh. 1980. "The Tipping Point Model: Prediction of Change in the Racial Composition of Cleveland, Ohio's Neighborhoods, 1940–1970." *Environment and Planning* 12: 385–98.

Schwirian, Kent P. 1983. "Models of Neighborhood Change." *Annual Review of Sociology* 9: 83–102.

Seligman, Amanda. 2005. *Block by Block: Neighborhoods and Public Policy on Chicago's West Side*. Chicago: University of Chicago Press.

Sewell, William F. 1992. "A Theory of Structure: Duality, Agency, and Transformation." *American Journal of Sociology* 98(1): 1–29.

Shapiro, Thomas M. 2004. *The Hidden Cost of Being African American: How Wealth Perpetuates Inequality*. New York: Oxford University Press.

Shaw, Clifford R., and Henry D. McKay. 1942. *Juvenile Delinquency in Urban Areas*. Chicago: University of Chicago Press.

Sherman, Susan R., Russell A. Ward, and Mark LaGory. 1988. "Women as Caregivers of the Elderly." *Social Work* 33(2): 164–67.

Singh, Nakhil Pal. 2004. *Black Is a Country: Race and the Unfinished Struggle for Democracy*. Cambridge: Harvard University Press.

Skogan, Wesley. 1990. *Disorder and Decline: Crime and the Spiral of Decay in American Neighborhoods*. New York: Free Press.

South, Scott J., and Glenn D. Deane. 1993. "Race and Residential Mobility: Individual Determinants and Structural Constraints." *Social Forces* 72: 147–67.

Speare, Alden, Jr. 1974. "Residential Satisfaction as an Intervening Variable in Residential Mobility." *Demography* 11(2): 173–88.

Stack, Carol B. 1974. *All Our Kin: Strategies for Survival in a Black Community*. New York: Harper and Row.

Suarez, Ray. 1999. *The Old Neighborhood: What We Lost in the Great Suburban Migration, 1966–1999*. New York: Free Press.

Suttles, Gerald. 1972. *The Social Construction of Communities*. Chicago: University of Chicago Press.

Taub, Robert P., Garth Taylor, and Jan D. Dunham. 1984. *Paths of Neighborhood Change: Race and Crime in Urban America*. Chicago: University of Chicago Press.

Taylor, Paul, Cary Funk, and Peyton Craighill. 2006. "Are We Happy Yet?" Pew Research Center Social Trends Report, http://pewresearch.org/assets/social/pdf/AreWeHappyYet.pdf.

Taylor, Ralph B. 2001. *Breaking Away from Broken Windows: Baltimore Neighborhoods and the Nationwide Fight against Crime, Grime, Fear, and Decline*. Boulder: Westview Press.

Teitler, Julian O., and Christopher C. Weiss. 1996. "Contextual Sex: The Effect of School and Neighborhood Environments on the Timing of First Intercourse." Paper presented at the Annual Meetings of the Population Association of America, New Orleans, May.

Thomas, William Isaac, and Florian Znaniecki. 1995. *The Polish Peasant in Europe and America: A Classic Work in Immigration History*. Champaign: University of Illinois Press.

Tinker, Anthea. 1997. "Housing and Household Movement in Later Life: Developing the Range of Housing Options in the United Kingdom." *Journal of Housing for the Elderly* 12 (1–2): 9–17.

Trice, Dawn Turner. 1997. *Only Twice I've Wished for Heaven.* New York: Crown.

Turner, William L., Beverly R. Wallace, Jared R. Anderson, and Carolyn Bird. 2004. "The Last Mile of the Way: Understanding Care Giving in African American Families at the End-of-Life." *Journal of Marital and Family Therapy* 30(4): 427–38.

U.S. Department of Housing and Urban Development. 1999. "Housing Our Elders." Washington, D.C.: U.S. Department of Housing and Urban Development.

Venkatesh, Sudhir Alladi. 1997. "The Social Organization of Street Gang Activity in an Urban Ghetto." *American Journal of Sociology* 103: 82–111.

Wacquant, Loïc J. D. 1997. "Three Pernicious Premises in the Study of the American Ghetto." *International Journal of Urban & Regional Research* 21(2): 341–53.

Wacquant, Loïc J. D., and William Julius Wilson. 1989. "The Cost of Racial and Class Exclusion in the Inner City." *The Annals of the American Academy of Political and Social Science* 501(January): 8–25.

Ward, Russell A., Mark LaGory, and Susan R. Sherman. 1988. *The Environment for Aging: Social, Interpersonal, and Spatial Contexts.* Tuscaloosa: University of Alabama Press.

White, Michael. 1984. "Racial and Ethnic Succession in Four Cities." *Urban Affairs Quarterly* 20: 165–83.

White-Means, Shelley I. 1993. "Informal Home Care for Frail Black Elderly." *Journal of Applied Gerontology* 12(1): 18–33.

Wilson, James Q., and George Kelling. 1982. "Broken Windows." *Atlantic Monthly* (March): 29–38.

Wilson, William J. 1987. *The Truly Disadvantaged: The Inner City, the Underclass, and Public Policy.* Chicago: University of Chicago Press.

——. 2009. *More Than Just Race: Being Black and Poor in the Inner City.* New York: W. W. Norton.

Wilson, William J., and Richard P. Taub. 2006. *There Goes the Neighborhood: Racial, Ethnic, and Class Tensions in Four Chicago Neighborhoods and Their Meaning for America.* New York: Random House.

Woldoff, Rachael A. 2002. "The Effects of Local Stressors on Neighborhood Attachment." *Social Forces* 81(1): 87–116.

——. 2006a. "Living Where the Neighbors Are Invested: Wealth and Racial/Ethnic Differences in Individuals' Neighborhood Homeownership Rate." In *Wealth Accumulation and Communities of Color in the United States: Current Issues,* edited by Jessica Gordon Nembhard and Ngina Chiteji, 267–93. Ann Arbor: University of Michigan Press.

——. 2006b. "Emphasizing Fear of Crime in Models of Neighborhood Social Disorganization." *Crime Prevention and Community Safety* 8(4): 228–47.

——. 2008. "Wealth, Human Capital, and Family across Racial/Ethnic Groups: Integrating Models of Wealth and Locational Attainment." *Urban Studies* 45(3): 527–51.

Woldoff, Rachael A., and Brian J. Gerber. 2007. "Protect or Neglect? Social Structure, Decision Making, and the Risk of Living in African American Places in New Orleans." In *Racing the Storm: Racial Implications and Lessons Learned from Hurricane Katrina,* edited by H. Potter, 171–96. Lanham, Md.: Lexington Books.

Woldoff, Rachael A., and Seth Ovadia. 2009. "Not Getting Their Money's Worth: African American Disadvantages in Converting Income, Wealth, and Education into Residential Quality." *Urban Affairs Review* 45(1): 66–91. '

Woldoff, Rachael A., and Karen Weiss. 2010. "Stop Snitchin': Exploring Definitions of the Snitch and Implications for Urban Black Communities." *Journal of Criminal Justice and Popular Culture* 17(1): 184–223.

Yinger, John. 1995. *Closed Doors, Opportunities Lost: The Continuing Costs of Housing Discrimination.* New York: Russell Sage Foundation.

Young, Heather M. 1998. "Moving to Congregate Housing: The Last Chosen Home." *Journal of Aging Studies* 12(2): 149–65.

Zielenbach, Sean. 2000. *The Art of Revitalization: Improving Conditions in Distressed Inner-City Neighborhoods.* New York: Garland.

Index

Adelman, Robert M., 220n12

adult children of stayers, 27, 48, 87–88, 94–96, 109, 139. *See also* pressure to move

African Americans. *See* blacks

age: ageism, 39, 39n30, 61; differences of, between white stayers and black pioneers, 109–10; segregation by, 61

agency, 39–40, 67, 213, 215–16. *See also* residential mobility decision-making

aging in place: advantages of Parkmont for, 54; agency and, 216; debility and death and, 62–63, 76; desire for, 27, 33–34, 75; and importance of cross-racial neighboring, 94–95; as preferred to a retirement community, 60–61, 71, 77; pressure to move and, 48. *See also* pressure to move

Aldrich, Howard E., 38n27

Anderson, Elijah, 35–36, 35n16, 56n41, 89n1. *See also* "street" vs. "decent"

assimilationist attitudes, 150–56, 202, 211, 219. *See also* socialization

Bach, Robert L., 149n21

Barsky, Morris (pseud.), 62–63, 93, 105

black church in Parkmont, 21, 100, 170, 225

black flight: defined, 2–3, 137; and instability of neighborhood, 221–24, 227–28; intraracial conflict as factor in, 137–38, 146, 158, 214–15, 222–24, 228; and mobility intentions of second wave, 157–58; and resegregation, 223; retirement and, 131–32, 133; schools as factor in, 198–99, 204–05, 211–12; and timing of arrival, 138; white flight and, 5, 13–14, 24, 213

black pioneers, 6–7, 28–30; agency and, 39–40, 67, 213; and civic associations, 20, 130, 171–72, 221; defined, 4, 28; financial investment in Parkmont, 36, 40–42; integration as factor in entry decisions, 6, 15–16, 39, 42–45, 59, 150, 151, 218–19; mortgages and, 42; real estate searches by, 42; and relative safety of Parkmont, 22–23, 28–29, 128, 171–72; residential satisfaction of, 10, 28–29; socioeconomic status of, 36, 45, 55–56, 57, 137–38, 219; as strivers, 34; as term, 34; and white flight, 45, 55, 59–60, 67–70. *See also* black flight; cross-racial neighboring; cultural differences between pioneers and second wavers; cultural similarities between stayers and pioneers; disorder; neighbor networks and social structures; occupations of black pioneers; resegregation of Parkmont; residential mobility decision-making; schools; social control; socialization

blacks: assumptions about residential preferences of, 32, 227; assumptions of close-knit communities of, 169–70, 170n27, 229; attitudes toward racial integration, 218, 220, 220n12; caregiving culture of, 98–100; cultural values of, in U.S., 99; diversity within communities, 148; fear of, 14–17, 60, 80, 81; as homeowners, 18–19, 23, 40–42; institutions for, lack of, 25, 225, 228; religious/spiritual beliefs of, 99, 100; reverence for the elderly of, 69, 98–100, 100n9; as term in text, 1n1; working class, 137–38. *See also* black pioneers; black second wavers; culture; racial prejudice

black second wavers, 7, 10–11, 30–31; defined, 4, 30; homeownership by, 23–24; mobility intentions of, 157–58, 161–62; as percentage of population, 80; on relative integration, 21; and relative safety of Parkmont, 158, 160, 174, 187; and segregation of Parkmont, acceptance of, 144, 150; as short-term residents, 156–58; socioeconomic status of, 30–31, 137–38, 152–56; as stage in racial turnover, 5. *See also* cultural differences; disorder; Lombard school; social control; socialization

block parties, 93, 122–24, 160–61

block watch groups, 20, 124, 129, 226–27

Bobo, Lawrence, 13n3

broken windows theory, 117–18n1, 127n2, 158, 223

Bryan, Thomas M., 38n27

Burgess, Ernest W., 149

housing market *(cont.)*
114; subprime mortgages, 19, 23, 138–39;
timing of arrival and, 138–39. *See also*
government policies; mortgage assistance
programs
housing satisfaction, amenities, 14, 25, 114–15
human ecology perspective, 38–39, 40

institutional memory, 10, 105–06, 106n12, 107,
108, 174, 217
institutions for black residents, lack of, 5–6
integration *See* racial integration
interracial cooperation. *See* cross-racial neighboring
intraracial conflict (pioneers and second
wavers): perception of, by pioneers, 9–10;
as push factor, 5–7, 136–38, 146–47, 149,
152–53, 158, 161–62, 173–74, 190, 214–15,
222–24, 228. *See also* cross-racial neighboring; cultural differences; "street" vs. "decent"
Irish Americans, 15, 116, 206
Italian Americans, 8, 15, 19, 27–28, 53, 58, 65,
75, 98, 107, 151, 206, 211, 225

Jackson, Anne (pseud.), 40–41, 60, 69–70, 101,
107, 151, 170–72
Jackson, Carla (pseud.), 155, 165–66, 171,
206–07
Jewish Community Center (JCC), 27, 52, 68, 225
Jewish residents of Parkmont, 14–18, 21,
72–73, 82–84, 225. *See also* white stayers
Jones, Nina and Daryl (pseud.), 43–44, 70,
104–05, 147, 163, 165, 196–97, 199–200,
201–02, 203, 209

Kaiser, Edward J., 32n1
Katz, Leo and Gladys (pseud.), 51–52, 57–58,
62, 93, 97–98, 102–04
Kelling, George, 117n1
Kennedy, Maureen, 89n1
Krase, Jerome, 137
Krysan, Maria, 13n4

LaGory, Mark, 92n5
Lamont, Michèle, 136n6
Laundromat, 25, 164–65, 172
Lauria, Mickey, 38n27
Ledwith, Valerie, 149n21
Leonard, Paul, 89n1
Lewis, Oscar, 136n6
library, 27, 52, 81–82, 164
Linde, Charlotte, 106n12
Lofland, Lyn H., 79n3
Lombard school: absence of pioneer children
affecting second wave children, 193, 211;

behavior problems in, 194, 199, 200–203;
and black flight, 11, 198–99, 204–05,
211–12; as black segregated school, 17,
116–17, 180, 183, 194, 211–12; busing program as integrating, 16, 183, 205, 209–11;
crime and, 200–202, 208; dress code, 208;
facilities of, 194, 197; as factor in entry decision for black pioneers, 195–97, 212; and
intraracial conflict, 199–203, 210–12; local
nature of problems, 207–09; as low-income
school, 194, 201; nonresidents, presence in,
182–85, 193–94, 201, 205–12; overcrowding in, 180–81, 206, 209; parenting styles
and family structure and, 199–201, 208–09;
police presence in, 194, 199–200; preschool
of, 201; quality of, 15, 116, 164, 180–82,
194, 225; race and establishment of, 15, 211;
relative safety of, 201; reputation of, 181–82,
195–97, 212; second wave children attending, 30, 164, 180–85, 190, 199–203, 210–11;
vandalism of, 193–94; violence in, 29, 183,
184, 193, 200–201, 203; and white flight, 17,
198–99, 211. *See also* schools
low-income housing programs, 19, 23–24, 29,
115

McAllister, Ronald J., 32n1
McCall, George (pseud.), 151–52, 162–63
McCall, Sonya (pseud.), 44–45, 59–60, 67–68,
141, 146, 151–52, 159, 165, 172–73, 196,
203–04
McPherson, Miller, 90n2
Meadows, Gene and Margaret (pseud.), 6–7,
69, 95, 150–51, 156, 159, 162, 172, 198, 207
Meyer, Stephen Grant, 38n27
military, mortgage assistance and, 41, 42, 115
mobility constraints on black pioneers: family
obligations, 24; finances, 24, 30; job residency
requirements, 22, 24, 30, 41, 44, 113, 114, 150,
198; relative safety of Parkmont, 22–23
mobility thoughts and intentions of black
pioneers: crime as factor in, 173; disorder as
factor in, 6, 117–18n1, 158, 223–24; drugs as
factor in, 151; and intraracial conflict, 5–7,
136–37, 147, 149, 152–53, 161–62, 173, 174,
190, 222, 223–24; suburbs as goal, 131–32,
174–75, 204–05; white flight as factor in, 24.
See also mobility constraints on black pioneers; residential mobility decision-making
Molotch, Harvey, 13n5
Morrison, Peter A., 38n27
mortgage assistance programs: down payment
assistance programs, 19; enabling black in-
migration, 18–19, 23–24, 41, 42; first-time
homeowner programs, 18, 41; low-income